OPC

RAIL ATLAS

GREAT BRITAIN & IRELAND

8th edition

by S. K. Baker

OPC

Oxford Publishing Co.

1st edition published 1977
2nd edition published 1978
3rd edition published 1980
4th edition published 1984
Reprinted 1985
5th edition published 1988
Reprinted 1988 and 1989
6th edition published 1990
7th edition published 1992
Reprinted 1995
8th edition published 1996

Cartography by Map Creation Ltd, Maidenhead, Berks

A catalogue record for this book is available from the British Library.

ISBN 0-86093-534-5

Library of Congress Catalog Card Number: 96-77284

Oxford Publishing Co. is an imprint of Haynes Publishing, Sparkford,
Nr Yeovil, Somerset BA22 7JJ

Printed and bound in France by imprimerie pollina s.a., Luçon n° 67655

Typeset in Univers Roman Medium

Front cover illustrations:
Top: Three Eurostars at London Waterloo International station, 17th August 1995.
Below, left: Irish Rail No. 154 at Limerick Junction on the 15.55 Limerick-Rosslare
train, 6th May 1995.
Below, right: South Yorkshire Supertram No. 01 at Woodbourn Road, Sheffield,
25th June 1994.

(All *Stuart Baker*)

GLOSSARY OF ABBREVIATIONS

ABM	Associated British Maltsters		LIFT	London International Freight Terminal
ABP	Associated British Ports		L.L.	Low Level
ARC	Amey Roadstone Company		LUL	London Underground Limited
ASW	Allied Steel & Wire		MDHC	Mersey Docks & Harbour Company
B & I	British & Irish Line		M&EE	Mechanical and Electrical Engineer
BIS	British Industrial Sand		MoD	Ministry of Defence
BOC	British Oxygen Company		MSC	Manchester Ship Canal
BP	British Petroleum		NIR	Northern Ireland Railways
BR	British Rail		OLE	Overhead Line Equipment
BWB	British Waterways Board		PO	Post Office
C. & W.	Carriage and Wagon		P.S.	Power Station
Cal-Mac	Caledonian MacBrayne		PTE	Passenger Transport Executive
C.C.	County Council		P.W.	Permanent Way
CE	Civil Engineer		RJB	R. J. Budge Mining
C.S.	Carriage Sidings		RMC	Ready Mix Concrete (Marcon)
DCL	Distillers Company Limited		RPSI	Railway Preservation Society of Ireland
Dist	Distribution		RTK	Railtrack
D.P.	Disposal Point (Opencast Coal)		S. & T.	Signal & Telegraph
ECC	English China Clays International		SAI	Scottish Agricultural Industries
EMU	Electric Multiple Unit		SGD	Scottish Grain Distillers
FLT	Freightliner Terminal		SMD	Scottish Malt Distillers
GEC	General Electric Company		Term.	Terminal
H.L.	High Level		UES	United Engineering Steels
ICI	Imperial Chemical Industries		UKAEA	United Kingdom Atomic Energy Authority
IE	Iarnrod Eireann (Irish Rail)			

PREFACE TO FIRST EDITION

The inspiration for this atlas was two-fold; firstly a feeling of total bewilderment by 'Llans' and 'Abers' on first visiting South Wales four years ago, and secondly a wall railway map drawn by a friend, Martin Bairstow. Since then, at university, there has been steady progress in drawing the rail network throughout Great Britain. The author feels sure that this atlas as it has finally evolved will be useful to all with an interest in railways, whether professional or enthusiast. The emphasis is on the current network since it is felt that this information is not published elsewhere.

Throughout, the main aim has been to show clearly, using expanded sheets where necessary, the railways of this country, including the whole of London Transport and light railways. Passenger lines are distinguished by colour according to operating company and all freight-only lines are depicted in red. The criterion for a British Rail passenger line has been taken as at least one advertised passenger train per day in each direction. On passenger routes, to assist the traveller, single and multiple track sections, with crossing loops on single lines have been shown. Symbols are used to identify both major centres of rail freight, such as collieries and power stations, and railway installations such as locomotive depots and works. Secondary information, for example junction names and tunnels over 100 yards long, with lengths if over one mile has been shown.

The author would like to express his thanks to members of the Oxford University Railway Society and to Nigel Bird, Chris Hammond and Richard Warson in particular for help in compiling and correcting the maps. His cousin, Dr Tony McCann deserves special thanks for removing much of the tedium by computer sorting the index, as do Oxford City Libraries for providing excellent reference facilities.

June 1977

PREFACE TO EIGHTH EDITION

This eighth edition of the *Rail Atlas* has been fully revised and expanded. There is an increasing interest in the railways of Ireland and there are 14 new maps covering the full Irish main line network as well as the numerous narrow gauge peat bog railways.

The national rail network is evolving and expanding at quite a rate so there are many changes on the maps since the previous edition. The various network development proposals are included: the main line proposals, preservation schemes, Light Rail Transit proposals and new links for the Channel Tunnel freight and high speed passenger services are all most positive initiatives.

This edition is published at two milestones for the *Rail Atlas* – it is 20 years since preparation for the first edition commenced, and the seventh edition saw the 100,000th copy sold.

The author would like to thank the many people who have contacted him to supply material for this new edition. Thanks are also due to his family for their patience and support.

Stuart K. Baker
York
August 1996

CONTENTS

Publisher's Note

Although situations are constantly changing on the railways of Britain, every effort has been made by the author to ensure complete accuracy of the maps in the book at the time of going to press.

KEY TO ATLAS

		Surface	Tunnel	Tube
Passenger Rail Network *(With gauge where other than standard gauge: i. e. 4' 8½" Britain/ 5' 3" Ireland)*	Multiple Track	———————	—)----(—	- - - - - - - - - -
	Single Track	+++++++++++++++	+++)----(+++	- - - - - - - - - -
Municipal/ Urban Railways or Irish Peat Railways. *(London Underground Ltd lines indicated by code. Irish Peat lines are 3' gauge unless shown).*	Multiple Track	—— C ——	—)- C -(—	- - C - -
	Single Track	+++ C +++	+++)- C -(+++	- - C - -
Preserved & Minor Passenger Railways *(With name, and gauge where other than standard gauge).*	Multiple Track	———————	—)----(—	
	Single Track	+++++++++++++++	+++)----(+++	
Freight only lines	No Single/ Multiple Distinction	———————	—)----(—	

Advertised Passenger Station:

Saltburn
————————●————————

Crossing Loop at Passenger Station:

Newtown
++++++++++✖++++++++++

Crossing Loop on Single Line:

Kincraig
++++++++++✗++++++++++

Unadvertised/ Excursion Station:

Dunleer*
————————●————————

Major Power Signal boxes	**PRESTON**	Line Ownership Boundaries	RTK ┃ LUL
Carriage Sidings	———————┤C. S.	Colliery (incl. Washery & Opencast site)	——————▲
Freight Marshalling Yard	▱	Power Station	——————△
Freightliner Terminal	———————┤FLT	Oil Refinery	——————●
Locomotive Depot/ Stabling Point	■ BS	Oil Terminal	——————○
Railway Works	▨	Cement Works or Terminal	——————■
Junction Names		Quarry	——————□
	Haughley Junc.		
Country Border (Britain)	/////////////	Other Freight Terminal	———————
Country Border (Ireland)	— · — · — · — ·	County Boundary	— · — · — · — ·
Shipping Service	- - - - - - - - - -	Proposed Railway	===========

IV

DIAGRAM OF MAPS

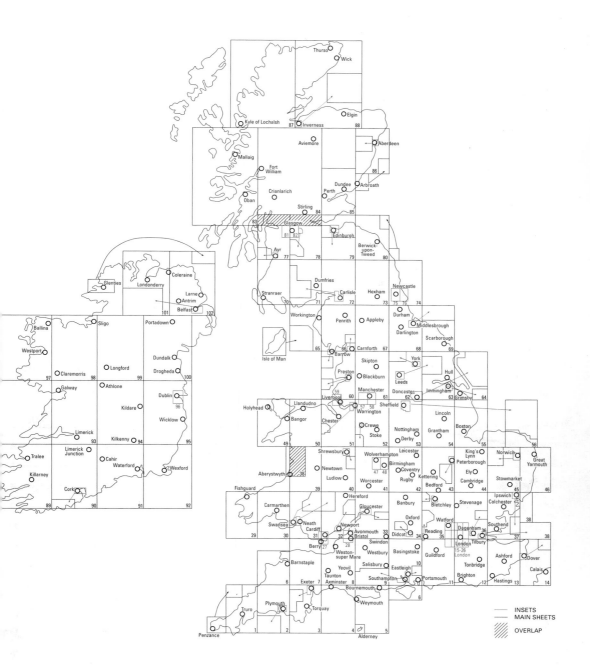

INSETS
MAIN SHEETS
OVERLAP

V

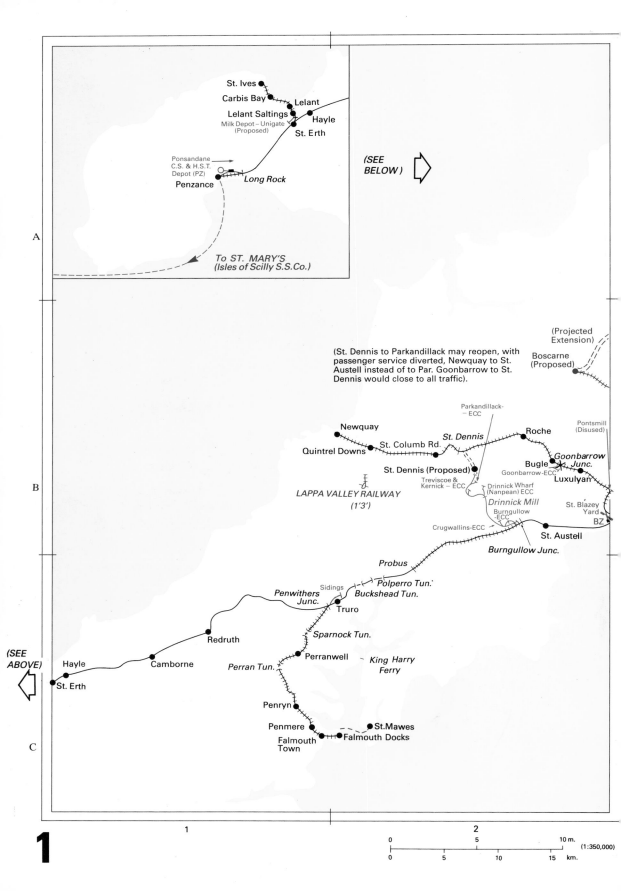

(SEE BELOW)

St. Ives
Carbis Bay
Lelant
Lelant Saltings
Hayle
Milk Depot – Unigate
(Proposed)
St. Erth

Ponsandane
C.S. & H.S.T.
Depot (PZ)
Long Rock
Penzance

To ST. MARY'S
(Isles of Scilly S.S.Co.)

A

(Projected
Extension)

Boscarne
(Proposed)

(St. Dennis to Parkandillack may reopen, with
passenger service diverted, Newquay to St.
Austell instead of to Par. Goonbarrow to St.
Dennis would close to all traffic).

Parkandillack–
ECC

Pontsmill
(Disused)

Newquay
St. Columb Rd.
St. Dennis
Roche
*Goonbarrow
Junc.*

Quintrel Downs
Bugle
Goonbarrow–ECC
Luxulyan

St. Dennis (Proposed)
Treviscoe &
Kernick – ECC
Drinnick Wharf
(Nanpean) ECC
St. Blazey
Yard

B
LAPPA VALLEY RAILWAY
(1'3")
Drinnick Mill
Burngullow
–ECC
BZ

Crugwallins–ECC
St. Austell

Burngullow Junc.

Probus

Polperro Tun.
Sidings
*Penwithers
Junc.*
Buckshead Tun.
Truro

Sparnock Tun.

Redruth
Perranwell
*King Harry
Ferry*

*(SEE
ABOVE)*
Hayle
Camborne
Perran Tun.

St. Erth
Penryn

Penmere
St.Mawes
Penmere
Falmouth Docks
Falmouth
Town

C

1
2

0   5   10 m.

(1:350,000)

0   5   10   15   km.

1

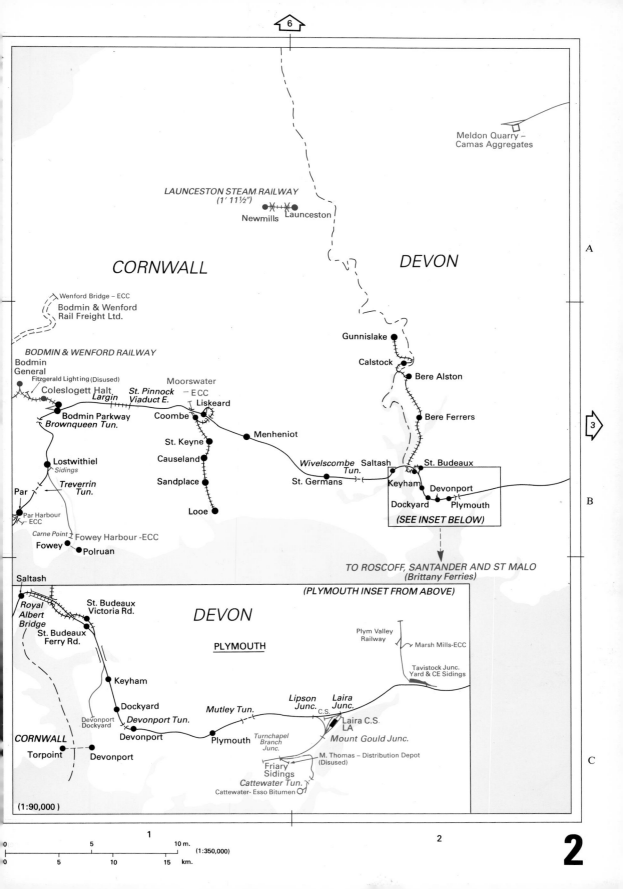

Meldon Quarry –
Camas Aggregates

LAUNCESTON STEAM RAILWAY
(1' 11½")
Newmills   Launceston

A

CORNWALL   *DEVON*

Wenford Bridge – ECC
Bodmin & Wenford
Rail Freight Ltd.

BODMIN & WENFORD RAILWAY

Bodmin   Gunnislake
General
Fitzgerald Lighting (Disused)   Calstock
Coleslogett Halt   Moorswater
         Largin – ECC   Bere Alston
              St. Pinnock
              Viaduct E. Liskeard
Bodmin Parkway   Coombe   Bere Ferrers
Brownqueen Tun.
                     St. Keyne   Menheniot
Lostwithiel   Saltash   St. Budeaux
   Sidings   Causeland   *Wivelscombe*
Par   *Tun.*   Keyham   Devonport
   Treverrin   Sandplace   St. Germans
   Tun.   Dockyard   Plymouth
Par Harbour   *(SEE INSET BELOW)*
– ECC
  Carne Point   Looe
Fowey   Fowey Harbour – ECC
   Polruan

B

3

TO ROSCOFF, SANTANDER AND ST MALO
(Brittany Ferries)

(PLYMOUTH INSET FROM ABOVE)

Saltash
Royal   St. Budeaux   *DEVON*
Albert   Victoria Rd.
Bridge   **PLYMOUTH**
        St. Budeaux   Plym Valley
        Ferry Rd.   Railway   Marsh Mills–ECC

                                                       Tavistock Junc.
              Keyham   Yard & CE Sidings

              Dockyard   *Mutley Tun.* *Lipson*   *Laira*
   Devonport   *Devonport Tun.*   *Junc.*   *Junc.*
   Dockyard   C.S.
CORNWALL   Devonport   Plymouth   Laira C.S.
                                     Turnchapel   LA
Torpoint   Devonport   Branch   *Mount Gould Junc.*
                                     Junc.
                                          M. Thomas – Distribution Depot
                                     Friary   (Disused)
                                     Sidings
                                     Cattewater Tun.
(1:90,000)   Cattewater– Esso Bitumen

C

0   5   10 m.
     (1:350,000)
1   2
0   5   10   15   km.

2

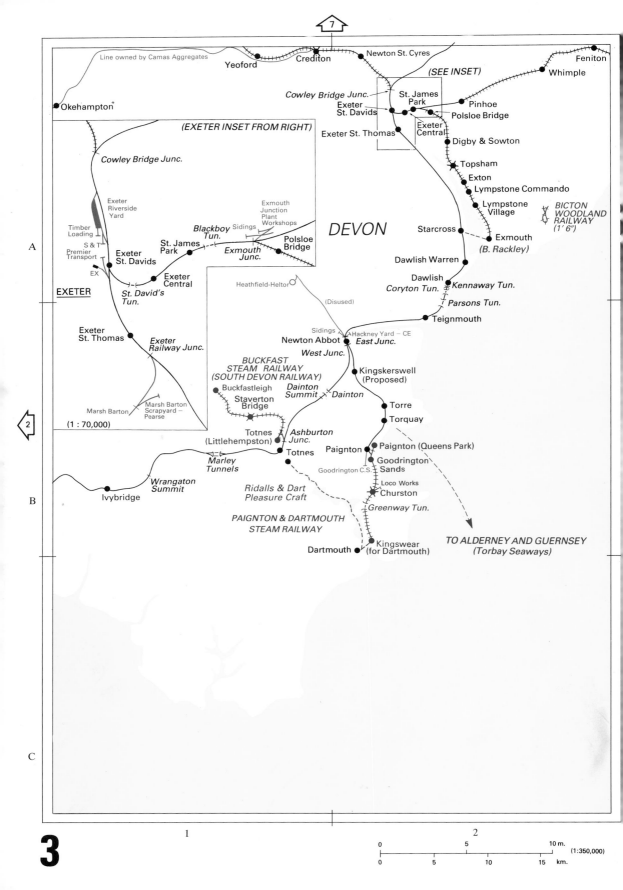

Line owned by Camas Aggregates

Yeoford

Crediton

Newton St. Cyres

Feniton

Whimple

(SEE INSET)

Cowley Bridge Junc.

St. James Park

Exeter St. Davids

Pinhoe

Polsloe Bridge

Okehampton*

Exeter St. Thomas

Exeter Central

Digby & Sowton

(EXETER INSET FROM RIGHT)

Cowley Bridge Junc.

Topsham

Exton

Lympstone Commando

Exeter Riverside Yard

Exmouth Junction Plant Workshops

Lympstone Village

BICTON WOODLAND RAILWAY (1' 6")

Timber Loading

S & T

Blackboy Tun.

Sidings

Polsloe Bridge

Starcross

DEVON

Premier Transport

St. James Park

Exmouth Junc.

Exmouth
(B. Rackley)

A

EX

Exeter St. Davids

Exeter Central

Dawlish Warren

Dawlish

Kennaway Tun.

EXETER

St. David's Tun.

Heathfield-Heltor

Coryton Tun.

Parsons Tun.

(Disused)

Exeter St. Thomas

Exeter Railway Junc.

Sidings

Hackney Yard – CE

Teignmouth

Newton Abbot   *East Junc.*

West Junc.

BUCKFAST STEAM RAILWAY (SOUTH DEVON RAILWAY)

Kingskerswell
(Proposed)

Buckfastleigh

Dainton Summit

Dainton

Torre

Marsh Barton Scrapyard – Pearse

Staverton Bridge

Torquay

Marsh Barton

(1 : 70,000)

Totnes
(Littlehempston)

Ashburton Junc.

Paignton

Paignton (Queens Park)

Totnes

Goodrington C.S.

Goodrington Sands

Marley Tunnels

Wrangaton Summit

Ridalls & Dart Pleasure Craft

Loco Works
Churston

B

Ivybridge

Greenway Tun.

PAIGNTON & DARTMOUTH STEAM RAILWAY

Dartmouth

Kingswear
(for Dartmouth)

TO ALDERNEY AND GUERNSEY
(Torbay Seaways)

C

3

1

2

0   5   10 m.

(1:350,000)

0   5   10   15   km.

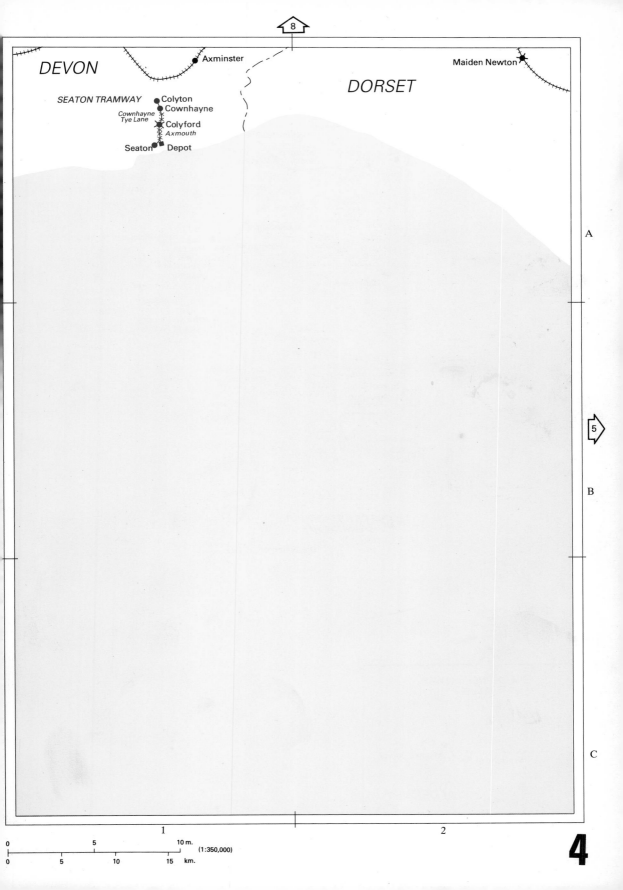

DEVON

Axminster

SEATON TRAMWAY • Colyton
• Cownhayne
Cownhayne
Tye Lane ✕ Colyford
✕ Axmouth
Seaton • ✕ Depot

DORSET

Maiden Newton

A

5

B

C

1

2

0   5   10 m.
(1:350,000)
0   5   10   15   km.

4

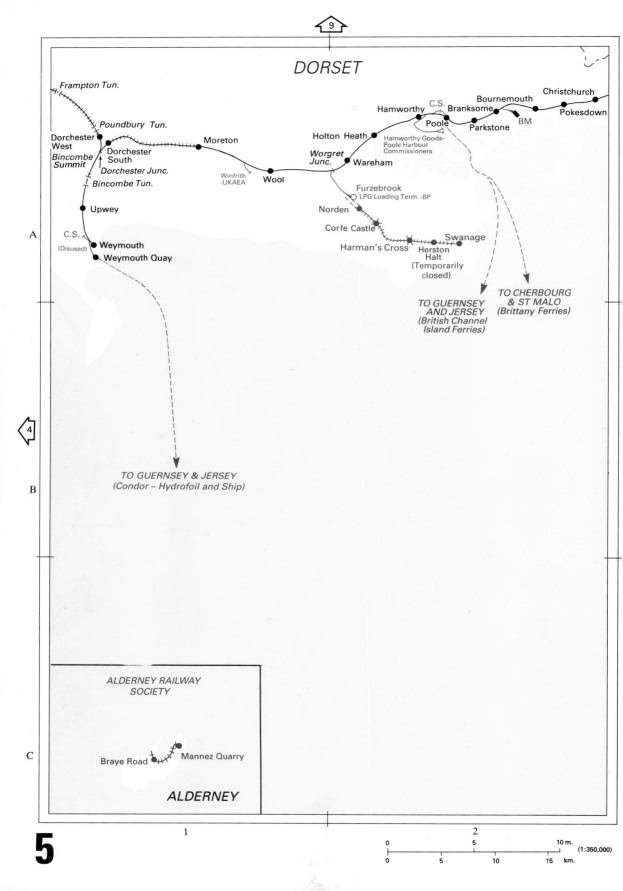

DORSET

Frampton Tun.

Poundbury Tun.

Dorchester
West

Bincombe
Summit

Dorchester
South

Dorchester Junc.

Bincombe Tun.

Moreton

Winfrith
-UKAEA

Wool

Holton Heath

Worgret
Junc.

Wareham

Hamworthy

C.S.

Poole

Hamworthy Goods-
Poole Harbour
Commissioners

Branksome

Parkstone

Bournemouth

BM

Christchurch

Pokesdown

Upwey

C.S.
(Disused)

Weymouth

Weymouth Quay

Furzebrook
LPG Loading Term.-BP

Norden

Corfe Castle

Harman's Cross

Herston
Halt
(Temporarily
closed)

Swanage

TO GUERNSEY
AND JERSEY
(British Channel
Island Ferries)

TO CHERBOURG
& ST MALO
(Brittany Ferries)

TO GUERNSEY & JERSEY
(Condor – Hydrofoil and Ship)

A

4

B

C

ALDERNEY RAILWAY
SOCIETY

Braye Road

Mannez Quarry

ALDERNEY

5

1

2

0   5   10 m.

0   5   10   15   km.

(1:350,000)

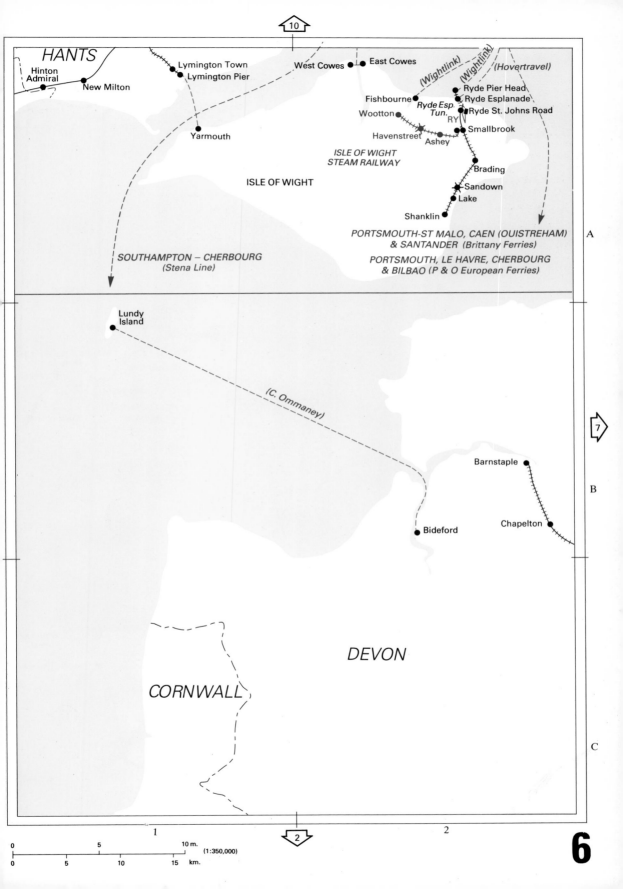

HANTS

Hinton
Admiral
New Milton

Lymington Town
Lymington Pier

West Cowes East Cowes

(Wightlink) *(Wightlink)* *(Hovertravel)*

Yarmouth

Fishbourne
Wootton

Ryde Pier Head
Ryde Esplanade
Ryde Esp. Ryde St. Johns Road
Tun. RY
Smallbrook

Havenstreet
Ashey

*ISLE OF WIGHT
STEAM RAILWAY*

ISLE OF WIGHT

Brading

Sandown
Lake

Shanklin

A

**PORTSMOUTH-ST MALO, CAEN (OUISTREHAM)
& SANTANDER (Brittany Ferries)**

**PORTSMOUTH, LE HAVRE, CHERBOURG
& BILBAO (P & O European Ferries)**

SOUTHAMPTON – CHERBOURG
(Stena Line)

Lundy
Island

(C. Ommaney)

7

Barnstaple

B

Bideford

Chapelton

DEVON

CORNWALL

C

0   5   10 m.
(1:350,000)
0   5   10   15   km.

1   2   2

6

10

2

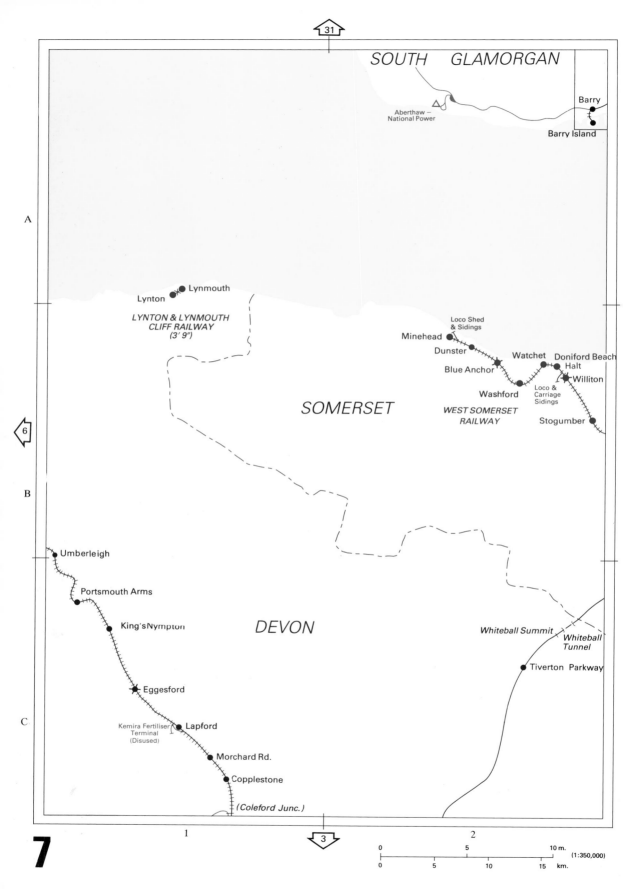

SOUTH GLAMORGAN

Barry

Aberthaw –
National Power

Barry Island

A

Lynmouth

Lynton

*LYNTON & LYNMOUTH
CLIFF RAILWAY
(3' 9")*

Loco Shed
& Sidings

Minehead

Dunster

Watchet

Doniford Beach
Halt

Blue Anchor

Williton

SOMERSET

Washford

Loco &
Carriage
Sidings

*WEST SOMERSET
RAILWAY*

Stogumber

6

B

Umberleigh

Portsmouth Arms

King's Nympton

DEVON

Whiteball Summit

*Whiteball
Tunnel*

Tiverton Parkway

Eggesford

C

Kemira Fertiliser
Terminal
(Disused)

Lapford

Morchard Rd.

Copplestone

(Coleford Junc.)

7

2

0   5   10 m.
|——————|——————|
0   5   10   15   km.

(1:350,000)

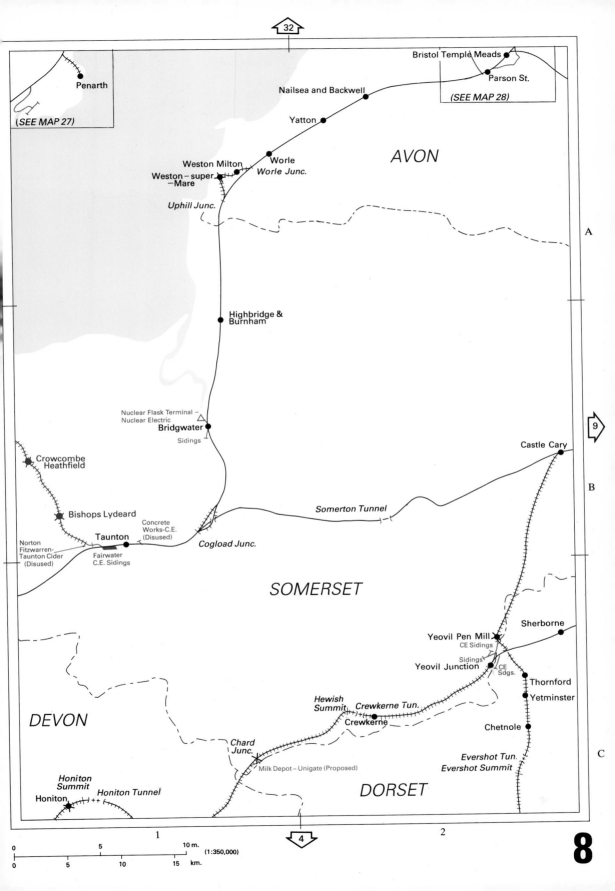

32

Penarth

(SEE MAP 27)

Bristol Temple Meads

Parson St.

(SEE MAP 28)

Nailsea and Backwell

Yatton

AVON

Worle

Weston Milton

Weston – super
– Mare

Worle Junc.

Uphill Junc.

A

Highbridge &
Burnham

Nuclear Flask Terminal –
Nuclear Electric

Bridgwater

Sidings

Castle Cary

9

Crowcombe
Heathfield

B

Bishops Lydeard

Somerton Tunnel

Concrete
Works-C.E.
(Disused)

Taunton

Norton
Fitzwarren-
Taunton Cider
(Disused)

Fairwater
C.E. Sidings

Cogload Junc.

SOMERSET

Sherborne

Yeovil Pen Mill

CE Sidings

Sidings

Yeovil Junction

CE
Sdgs.

Thornford

Yetminster

DEVON

*Hewish
Summit*

Crewkerne Tun.

Crewkerne

Chetnole

*Chard
Junc.*

Milk Depot – Unigate (Proposed)

Evershot Tun.

Evershot Summit

C

*Honiton
Summit*

Honiton Tunnel

Honiton

DORSET

0		5		10 m.

(1:350,000)

0	5	10	15	km.

1

4

2

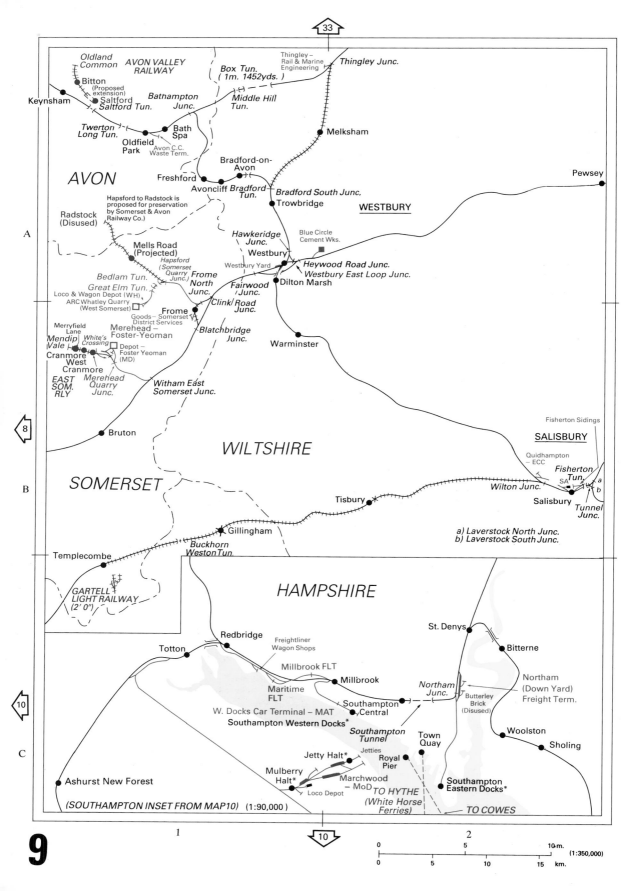

Oldland Common
AVON VALLEY RAILWAY
*Thingley –
Rail & Marine
Engineering*
Thingley Junc.

Bitton
(Proposed
extension)
*Box Tun.
(1m. 1452yds.)*

Keynsham
Saltford
Saltford Tun.
*Batnampton
Junc.*
*Middle Hill
Tun.*

Melksham

*Twerton
Long Tun.*
Bath
Spa
Oldfield
Park
*Avon C.C.
Waste Term.*
*Bradford-on-
Avon*

AVON
Freshford
Avoncliff *Bradford
Tun.*
Bradford South Junc.
Trowbridge
Pewsey

WESTBURY

*Hawkeridge
Junc.*
Blue Circle
Cement Wks.

Radstock
(Disused)
*Hapsford to Radstock is
proposed for preservation
by Somerset & Avon
Railway Co.)*
Mells Road
(Projected)
*Hapsford
(Somerset
Quarry Junc.)*
*Frome
North
Junc.*
Westbury
Westbury Yard
Heywood Road Junc.
Westbury East Loop Junc.

Bedlam Tun.
Great Elm Tun.
Loco & Wagon Depot (WH)
*ARC Whatley Quarry
(West Somerset)*
*Fairwood
Junc.*
Dilton Marsh

*Merryfield
Lane*
*White's
Crossing*
*Clink/ Road
Junc.*
Goods – Somerset
District Services
Merehead –
Foster-Yeoman

*Mendip
Vale*
Cranmore
West
Cranmore
*Depot –
Foster Yeoman (MD)*
*Blatchbridge
Junc.*

EAST
SOM.
RLY
*Merehead
Quarry
Junc.*
Warminster

Fisherton Sidings

*Witham East
Somerset Junc.*

SALISBURY

WILTSHIRE
*Quidhampton
– ECC*
*Fisherton
Tun.*

Bruton
SA
a
b

SOMERSET
Wilton Junc.
*Tunnel
Junc.*

B
Tisbury
Salisbury

Gillingham
*a) Laverstock North Junc.
b) Laverstock South Junc.*

Templecombe
*Buckhorn
Weston Tun.*

HAMPSHIRE

*GARTELL
LIGHT RAILWAY
(2' 0")*

St. Denys
Bitterne

Redbridge
*Freightliner
Wagon Shops*
Northam
(Down Yard)
Freight Term.

Totton
Millbrook FLT
*Northam
Junc.*
Butterley
Brick
(Disused)

Maritime
FLT
Millbrook
Woolston

W. Docks Car Terminal – MAT
*Southampton Western Docks**
Southampton
Central
Sholing

*Southampton
Tunnel*
Town
Quay

Jetties
Jetty Halt*
Royal
Pier

Ashurst New Forest
Mulberry
Halt*
Marchwood
– MoD
Southampton
Eastern Docks*

Loco Depot
TO HYTHE
(White Horse
Ferries)

(SOUTHAMPTON INSET FROM MAP10) (1:90,000)
TO COWES

9

1
10
2

0   5   10 m.
(1:350,000)
0   5   10   15   km.

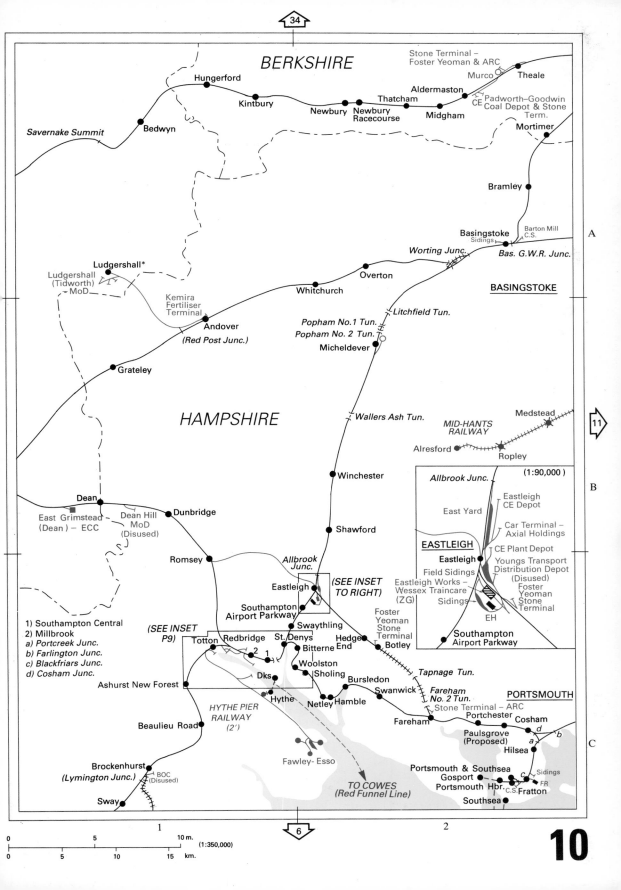

BERKSHIRE

Stone Terminal –
Foster Yeoman & ARC

Murco

Theale

Hungerford

Kintbury

Thatcham

Aldermaston

Newbury

Newbury
Racecourse

Midgham

CE

Padworth–Goodwin
Coal Depot & Stone
Term.

Savernake Summit

Bedwyn

Mortimer

Bramley

Basingstoke

Barton Mill
C.S.

Sidings

BASINGSTOKE

Worting Junc.

A

Bas. G.W.R. Junc.

Ludgershall*

Ludgershall
(Tidworth)
MoD

Kemira
Fertiliser
Terminal

Overton

Whitchurch

Litchfield Tun.

Popham No.1 Tun.
Popham No.2 Tun.

Andover

(Red Post Junc.)

Micheldever

Grateley

HAMPSHIRE

Wallers Ash Tun.

*MID-HANTS
RAILWAY*

Medstead

Alresford

Ropley

11

Winchester

(1:90,000)

Allbrook Junc.

B

Dean

East Grimstead
(Dean) – ECC

Dean Hill
MoD
(Disused)

Dunbridge

East Yard

Eastleigh
CE Depot

Car Terminal –
Axial Holdings

Shawford

EASTLEIGH

Eastleigh

CE Plant Depot

Romsey

*Allbrook
Junc.*

Eastleigh

*(SEE INSET
TO RIGHT)*

Field Sidings

Youngs Transport
Distribution Depot
(Disused)

Eastleigh Works –
Wessex Traincare
(ZG)

Foster
Yeoman
Stone
Terminal

Southampton
Airport Parkway

Swaythling

EH

*(SEE INSET
P9)*

Totton

Redbridge

St. Denys

Hedge
End

Botley

Foster
Yeoman
Stone
Terminal

Sidings

Southampton
Airport Parkway

1) Southampton Central
2) Millbrook
a) Portcreek Junc.
b) Farlington Junc.
c) Blackfriars Junc.
d) Cosham Junc.

Bitterne

Woolston

Sholing

Bursledon

Swanwick

Tapnage Tun.

PORTSMOUTH

Dks

Netley

Hamble

*Fareham
No.2 Tun.*

Ashurst New Forest

*HYTHE PIER
RAILWAY
(2')*

Hythe

Stone Terminal – ARC

Portchester

Cosham

d

Beaulieu Road

Fareham

Paulsgrove
(Proposed)

a

b

Hilsea

C

Fawley- Esso

Brockenhurst
(Lymington Junc.)

BOC
(Disused)

*TO COWES
(Red Funnel Line)*

Portsmouth & Southsea

Gosport

Portsmouth Hbr.

Sidings

c

FR

Sway

C.S.

Fratton

Southsea

1

5

10 m.

(1:350,000)

6

2

10

0   5   10   m.

0   5   10   15   km.

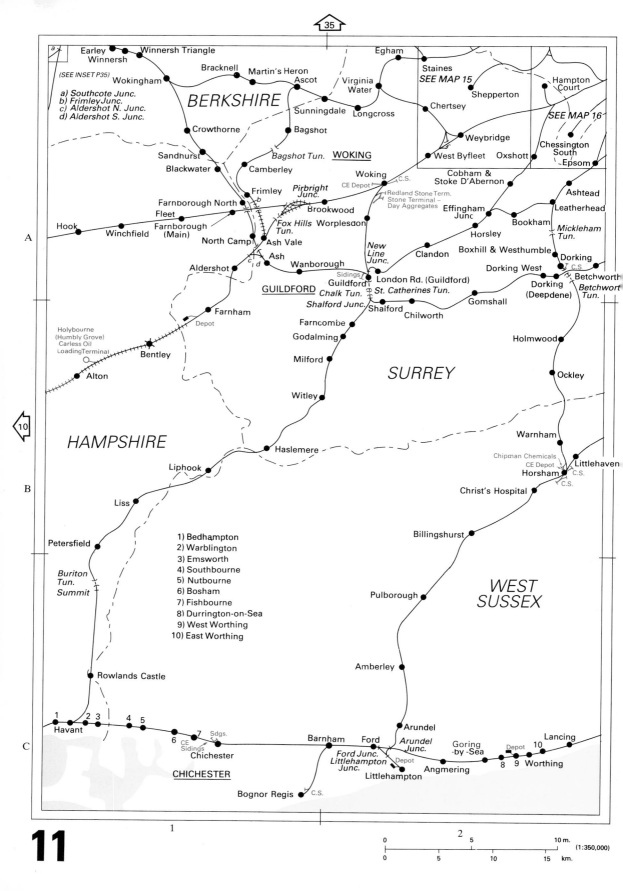

a
(SEE INSET P35)

a) Southcote Junc.
b) Frimley Junc.
c) Aldershot N. Junc.
d) Aldershot S. Junc.

Earley
Winnersh
Winnersh Triangle
Bracknell
Martin's Heron
Ascot
Egham
Staines
SEE MAP 15
Shepperton
Hampton
Court
Wokingham
BERKSHIRE
Virginia
Water
Chertsey
SEE MAP 16
Crowthorne
Sunningdale
Longcross
Weybridge
Chessington
South
Sandhurst
Bagshot
Epsom
Blackwater
Bagshot Tun.
WOKING
West Byfleet
Oxshott
Camberley
Woking
C.S.
Cobham &
Stoke D'Abernon
Ashtead
Frimley
Pirbright
Junc.
CE Depot
Leatherhead
Farnborough North
b
Brookwood
Redland Stone Term.
Stone Terminal –
Day Aggregates
Effingham
Junc.
Bookham
Mickleham
Tun.
Fleet
Fox Hills
Worplesdon
Horsley
Hook
Farnborough
(Main)
Tun.
Boxhill & Westhumble
Dorking
A
Winchfield
North Camp
Ash Vale
New
Line
Junc.
Clandon
Dorking West
C.S.
Aldershot
c
d
Ash
Wanborough
Betchworth
Sidings
London Rd. (Guildford)
Dorking
(Deepdene)
Betchwort
Tun.
GUILDFORD
Guildford
Chalk Tun.
St. Catherines Tun.
Gomshall
Farnham
Shalford Junc.
Shalford
Chilworth
Depot
Farncombe
Holmwood
Holybourne
(Humbly Grove)
Carless Oil
LoadingTerminal
Godalming
Bentley
Milford
SURREY
Ockley
Alton
Witley
Warnham
HAMPSHIRE
Chipman Chemicals
CE Depot
Littlehaven
Haslemere
Horsham
C.S.
Liphook
C.S.
B
Christ's Hospital
Liss
Billingshurst
Petersfield
1) Bedhampton
2) Warblington
3) Emsworth
4) Southbourne
5) Nutbourne
6) Bosham
7) Fishbourne
8) Durrington-on-Sea
9) West Worthing
10) East Worthing
Buriton
Tun.
Summit
Pulborough
WEST
SUSSEX
Amberley
Rowlands Castle
1
2 3
4 5
7
Sdgs.
Arundel
Lancing
Havant
6
CE
Sidings
Barnham
Ford
Arundel
Junc.
Goring
-by-Sea
Depot
10
Chichester
Ford Junc.
Littlehampton
Junc.
Depot
8 9
Worthing
C
CHICHESTER
Littlehampton
Angmering
Bognor Regis
C.S.

10

11

1

0   2   10 m.
                  5   (1:350,000)
0   5   10   15   km.

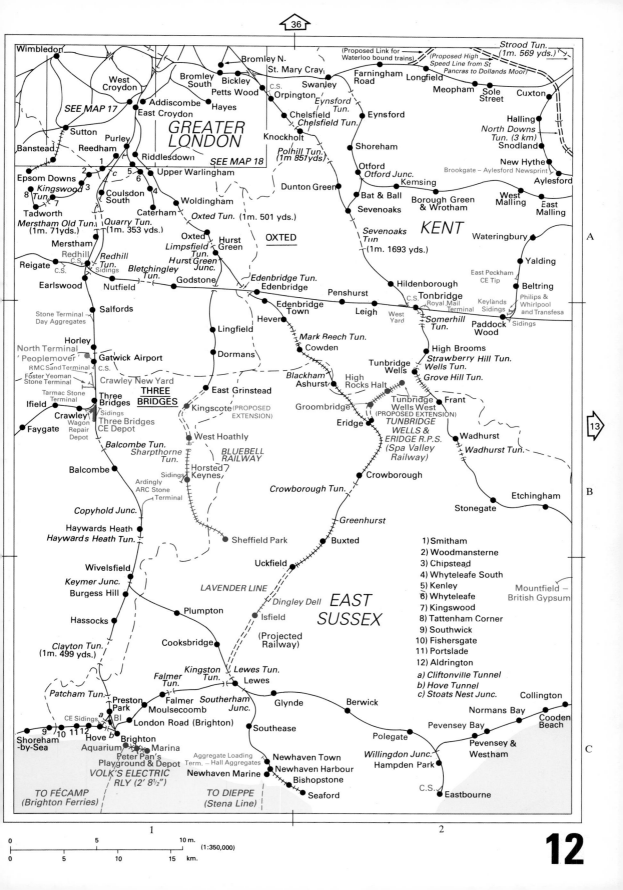

Wimbledon

West Croydon

SEE MAP 17

Sutton

Banstead

Purley

Reedham

Epsom Downs

Kingswood Tun.

Tadworth

Merstham Old Tun. (1m. 71yds.)

Coulsdon South

Caterham

Merstham

Reigate

Redhill C.S.

Redhill Tun.

Sidings

Earlswood

Nutfield

Salfords

Stone Terminal Day Aggregates

Horley

North Terminal 'Peoplemover'

RMC Sand Terminal

Foster Yeoman Stone Terminal

Tarmac Stone Terminal

Ifield

Crawley

Faygate

Three Bridges

THREE BRIDGES

Sidings

Wagon Repair Depot

Three Bridges CE Depot

Balcombe Tun.

Balcombe

Sharpthorne Tun.

Ardingly ARC Stone Terminal

Copyhold Junc.

Haywards Heath

Haywards Heath Tun.

Wivelsfield

Keymer Junc.

Burgess Hill

Hassocks

Clayton Tun. (1m. 499 yds.)

Patcham Tun.

CE Sidings

Shoreham -by-Sea

9 10 11 12

Hove

Aquarium

Peter Pan's Playground & Depot

VOLK'S ELECTRIC RLY (2' 8½")

TO FÉCAMP (Brighton Ferries)

Preston Park

London Road (Brighton)

Moulsecoomb

Brighton

Marina

Bromley N.

St. Mary Cray

Bromley South

Bickley

Petts Wood

Hayes

Addiscombe

East Croydon

GREATER LONDON

SEE MAP 18

Upper Warlingham

Woldingham

Oxted Tun. (1m. 501 yds.)

Oxted

Limpsfield Tun.

Hurst Green

Hurst Green Junc.

OXTED

Godstone

Bletchingley Tun.

Edenbridge Tun.

Edenbridge

Edenbridge Town

Hever

Lingfield

Dormans

East Grinstead

Kingscote (PROPOSED EXTENSION)

West Hoathly

BLUEBELL RAILWAY

Horsted Keynes

Sidings

Sheffield Park

LAVENDER LINE

Plumpton

Cooksbridge

Dingley Dell

Isfield

(Projected Railway)

EAST SUSSEX

Kingston Tun.

Falmer Tun.

Falmer

Southerham Junc.

Lewes Tun.

Lewes

Glynde

Southease

Newhaven Town

Newhaven Harbour

Aggregate Loading Term. – Hall Aggregates

Newhaven Marine

Bishopstone

Seaford

TO DIEPPE (Stena Line)

Orpington

Swanley

Chelsfield

Chelsfield Tun.

Knockholt

C.S.

Polhill Tun. (1m 851yds.)

Eynsford Tun.

Eynsford

Shoreham

Otford

Otford Junc.

Dunton Green

Bat & Ball

Sevenoaks

Sevenoaks Tun. (1m. 1693 yds.)

Penshurst

Leigh

West Yard

Hildenborough

C.S.

Tonbridge

Royal Mail Terminal

Somerhill Tun.

Paddock Wood

Cowden

Mark Beech Tun.

Blackham

Ashurst

High Rocks Halt

Groombridge

Eridge

Tunbridge Wells West (PROPOSED EXTENSION)

TUNBRIDGE WELLS & ERIDGE R.P.S. (Spa Valley Railway)

High Brooms

Strawberry Hill Tun.

Tunbridge Wells

Wells Tun.

Grove Hill Tun.

Frant

Wadhurst

Wadhurst Tun.

Crowborough

Crowborough Tun.

Greenhurst

Buxted

Uckfield

Stonegate

Etchingham

Berwick

Polegate

Willingdon Junc.

Hampden Park

C.S.

Eastbourne

Normans Bay

Pevensey Bay

Pevensey & Westham

Cooden Beach

Collington

KENT

Farningham Road

Longfield

Meopham

Sole Street

Cuxton

Halling

North Downs Tun. (3 km)

Snodland

New Hythe

Brookgate – Aylesford Newsprint

Aylesford

West Malling

East Malling

Wateringbury

Yalding

Beltring

East Peckham CE Tip

Philips & Whirlpool and Transfesa

Keylands Sidings

Sidings

(Proposed Link for Waterloo bound trains)

(Proposed High Speed Line from St Pancras to Dollands Moor)

Strood Tun. (1m. 569 yds.)

Kemsing

Borough Green & Wrotham

A

B

13

C

1

2

1) Smitham
2) Woodmansterne
3) Chipstead
4) Whyteleafe South
5) Kenley
6) Whyteleafe
7) Kingswood
8) Tattenham Corner
9) Southwick
10) Fishersgate
11) Portslade
12) Aldrington
a) Cliftonville Tunnel
b) Hove Tunnel
c) Stoats Nest Junc.

Mountfield – British Gypsum

0   5   10 m.
(1:350,000)
0   5   10   15   km.

12

Strood
Rochester
a
Fort
Pitt Tun.
Chatham
Chatham Tun.
Gillingham Tun.
Gillingham
Gl
Rainham
Newington
Kemsley
d
b
2
c
2
Kemsley Down
Sittingbourne
Sittingbourne
Teynham

GILLINGHAM
Swale
King's Ferry Bridge
Ridham Dock Scrapyard – Ridham Sea Terminals
2

SITTINGBOURNE & KEMSLEY LT.RLY. (2'6")

Chestfield & Swalecliffe
Herne Bay
Whitstable
Seasalter (Projected)
Sturry

1) Freight Terminals – Wood & Victa Railfreight
2) Grovehurst Paper Mill
3) Maintenance Depot

Faversham
C.S.

Canterbury West
Canterbury East
Bekesbourne

a) Rochester Bridge Junc.
b) Western Junc.
c) Eastern Junc.
d) Middle Junc.
e) Saltwood Junc.
f) Continental Junc.

Selling
Selling Tun.
Chartham
Chilham
Adisham
Aylesham
Snowdown

Allington – ARC Stone Terminal
Barming
Maidstone East
Bearsted
Wheeler St. Tun.
Hollingbourne Tun.
Hollingbourne
Harrietsham
East Farleigh
Maidstone West
Maidstone Barracks
Harrietsham Tun.
Sandway Tun.
Lenham

A

MAIDSTONE WEST
Charing

(Proposed High Speed Line from St Pancras to Dollands Moor)

Hothfield – Tarmac Stone Term.
Wye
Ashford Tun.
ARC Stone Term.
C.S.
CE Depot

Marden
Staplehurst
Headcorn
Pluckley
Chart Leacon Works – ABB (AF)
Ashford International
Kimberley C.S.

KENT

ASHFORD

CE Plant Depot
Sevington (Disused)

Dollands Moor Sidings
Cheriton Shuttle Terminal
Depot
Martello Tun.
Sandling Tun.
Westenhanger
Sandling
e Maint. Depot.
Saltwood Tun.
Hythe
Folkestone Harbour

12

KENT & EAST SUSSEX RAILWAY
Depot
Rolvenden
Tenterden Town

Ham Street

Burmarsh Road Halt *
Dymchurch
Jefferstone Lane

Folkestone Central
Folkestone West
Folkestone East Junc.

B

ROTHER VALLEY RLY. (PROPOSED EXTENSION)
Bodiam
Wittersham Road
Northiam
Dixter (Not in regular use)
Appledore

ROMNEY, HYTHE & DYMCHURCH RAILWAY (1'3")

C.S.
Loco Depot
New Romney
P. W. Depot

Robertsbridge
Mountfield Tun.
Mountfield Sidings

EAST SUSSEX

Rye
Winchelsea
Romney Sands

Dungeness-Nuclear Electric
Dungeness

Battle
Doleham
Three Oaks
Mount Pleasant Tun.
C.S. (Disused)
Ore Tun.
Crowhurst
West St.
Hastings Tun.
C.S.
Ore
Hastings
St. Leonards Warrior Sq.
Bopeep Junc. & Tun.
St. Leonards Depot – St. Leonards Rail Engineering Ltd.
Bexhill

C

1
2
0   5   10 m.
(1:350,000)
0   5   10   15 km.

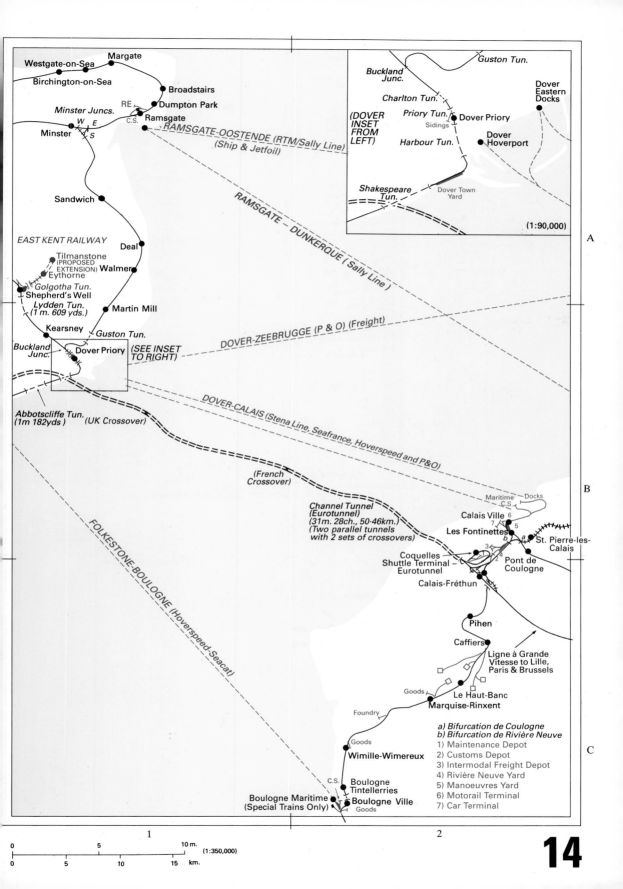

Margate
Westgate-on-Sea
Birchington-on-Sea
Broadstairs
Dumpton Park
Minster Juncs. RE
W E Ramsgate
Minster N S C.S.
RAMSGATE-OOSTENDE (RTM/Sally Line)
(Ship & Jetfoil)

RAMSGATE – DUNKERQUE (Sally Line)

Sandwich

EAST KENT RAILWAY
Deal
Tilmanstone (PROPOSED EXTENSION) Walmer
Eythorne
Golgotha Tun.
Shepherd's Well
Lydden Tun.
(1 m. 609 yds.) Martin Mill
Kearsney Guston Tun.
Buckland Junc. Dover Priory (SEE INSET TO RIGHT)

DOVER-ZEEBRUGGE (P & O) (Freight)

Abbotscliffe Tun.
(1m 182yds) (UK Crossover)

DOVER-CALAIS (Stena Line, Seafrance, Hoverspeed and P&O)

(French Crossover)

Channel Tunnel
(Eurotunnel)
(31m. 28ch., 50.46km.)
(Two parallel tunnels
with 2 sets of crossovers)

FOLKESTONE-BOULOGNE (Hoverspeed-Seacat)

Maritime Docks
C.S.
Calais Ville 6
7 5
Les Fontinettes b a
3 St. Pierre-les-Calais
2 Pont de Coulogne
Coquelles 4
Shuttle Terminal – Eurotunnel
Calais-Fréthun

Pihen

Caffiers
Ligne à Grande Vitesse to Lille, Paris & Brussels

Goods
Le Haut-Banc
Foundry Marquise-Rinxent

a) Bifurcation de Coulogne
b) Bifurcation de Rivière Neuve
1) Maintenance Depot
2) Customs Depot
3) Intermodal Freight Depot
4) Rivière Neuve Yard
5) Manoeuvres Yard
6) Motorail Terminal
7) Car Terminal

Goods

Wimille-Wimereux

C.S.
Boulogne Tintellerries
Boulogne Maritime
(Special Trains Only) Boulogne Ville
Goods

Dover Inset

Guston Tun.
Buckland Junc.
Charlton Tun.
Priory Tun. Dover Priory
Sidings
Harbour Tun.
Dover Eastern Docks
Dover Hoverport
(DOVER INSET FROM LEFT)
Shakespeare Tun.
Dover Town Yard
(1:90,000)

A

B

C

1 10 m.
0 5 (1:350,000)
0 5 10 15 km.
2

14

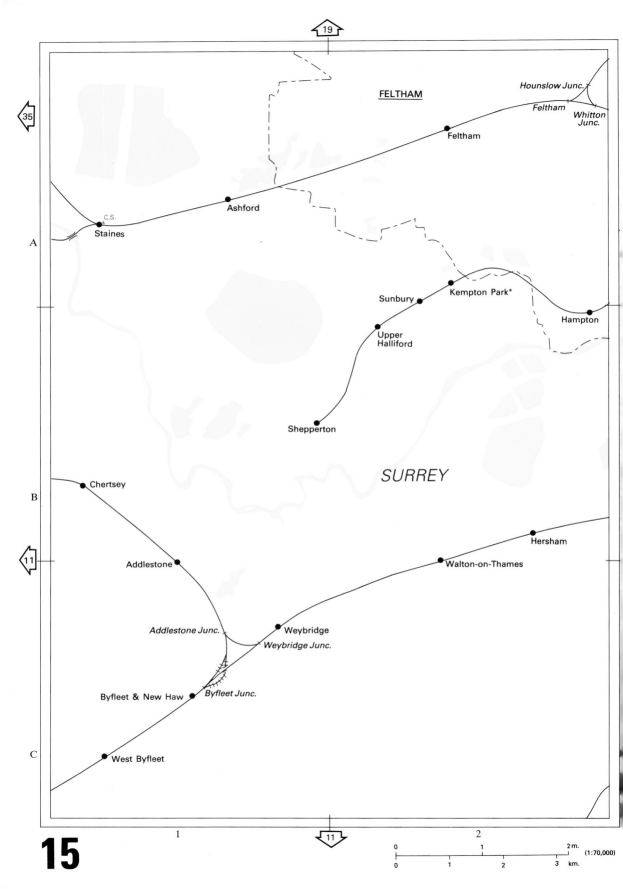

19

35

FELTHAM

Hounslow Junc.

Feltham

Whitton Junc.

Feltham

C.S.

Staines

Ashford

A

Sunbury

Kempton Park*

Hampton

Upper
Halliford

Shepperton

SURREY

Chertsey

B

Hersham

11

Addlestone

Walton-on-Thames

Addlestone Junc.

Weybridge

Weybridge Junc.

Byfleet & New Haw

Byfleet Junc.

C

West Byfleet

11

15

1

2

0   1   2 m.

0   1   2   3   km.

(1:70,000)

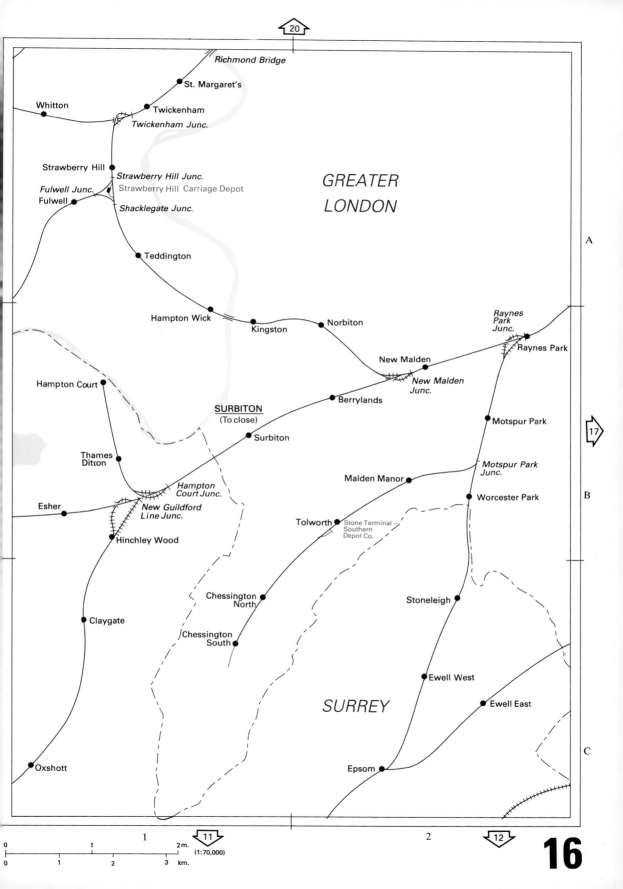

20

Richmond Bridge

St. Margaret's

Whitton

Twickenham

Twickenham Junc.

Strawberry Hill

Strawberry Hill Junc.

Strawberry Hill Carriage Depot

Fulwell Junc.

Fulwell

Shacklegate Junc.

GREATER LONDON

A

Teddington

Hampton Wick

Kingston

Norbiton

Raynes Park Junc.

Raynes Park

New Malden

New Malden Junc.

Hampton Court

Berrylands

SURBITON
(To close)

Surbiton

Motspur Park

17

Thames Ditton

Esher

Hampton Court Junc.

New Guildford Line Junc.

Malden Manor

Motspur Park Junc.

Worcester Park

B

Tolworth

Stone Terminal — Southern Depot Co.

Hinchley Wood

Chessington North

Stoneleigh

Claygate

Chessington South

SURREY

Ewell West

Ewell East

C

Oxshott

Epsom

0   1   2 m.
0   1   2   3 km.

1   11
(1:70,000)

2   12

16

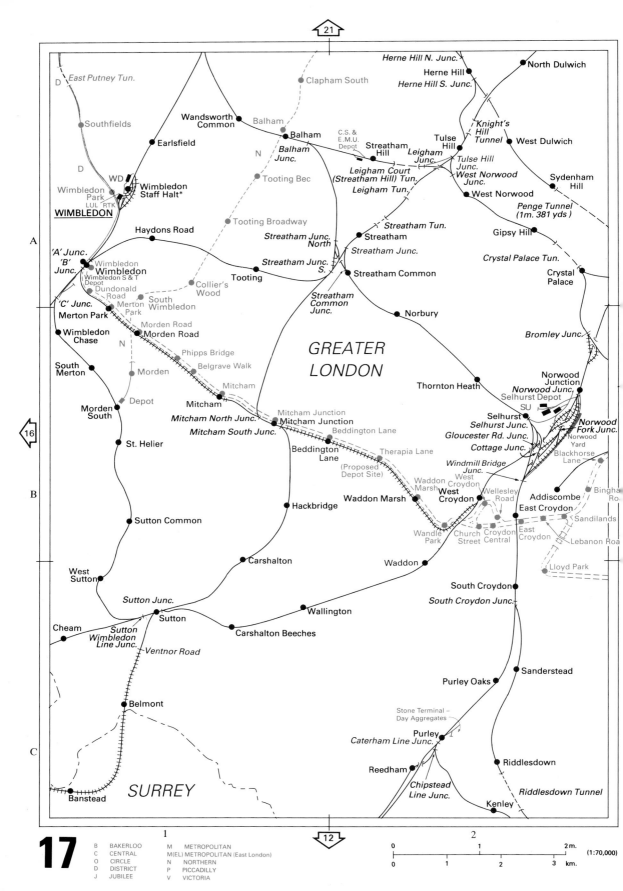

East Putney Tun.

D

Southfields

Clapham South

Herne Hill N. Junc.

Herne Hill

Herne Hill S. Junc.

North Dulwich

Wandsworth Common

Balham

Earlsfield

Balham

Balham Junc.

C.S. & E.M.U. Depot

Streatham Hill

Knight's Hill Tunnel

Tulse Hill

West Dulwich

Leigham Junc.

N

Tooting Bec

Leigham Court (Streatham Hill) Tun.

Tulse Hill Junc.

West Norwood Junc.

Sydenham Hill

WD

Wimbledon Park

Wimbledon Staff Halt*

Leigham Tun.

West Norwood

Penge Tunnel (1m. 381 yds)

Wimbledon Park

LUL RTK

WIMBLEDON

Tooting Broadway

Gipsy Hill

A

Haydons Road

Streatham Junc. North

Streatham

Streatham Tun.

Crystal Palace Tun.

'A' Junc.

'B' Junc.

Wimbledon

Wimbledon S & T Depot

Collier's Wood

Tooting

Streatham Junc. S.

Streatham Common

Crystal Palace

Dundonald Road

South Wimbledon

'C' Junc.

Merton Park

Merton Park

Streatham Common Junc.

Norbury

Wimbledon Chase

Morden Road

Morden Road

GREATER LONDON

Bromley Junc.

South Merton

N

Phipps Bridge

Belgrave Walk

Thornton Heath

Norwood Junction

Norwood Junc.

Morden

Mitcham

Selhurst Depot

Depot

Mitcham

Mitcham Junction

SU

Norwood Fork Junc.

Morden South

Mitcham North Junc.

Mitcham Junction

Selhurst

Selhurst Junc.

St. Helier

Mitcham South Junc.

Beddington Lane

Gloucester Rd. Junc.

Norwood Yard

Beddington Lane

Therapia Lane

Cottage Junc.

Blackhorse Lane

(Proposed Depot Site)

Windmill Bridge Junc.

West Croydon

Bingham Ro

Sutton Common

Hackbridge

Waddon Marsh

Waddon Marsh

West Croydon

Wellesley Road

Addiscombe

East Croydon

B

Carshalton

Waddon

Wandle Park

Church Street

Croydon Central

East Croydon

Sandilands

Lebanon Roa

West Sutton

Lloyd Park

Sutton Junc.

Wallington

South Croydon

Cheam

Sutton

South Croydon Junc.

Sutton Wimbledon Line Junc.

Carshalton Beeches

Ventnor Road

Sanderstead

Belmont

Purley Oaks

Stone Terminal – Day Aggregates

Purley

C

Caterham Line Junc.

Riddlesdown

SURREY

Reedham

Chipstead Line Junc.

Riddlesdown Tunnel

Banstead

Kenley

17

B	BAKERLOO	M	METROPOLITAN
C	CENTRAL	M(EL)	METROPOLITAN (East London)
O	CIRCLE	N	NORTHERN
D	DISTRICT	P	PICCADILLY
J	JUBILEE	V	VICTORIA

0 ... 1 ... 2 m.

0 ... 1 ... 2 ... 3 km.

(1:70,000)

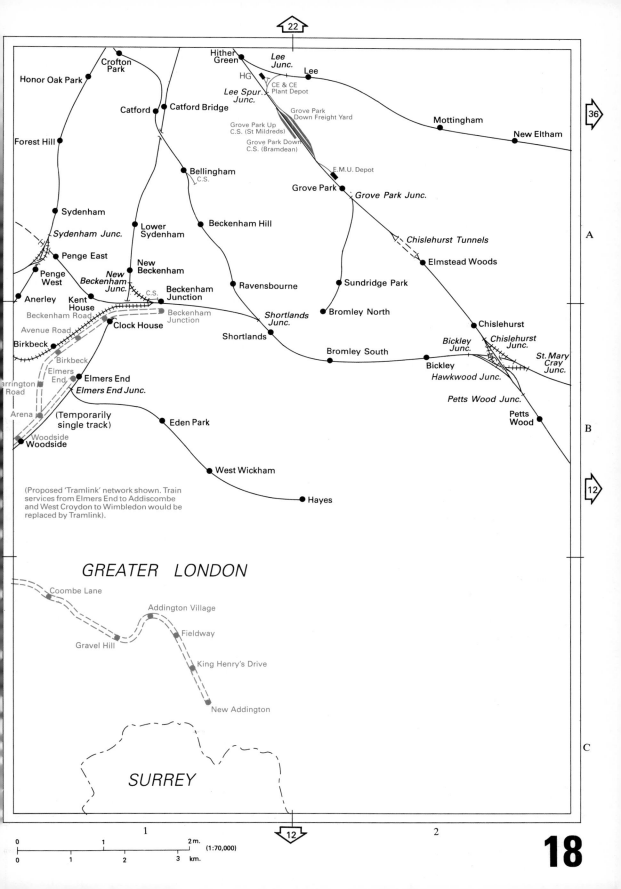

Hither Green
HG
Lee Junc.
Lee
Lee Spur Junc.
CE & CE Plant Depot
Crofton Park
Honor Oak Park
Catford
Catford Bridge
Grove Park Down Freight Yard
Mottingham
New Eltham
Grove Park Up C.S. (St Mildreds)
Grove Park Down C.S. (Bramdean)
Forest Hill
E.M.U. Depot
Bellingham
C.S.
Grove Park
Grove Park Junc.
Sydenham
Beckenham Hill
Sydenham Junc.
Chislehurst Tunnels
Lower Sydenham
Penge East
Elmstead Woods
New Beckenham
Penge West
New Beckenham Junc.
New Beckenham
C.S.
Beckenham Junction
Ravensbourne
Sundridge Park
Anerley
Kent House
Beckenham Junction
Bromley North
Chislehurst
Beckenham Road
Shortlands Junc.
Avenue Road
Clock House
Shortlands
Bickley Junc.
Chislehurst Junc.
Birkbeck
Bromley South
St. Mary Cray Junc.
Birkbeck
Bickley
Elmers End
Hawkwood Junc.
arrington Road
Elmers End
Elmers End
Elmers End Junc.
Petts Wood Junc.
Arena
(Temporarily single track)
Eden Park
Petts Wood
Woodside
Woodside
West Wickham
(Proposed 'Tramlink' network shown. Train services from Elmers End to Addiscombe and West Croydon to Wimbledon would be replaced by Tramlink).
Hayes

GREATER LONDON

Coombe Lane
Addington Village
Fieldway
Gravel Hill
King Henry's Drive
New Addington

SURREY

A

B

C

1
2

0   1   2 m.
0   1   2   3 km.
(1:70,000)

18

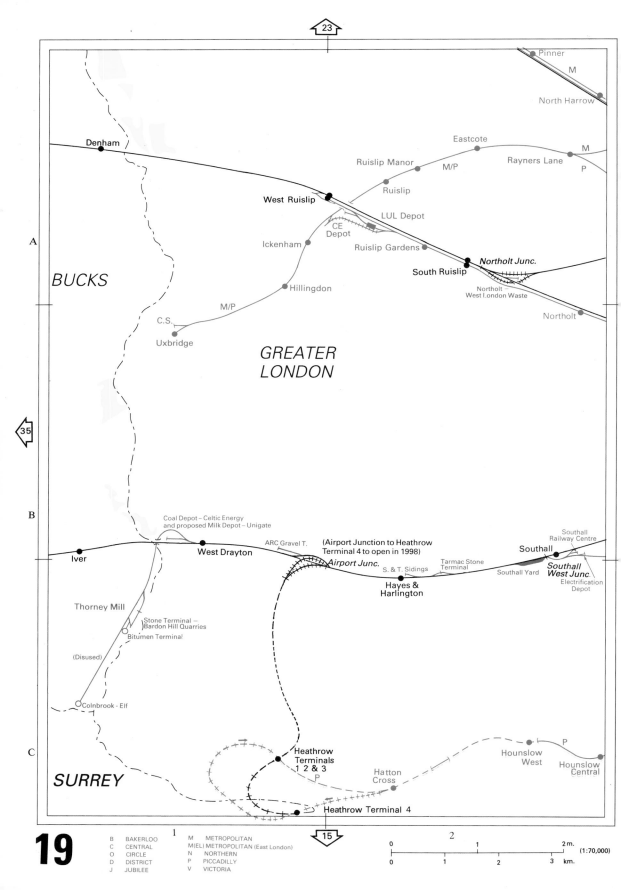

Pinner

M

North Harrow

Eastcote

Ruislip Manor

M/P

Rayners Lane

M

Ruislip

P

West Ruislip

LUL Depot

CE Depot

Northolt Junc.

A

Ruislip Gardens

South Ruislip

BUCKS

Ickenham

Northolt – West London Waste

Northolt

Hillingdon

M/P

C.S.

Uxbridge

GREATER LONDON

35

Coal Depot – Celtic Energy and proposed Milk Depot – Unigate

Southall Railway Centre

B

Iver

West Drayton

ARC Gravel T.

(Airport Junction to Heathrow Terminal 4 to open in 1998)

Airport Junc.

Southall

Tarmac Stone Terminal

Southall West Junc.

S. & T. Sidings

Southall Yard

Electrification Depot

Hayes & Harlington

Thorney Mill

Stone Terminal – Bardon Hill Quarries

Bitumen Terminal

(Disused)

Colnbrook - Elf

C

Heathrow Terminals 1 2 & 3

Hatton Cross

Hounslow West

Hounslow Central

P

SURREY

P

Heathrow Terminal 4

19

B	BAKERLOO	M	METROPOLITAN	
C	CENTRAL	M(EL)	METROPOLITAN (East London)	
O	CIRCLE	N	NORTHERN	
D	DISTRICT	P	PICCADILLY	
J	JUBILEE	V	VICTORIA	

1

2

0   1   2 m.

0   1   2   3 km.

(1:70,000)

Harrow & Wealdstone

a) Willesden H.L. Junc.
b) West London Junc.
c) Old Oak West Junc.
d) Cricklewood Curve Junc.
e) Mitre Bridge Junc.

1) Willesden S.W. Sidings – CE
2) Scrapyard – Mayer Parry Recycling
3) Brent Waste Terminal (Hendon)
   Shanks & McEwan
4) Acton – Foster Yeoman Stone term.
5) Willesden – FLT & Euroterminal
6) CE Yard
7) Shepherd's Bush (Proposed)

B

M

Harrow North Junc.

Harrow-on-the-Hill

West Harrow

LUL RTK

Northwick Park

M

Kenton

(Possible route for Crossrail to Aylesbury line trains shown at*)

J

Kingsbury

Silkstream Junc.

Burroughs Tun.

Hendon Central

Hendon

Brent Cross

Cricklewood C.S.

Brent Curve Junc.

Cricklewood Recess Sdgs.

Dudding Hill Junc.

d

Cricklewood

A

Redland Stone Term.

Preston Road

J/M

Depot

Wembley Park

South Kenton

South Harrow Sidings

Sudbury Hill Harrow

North Wembley

Sudbury & Harrow Road

Wembley Stadium

Neasden Freight Terminal – T.P. Dibden

Neasden Depot

Neasden

Dollis Hill

Willesden Green

J/M

S. Harrow Tun.

Northolt Park

Sudbury Hill

Sudbury Town

Wembley Central

C.S.

Neasden Junc.

Neasden Sidings

CE Sidings

WILLESDEN JUNC. (MAIN LINES)

P

B

Wembley Heavy Repair Shops

Wembley Central

LUL Depot

Wembley InterCity Carriage Depot (WB)

Stonebridge Park

Harlesden

WILLESDEN (LOCAL LINES)

Greenford W. Junc.

Greenford

E. Junc.

LTE Bay Junc. South Junc.

South Greenford (Southbound platform temporarily closed)

Alperton

Wembley European Freight Yard RFD

Willesden Royal Mail Terminal

Sudbury Junc.

Willesden Brent Yard

MG Gas Products

Willesden Junc.

Kensal Green Junc.

Kensal Rise

Perivale

C

Hanger Lane

Park Royal – Guinness (Disused)

Acton Canal Wharf Junc.

North Acton Junc.

5

WN

Kensal Green Tuns.

Kensal Green

Castle Bar Park

Castle Bar Tunnel

Drayton Green Junc.

Drayton Green

Plasser Wks

Park Royal

Marcon RMC Stone Term.

Park Royal Branch Junc.

North Acton

1

a

b

OC

e

Maintenance Depot

North Pole Road (Proposed)

Latimer Road

B

North Ealing

West Acton

4

Acton Wells Junc.

Acton East Junc.

Acton East

6

North Pole Junc.

North Pole Servicing Depot (European Services) (NP)

White City

C

Ealing Broadway

D

Hanger Lane Junc.

Acton Main Line

White City LUL Depot

Shepherd's Bush

7

Shepherd's Bush

Hanwell

West Ealing Junc.

West Ealing

West Ealing

Ealing Common

P/D

Acton Central

LUL Depot

Goldhawk Road

H

Depot

South Ealing

Northfields

P

LUL Acton Works

Acton Town North Junc.

Acton Town

South Acton

South Acton Junc.

Chiswick Park

Bedford Park Junc.

Stamford Brook

P/D

Ravenscourt Park

P/D

Hammersmith

Depot Boston Manor

LUL RTK

Turnham Green

H

Kew East Junc.

Gunnersbury Junc.

Gunnersbury

Old Kew Junc.

Stone Term – Day Aggregates

Brentford Goods

Brentford

Kew Bridge

New Kew Junc.

Kew Bridge

D

Osterley

Waste Terminal West London Waste

Syon Lane

Chiswick

Kew Gardens

Barnes Bridge

Barnes Bridge

C

P

Hounslow East

Isleworth

D

Mortlake

Barnes Junc.

Barnes

Hounslow

Richmond

North Sheen

Putney

0   1   2 m.   (1:70,000)
0   1   2   3 km.

2

B   BAKERLOO
C   CENTRAL
O   CIRCLE
D   DISTRICT
H   HAMMERSMITH & CITY

J   JUBILEE
M   METROPOLITAN
M(EL) METROPOLITAN (East London)
N   NORTHERN
P   PICCADILLY

20

21

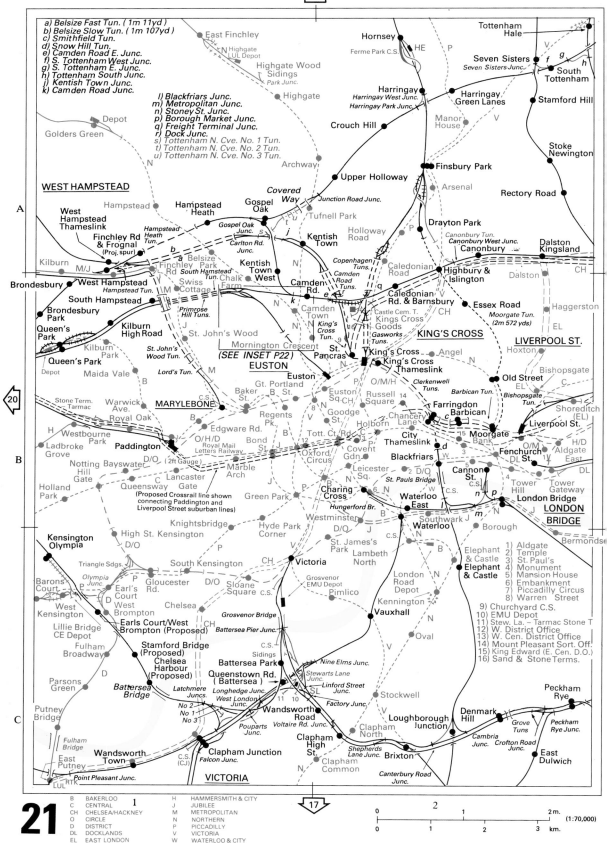

Blackhorse Rd.

Wood St.

V

V

St. James Street

Walthamstow Central
Walthamstow Queens Road

Snaresbrook

Barkingside

C

(Chelsea – Hackney line proposed would take over Fulham Broadway to Wimbledon and Leytonstone to Hainault via Newbury Park)

Wanstead

Redbridge

Gants Hill

C

Newbury Park

Copper Mill Junc.

Leyton Midland Road

CH
Leytonstone

GREATER LONDON

Clapton Junc.

Clapton

Leytonstone High Rd.

ZI
IL

Clapton Tun.

CH
Leyton

Temple Mills CE Sidings

Forest Gate Junc.

Wanstead Park

Manor Park

Ilford

Aldersbrook C.S.

A

Queens Road Tun.

Hackney Downs N. Junc.

Possible new depot for Eurostar Trains via a connection with a new route at Stratford

Temple Mills E. Junc.

Stratford FLT

High Meads LIFT & Junc. Isis Link

Forest Gate

Woodgrange Park

Barking Stn. Junc.

Hackney Downs

CH

C

SF

Homerton

Hackney Wick

Maryland

Woodgrange Park Junc.

EM

Barking

Hackney Central

Lea Junc.

g

d

Old Yard
Stratford

(Proposed Tunnel 20km with open section for possible Stratford station)

Barking Tilbury Line Junc. West

C.S.

Reading Lane Junc.

b

c

a

East Ham

Barking Tilbury Line Junc. East

London Fields

Thornton Fields C.S.

Upton Park

H/D

Cambridge Heath

Coal Depot (Disused)

Stratford Market Depot

Plaistow

a) Carpenters Rd. N. Junc.
b) Navarino Rd. Junc.
c) Channelsea N. Junc.
d) Stratford Central Junc.
e) Charlton Junc.
f) South Bermondsey Junc.
g) Channelsea S. Junc.

Bethnal Green

Bow Goods

Pudding Mill Lane

West Ham

Bethnal Green E. Junc.

ECC Stone Terminal
Bow Junc.

DL

Bow Rd.

Bow Church

West Ham

(Projected platforms)

C

H/D

Mile End

Bromley-by-Bow

Bethnal Green

Stepney Green

Devons Road

Gas Factory Junc.

DL

J

Whitechapel

Eastern District Office

DL

Canning Town

Prince Regent (Proposed)

Beckton

Beckton Depot

Limehouse

DL

Custom House

Royal Victoria (Proposed)

Royal Albert

Beckton Park

DL

Shadwell

Poplar Maintenance Depot

All Saints

East India

DL

Royal Victoria

Custom House

Prince Regent

Cyprus

Gallions Reach

B

EL

Wapping

Westferry
West India Quay

Blackwall

J

Silvertown Tun.

Rotherhithe

Canary Wharf

Poplar

Heron Quays

North Greenwich

Silvertown & City Airport

North Woolwich

J

South Quay

DL

Woolwich Free Ferry)

Canada Water (Proposed)

(Under Construction – due to open 1998)

Crossharbour & London Arena

Angerstein Wharf

Marcon RMC Stone Loading Terminal

Dock St. Tun.

Coleman St. Tun.

George IV Tun.

Calderwood St. Tun.

Cross St. Tun.

S & T Depot

Southwark Park Junc.

Surrey Quays

Mudchute

Island Gardens

(Mudchute and Island Gardens Stations to be moved)

Charlton

Bardon Stone Terminal

Mount St. Tun.

Charlton Tun.

Woolwich Dockyard

Woolwich Arsenal

Plumstead

Sdgs.

f

South Bermondsey

LUL Depot

Surrey Canal Junc.

North Kent East Junc.

EL

Pedestrian tunnel

Cutty Sark

Westcombe Park

Maze Hill

Angerstein Junc.

Camden Juncs.

Camden Road West Junc.

N

N

Camden Road

New Cross

Deptford

Greenwich College Tun.

Primrose Hill Tuns.

Camden Carriage Sidings

Up Empty Carriage Line Tun.

Camden Town

Morn. Cres.

Queens Road (Peckham)

New Cross Gate

Deptford Bridge

Greenwich

(Docklands Railway proposed extension)

Blackheath Tunnel

(INSET FROM MAP 21) (1:35,000)

Park St. Tuns.

N

Nunhead

St. John's

DL

Tanners Hill Junc.

Elverson Road

Blackheath Junc.

Kidbrooke Tun.

Up Empty Carriage Shed

EN

Lewisham Vale Junc.

Lewisham

Blackheath

(Mornington Crescent is temporarily closed – due to reopen in 1997)

Down Empty Carriage Shed

C

Nunhead Junc.

Brockley

Parks Bridge Junc.

Courthill Loop North

Kidbrooke

(TO EUSTON)

Falconwood

Ladywell Junc.

Courthill Loop Junc. South

Ladywell

Eltham

0   1   2 m.
0   1   2   3 km.

(1:70,000)

B BAKERLOO	EL EAST LONDON
C CENTRAL	H HAMMERSMITH & CITY
CH CHELSEA/HACKNEY	J JUBILEE
O CIRCLE	N NORTHERN
D DISTRICT	P PICCADILLY
DL DOCKLANDS	V VICTORIA

22

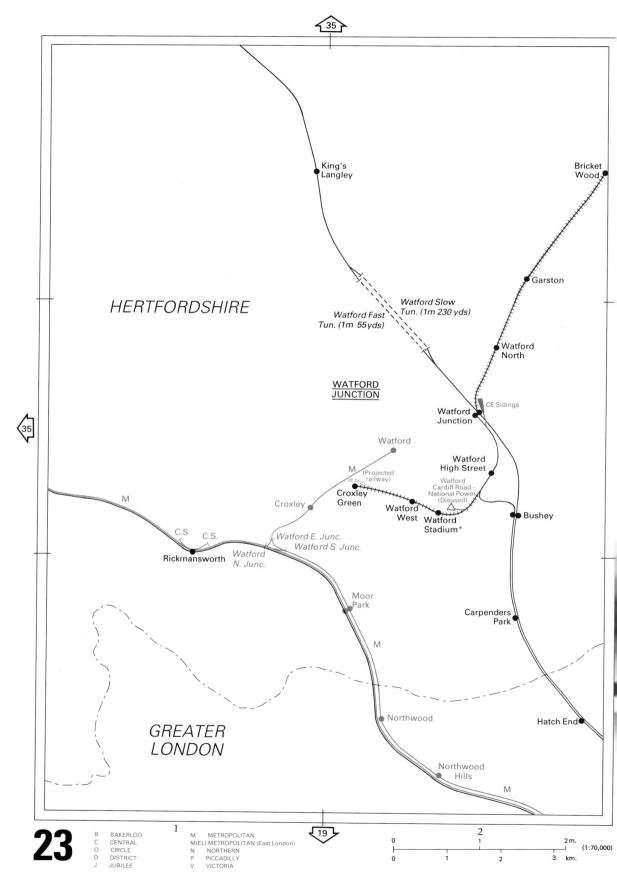

HERTFORDSHIRE

King's
Langley

Bricket
Wood

Garston

Watford Slow
Tun. (1m 230 yds)

Watford Fast
Tun. (1m 55 yds)

Watford
North

WATFORD
JUNCTION

CE Sidings

Watford
Junction

Watford
High Street

Watford
M   (Projected
              railway)

Watford
Cardiff Road –
National Power
(Disused)

Croxley
Green

Croxley

M

Watford
West

Watford
Stadium*

Bushey

C.S.   C.S.

Watford E. Junc.
Watford S. Junc.

Rickmansworth

Watford
N. Junc.

Moor
Park

Carpenders
Park

M

Northwood

Hatch End

GREATER
LONDON

Northwood
Hills

M

1

2

23

B	BAKERLOO	M	METROPOLITAN
C	CENTRAL	M(EL)	METROPOLITAN (East London)
O	CIRCLE	N	NORTHERN
D	DISTRICT	P	PICCADILLY
J	JUBILEE	V	VICTORIA

0   1   2 m.

0   1   2   3 km.

(1:70,000)

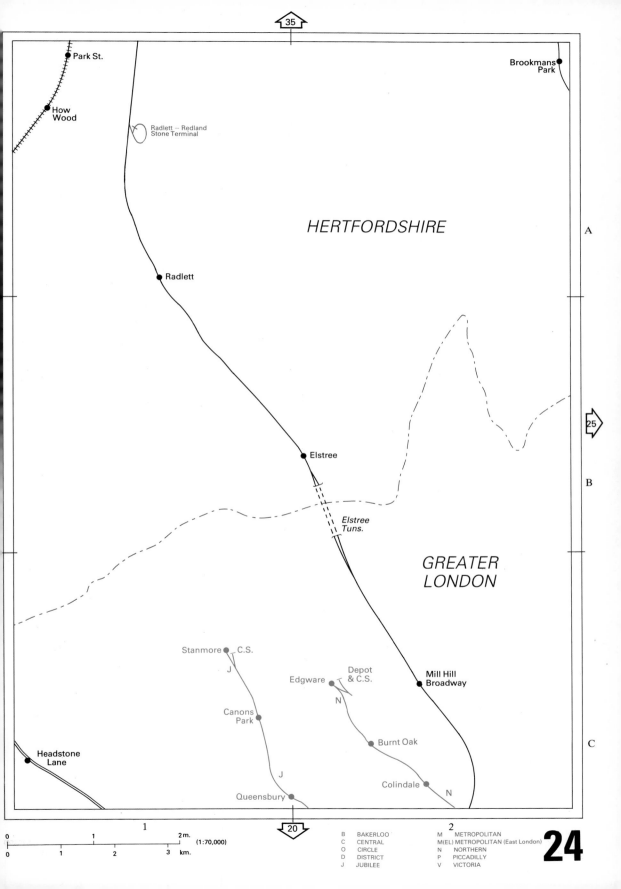

Park St.

Brookmans
Park

How
Wood

Radlett – Redland
Stone Terminal

HERTFORDSHIRE

A

Radlett

Elstree

B

Elstree
Tuns.

**GREATER
LONDON**

Stanmore C.S.

J

Depot
& C.S.

Mill Hill
Broadway

Edgware

N

Canons
Park

Burnt Oak

C

Headstone
Lane

J

Colindale

N

Queensbury

1			2	

0   1   2 m.

(1:70,000)

0   1   2   3 km.

B	BAKERLOO	M	METROPOLITAN
C	CENTRAL	M(EL)	METROPOLITAN (East London)
O	CIRCLE	N	NORTHERN
D	DISTRICT	P	PICCADILLY
J	JUBILEE	V	VICTORIA

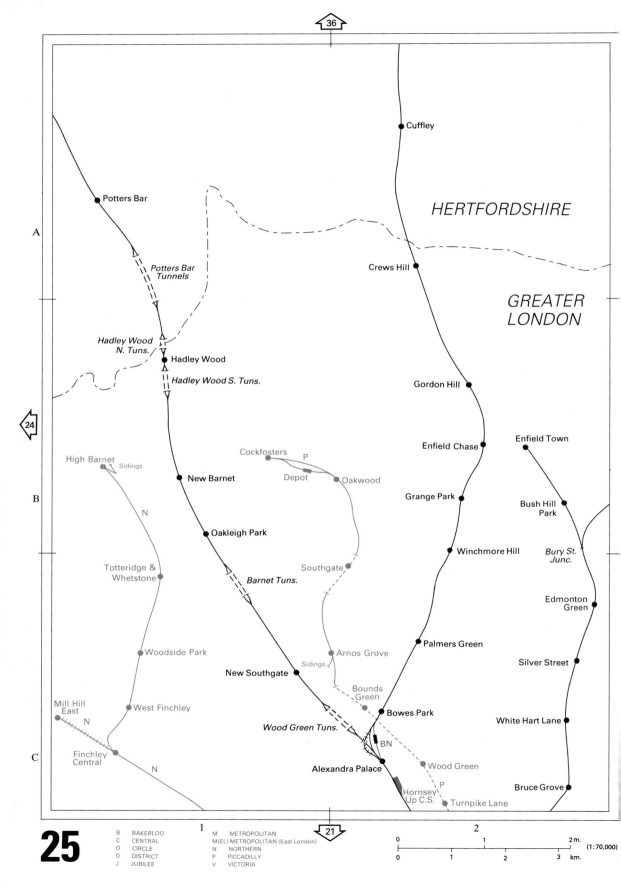

Cuffley

HERTFORDSHIRE

Potters Bar

A

Potters Bar
Tunnels

Crews Hill

*GREATER
LONDON*

Hadley Wood
N. Tuns.

Hadley Wood

Hadley Wood S. Tuns.

Gordon Hill

24

Enfield Chase

Enfield Town

High Barnet   Sidings

Cockfosters   P

Depot

Oakwood

New Barnet

Grange Park

Bush Hill
Park

B

N

Oakleigh Park

Winchmore Hill

*Bury St.
Junc.*

Totteridge &
Whetstone

Southgate

Barnet Tuns.

Edmonton
Green

Woodside Park

Arnos Grove

Palmers Green

Sidings

Silver Street

Mill Hill
East   N

West Finchley

New Southgate

Bounds
Green

Bowes Park

White Hart Lane

Finchley
Central   N

Wood Green Tuns.

BN

Wood Green

C

Alexandra Palace

Hornsey
Up C.S.   P

Bruce Grove

Turnpike Lane

25

B	BAKERLOO	M	METROPOLITAN
C	CENTRAL	M(EL)	METROPOLITAN (East London)
O	CIRCLE	N	NORTHERN
D	DISTRICT	P	PICCADILLY
J	JUBILEE	V	VICTORIA

1

2

0   1   2 m.

0   1   2   3 km.

(1:70,000)

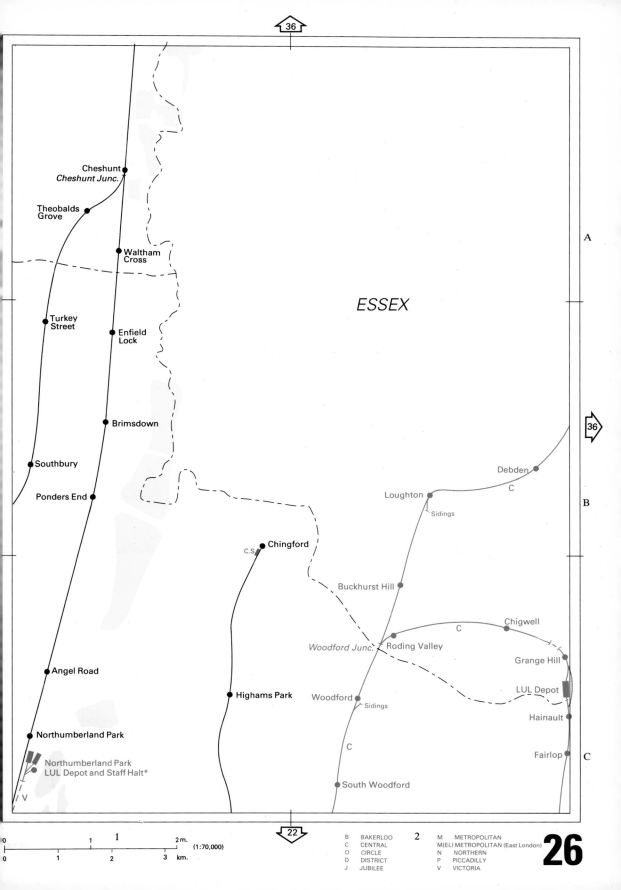

Cheshunt
Cheshunt Junc.

Theobalds
Grove

Waltham
Cross

ESSEX

Turkey
Street

Enfield
Lock

Brimsdown

Southbury

Debden

C

Loughton

B

Ponders End

Sidings

C.S. Chingford

Buckhurst Hill

Chigwell

C

Grange Hill

Woodford Junc. Roding Valley

Angel Road

LUL Depot

Highams Park

Woodford

Hainault

Sidings

C

Northumberland Park

Fairlop

C

Northumberland Park
LUL Depot and Staff Halt*

C

V

South Woodford

0	1	2 m.
1		

0   1   2   3 km.

(1:70,000)

B	BAKERLOO	2	M	METROPOLITAN
C	CENTRAL		M(EL)	METROPOLITAN (East London)
O	CIRCLE		N	NORTHERN
D	DISTRICT		P	PICCADILLY
J	JUBILEE		V	VICTORIA

26

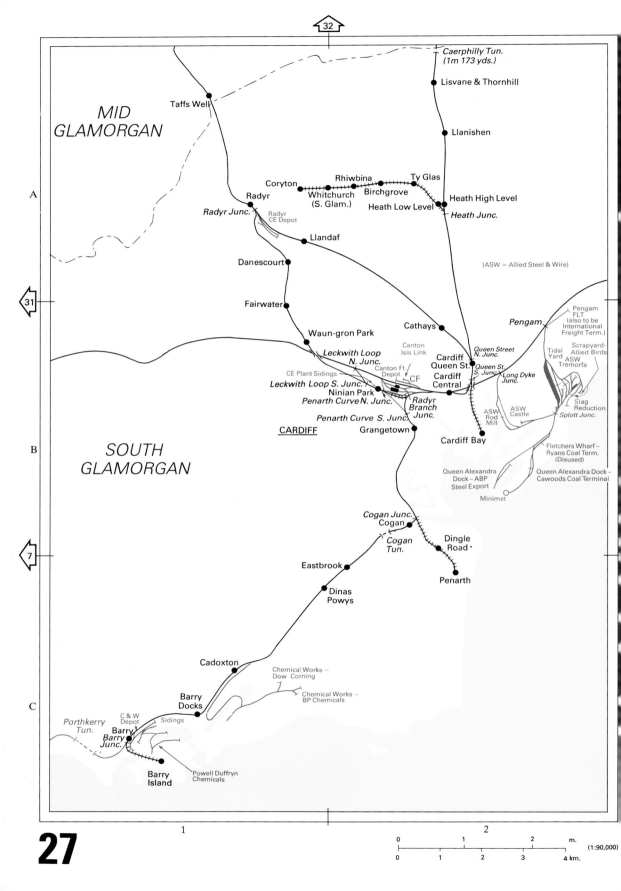

Caerphilly Tun.
(1m 173 yds.)

Lisvane & Thornhill

Llanishen

MID
GLAMORGAN

Taffs Well

A

Coryton
Rhiwbina
Ty Glas

Radyr
Whitchurch
(S. Glam.)
Birchgrove

Radyr Junc.
Heath High Level

Radyr
CE Depot
Heath Low Level

Heath Junc.

Llandaf

Danescourt

(ASW = Allied Steel & Wire)

31

Fairwater

Cathays

Pengam
FLT
(also to be
International
Freight Term.)

Pengam

Waun-gron Park

Canton
Isis Link

Scrapyard-
Allied Birds

Leckwith Loop
N. Junc.

Canton Ft.
Depot

Cardiff
Queen St.

Queen Street
N. Junc.

Tidal Yard

ASW
Tremorfa

CF

CE Plant Sidings

Leckwith Loop S. Junc.

Cardiff
Central

Queen St.
S. Junc.

Long Dyke
Junc.

Slag
Reduction

Ninian Park

B

Penarth Curve N. Junc.

Radyr
Branch
Junc.

Splott Junc.

SOUTH
GLAMORGAN

Penarth Curve S. Junc.

Grangetown

ASW
Rod
Mill

ASW
Castle

CARDIFF

Cardiff Bay

Fletchers Wharf –
Ryans Coal Term.
(Disused)

Queen Alexandra
Dock – ABP
Steel Export

Queen Alexandra Dock –
Cawoods Coal Terminal

Minimet

Cogan Junc.
Cogan

Dingle
Road

7

Cogan
Tun.

Eastbrook

Penarth

Dinas
Powys

Cadoxton

Chemical Works –
Dow Corning

C

Barry
Docks

Chemical Works –
BP Chemicals

Porthkerry
Tun.

C & W
Depot

Sidings

Barry
Barry
Junc.

Barry
Island

Powell Duffryn
Chemicals

27

1

2

0   1   2   m.

0   1   2   3   4 km.

(1:90,000)

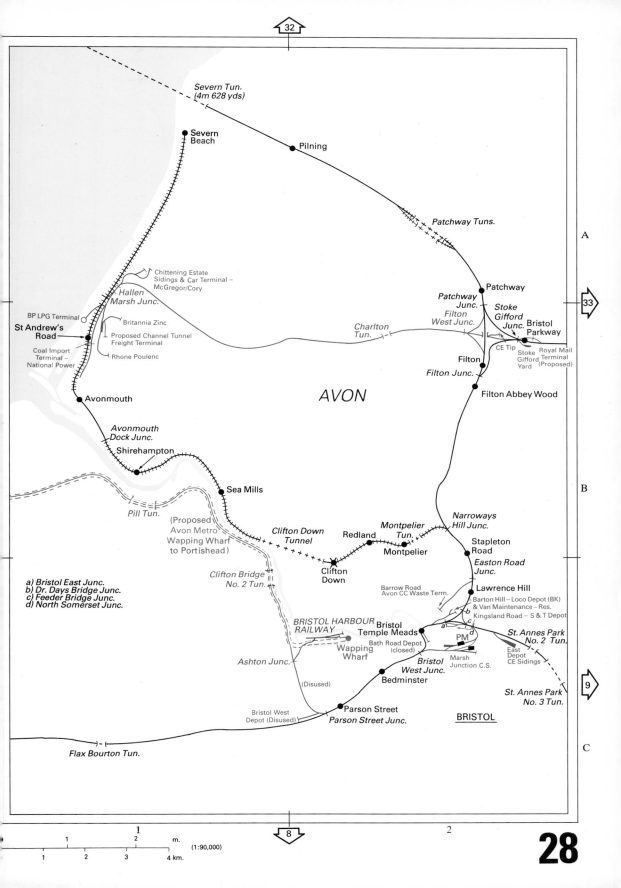

Severn Tun.
(4m 628 yds)

Severn
Beach

Pilning

Patchway Tuns.

Chittening Estate
Sidings & Car Terminal –
McGregor/Cory

Patchway

*Hallen
Marsh Junc.*

*Patchway
Junc.
Filton West Junc.*

*Stoke
Gifford
Junc.*

Bristol
Parkway

BP LPG Terminal

Britannia Zinc

*Charlton
Tun.*

CE Tip

**St Andrew's
Road**

Proposed Channel Tunnel
Freight Terminal

Stoke
Gifford
Yard

Royal Mail
Terminal
(Proposed)

Coal Import
Terminal –
National Power

Rhone Poulenc

Filton

Filton Junc.

AVON

Filton Abbey Wood

Avonmouth

*Avonmouth
Dock Junc.*

Shirehampton

Sea Mills

Pill Tun.

(Proposed
Avon Metro
Wapping Wharf
to Portishead)

*Clifton Down
Tunnel*

Redland

*Montpelier
Tun.*

*Narroways
Hill Junc.*

Stapleton
Road

Montpelier

*Easton Road
Junc.*

a) Bristol East Junc.
b) Dr. Days Bridge Junc.
c) Feeder Bridge Junc.
d) North Somerset Junc.

*Clifton Bridge
No. 2 Tun.*

Clifton
Down

Lawrence Hill

Barrow Road
Avon CC Waste Term.

Barton Hill – Loco Depot (BK)
& Van Maintenance – Res.
Kingsland Road – S & T Depot

*BRISTOL HARBOUR
RAILWAY*

Bristol
Temple Meads

St. Annes Park
No. 2 Tun.

PM

Ashton Junc.

*Wapping
Wharf*

Bath Road Depot
(closed)

Marsh
Junction C.S.

East
Depot
CE Sidings

*Bristol
West Junc.*

Bedminster

(Disused)

St. Annes Park
No. 3 Tun.

Bristol West
Depot (Disused)

Parson Street
Parson Street Junc.

BRISTOL

Flax Bourton Tun.

1
2

m.

1

2

(1:90,000)

1

2

3

4 km.

2

28

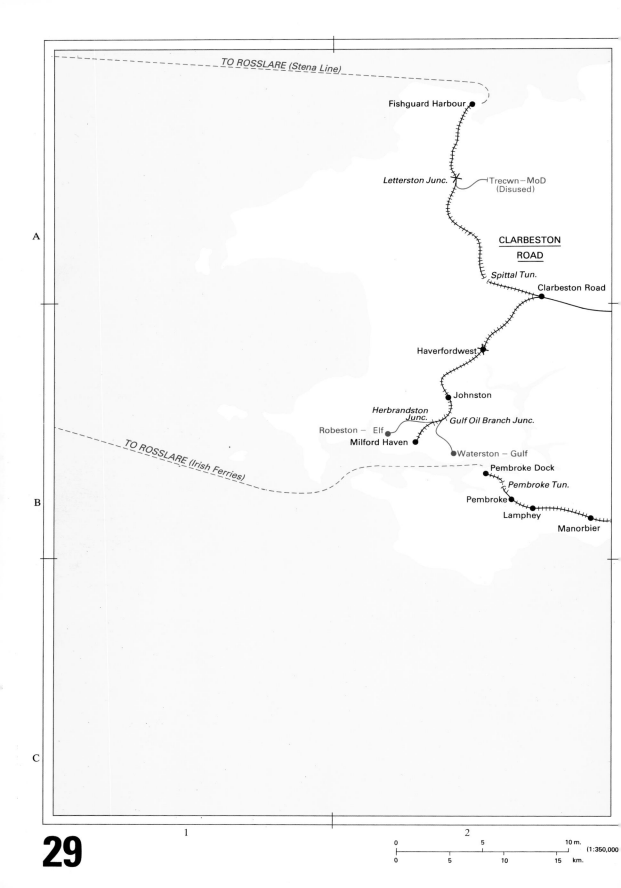

TO ROSSLARE (Stena Line)

Fishguard Harbour

Letterston Junc.
Trecwn — MoD
(Disused)

CLARBESTON
ROAD

Spittal Tun.
Clarbeston Road

Haverfordwest

Johnston

Herbrandston
Junc.
Gulf Oil Branch Junc.
Robeston — Elf
Milford Haven
Waterston — Gulf

TO ROSSLARE (Irish Ferries)

Pembroke Dock
Pembroke Tun.
Pembroke
Lamphey
Manorbier

29

0   5   10 m.
0   5   10   15   km.
(1:350,000)

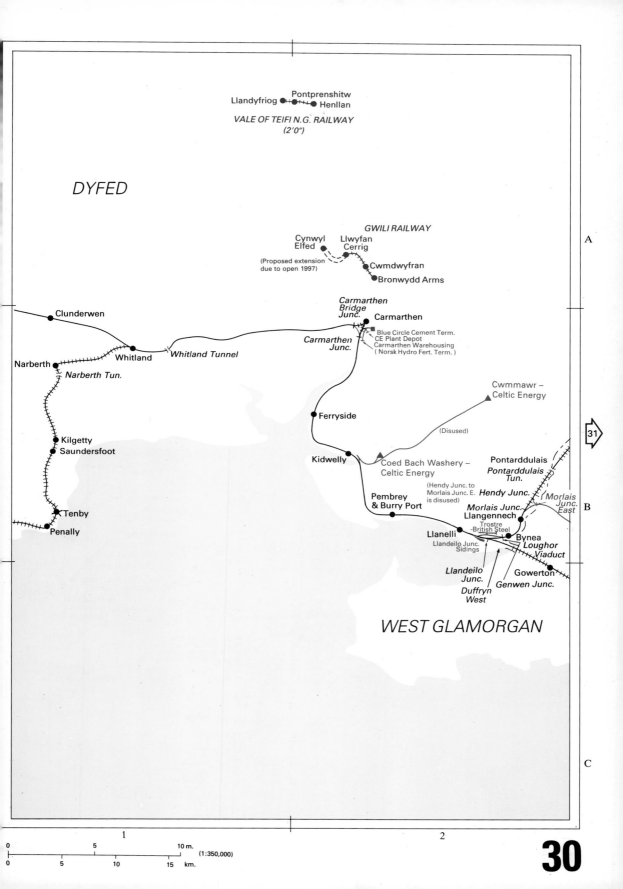

Llandyfriog ● ● ● Pontprenshitw
● Henllan
VALE OF TEIFI N.G. RAILWAY
(2'0")

DYFED

GWILI RAILWAY

Cynwyl
Elfed ●
Llwyfan
Cerrig

(Proposed extension
due to open 1997)

● Cwmdwyfran
● Bronwydd Arms

*Carmarthen
Bridge
Junc.*

Carmarthen

● Clunderwen

■ Blue Circle Cement Term.
CE Plant Depot
Carmarthen Warehousing
(Norsk Hydro Fert. Term.)

*Carmarthen
Junc.*

Narberth ●
● Whitland
↗ *Whitland Tunnel*

Narberth Tun.

Cwmmawr –
▲ Celtic Energy

● Ferryside

(Disused)

● Kilgetty
● Saundersfoot

Kidwelly ●

▲
Coed Bach Washery –
Celtic Energy

Pontarddulais ●

*Pontarddulais
Tun.*

▲ Tenby
● Penally

Pembrey
& Burry Port ●

(Hendy Junc. to
Morlais Junc. E.
is disused)

Hendy Junc.

Morlais Junc.
Llangennech ●

*Morlais
Junc.
East*

Trostre
-British Steel

Llanelli ●

● Bynea
● Loughor

Llandeilo Junc.
Sidings

*Loughor
Viaduct*

*Llandeilo
Junc.*

Genwen Junc.

● Gowerton

*Duffryn
West*

WEST GLAMORGAN

◀ 31

A

B

C

1

2

0 ─── 5 ─── 10 m.
(1:350,000)
0 ─── 5 ─── 10 ─── 15 km.

30

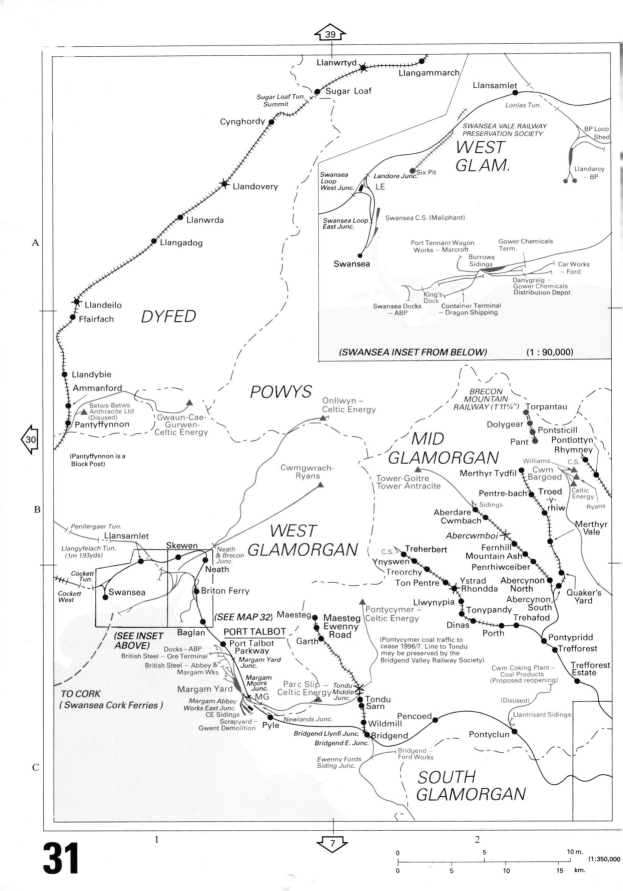

Llanwrtyd
Llangammarch
Llansamlet
Sugar Loaf
Sugar Loaf Tun. Summit
Cynghordy

Lonlas Tun.

SWANSEA VALE RAILWAY PRESERVATION SOCIETY

BP Loco Shed

WEST GLAM.

Llandovery

Six Pit
Swansea Loop West Junc.
Landore Junc.
LE
Llandarcy – BP

Llanwrda

Llangadog

A

Swansea Loop East Junc.
Swansea C.S. (Maliphant)

Port Tennant Wagon Works – Marcroft
Gower Chemicals Term.
Burrows Sidings
Car Works – Ford

Swansea

Danygraig – Gower Chemicals Distribution Depot

King's Dock

Llandeilo
Ffairfach

DYFED

Swansea Docks – ABP
Container Terminal – Dragon Shipping

(SWANSEA INSET FROM BELOW)   (1 : 90,000)

Llandybie
Ammanford

POWYS

BRECON MOUNTAIN RAILWAY (1'11¾")
Torpantau

Onllwyn – Celtic Energy

Dolygear
Pontsticill
Pant
Pontlottyn
Rhymney

30

Betws-Betws Anthracite Ltd (Disused)
Pantyffynnon

Gwaun-Cae-Gurwen-Celtic Energy

MID GLAMORGAN

Williams
Cwm Bargoed
C.S.
Celtic Energy

Merthyr Tydfil

(Pantyffynnon is a Block Post)

Cwmgwrach-Ryans

Tower-Goitre Tower Antracite

Pentre-bach
Troed-y-rhiw
Ryans

Merthyr Vale

B

Penllergaer Tun.
Llansamlet
Skewen
Neath & Brecon Junc.

WEST GLAMORGAN

Aberdare
Cwmbach
Sidings

Abercwmboi

Llangyfelach Tun. (1m 193yds)
Neath

C.S.
Treherbert
Ynyswen
Treorchy

Fernhill
Mountain Ash
Penrhiwceiber

Cockett Tun.

Cockett West
Swansea
Briton Ferry

Ton Pentre
Ystrad Rhondda
Abercynon North
Abercynon South
Quaker's Yard

Llwynypia
Tonypandy
Trehafod

(SEE MAP 32)
Maesteg
Maesteg Ewenny Road

Pontycymer – Celtic Energy
Dinas
Porth

Pontypridd
Trefforest

(SEE INSET ABOVE)
Baglan
PORT TALBOT
Garth

(Pontycymer coal traffic to cease 1996/7. Line to Tondu may be preserved by the Bridgend Valley Railway Society)

Trefforest Estate

Docks – ABP
British Steel – Ore Terminal
British Steel – Abbey & Margam Wks.
Port Talbot Parkway
Margam Yard Junc.

Parc Slip – Celtic Energy
Tondu Middle Junc.

Cwm Coking Plant – Coal Products (Proposed reopening)

TO CORK (Swansea Cork Ferries)

Margam Yard
Margam Moors Junc.
MG

Tondu
Sarn

(Disused)

Margam Abbey Works East Junc.
CE Sidings
Scrapyard – Gwent Demolition

Newlands Junc.
Pyle

Pencoed
Wildmill

Llantrisant Sidings

Pontyclun

Bridgend Llynfi Junc.
Bridgend E. Junc.
Bridgend

C

Ewenny Fords Siding Junc.

Bridgend – Ford Works

SOUTH GLAMORGAN

1   7   2

0   5   10 m.   (1:350,000)
0   5   10   15 km.

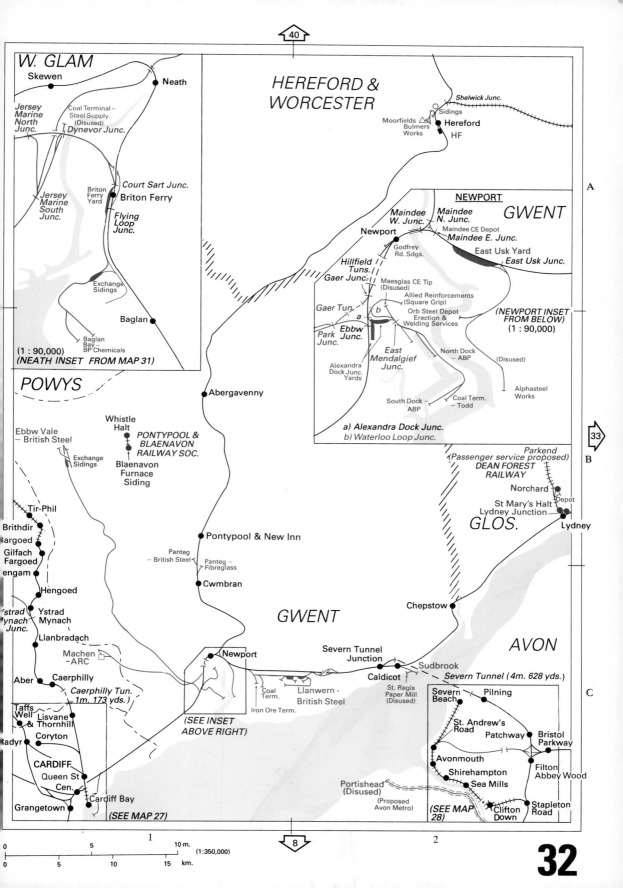

W. GLAM

Skewen Neath

Jersey
Marine
North
Junc.

Coal Terminal –
Steel Supply
(Disused)
Dynevor Junc.

Briton
Ferry
Yard Court Sart Junc.
Briton Ferry

Jersey
Marine
South
Junc. Flying
Loop
Junc.

Exchange
Sidings

Baglan

Baglan
Bay –
BP Chemicals

(1 : 90,000)
(NEATH INSET FROM MAP 31)

*HEREFORD &
WORCESTER*

Shelwick Junc.
Sidings
Moorfields Hereford
Bulmers
Works HF

GWENT

NEWPORT

Maindee
W. Junc. Maindee
N. Junc.
Maindee CE Depot
Newport *Maindee E. Junc.*

Godfrey
Rd. Sdgs. East Usk Yard
East Usk Junc.

Hillfield
Tuns.
Gaer Junc. Maesglas CE Tip
(Disused)
Allied Reinforcements
(Square Grip)
Gaer Tun. Orb Steel Depot
Erection &
Welding Services
a b
Park
Junc. **Ebbw
Junc.**

East
Mendalgief
Junc. North Dock
– ABP (Disused)

Alexandra
Dock Junc.
Yards Alphasteel
Works

South Dock –
ABP Coal Term.
– Todd

a) Alexandra Dock Junc.
b) Waterloo Loop Junc.

*(NEWPORT INSET
FROM BELOW)*
(1 : 90,000)

POWYS

Abergavenny

Whistle
Halt

Ebbw Vale
– British Steel

Exchange
Sidings

*PONTYPOOL &
BLAENAVON
RAILWAY SOC.*

Blaenavon
Furnace
Siding

Tir-Phil

Brithdir
argoed

Gilfach
Fargoed
engam

Hengoed

'strad
ynach
Junc. Ystrad
Mynach

Llanbradach

Machen
– ARC

Aber Caerphilly

*Caerphilly Tun.
1m. 173 yds.)*

Taffs
Well
Lisvane
& Thornhill

adyr Coryton

CARDIFF

Queen St
Cen.

Grangetown Cardiff Bay

(SEE MAP 27)

Pontypool & New Inn

Panteg
– British Steel
Panteg –
Fibreglass

Cwmbran

GWENT

Newport

(SEE INSET
ABOVE RIGHT)

Coal
Term.
Iron Ore Term. Llanwern –
British Steel

Severn Tunnel
Junction
Sudbrook
Caldicot *Severn Tunnel (4m. 628 yds.)*

St. Regis
Paper Mill
(Disused)

Chepstow

Parkend
(Passenger service proposed)
**DEAN FOREST
RAILWAY**

Norchard Depot
St Mary's Halt
Lydney Junction
Lydney

GLOS.

AVON

Severn
Beach Pilning

St. Andrew's
Road Patchway Bristol
Parkway

Avonmouth Filton
Abbey Wood
Shirehampton Sea Mills

Portishead
(Disused)
(Proposed
Avon Metro) Clifton
Down Stapleton
Road

**(SEE MAP
28)**

A

33
B

C

0   5   10 m.
0 5   10   15   km.
1 (1:350,000) 2

32

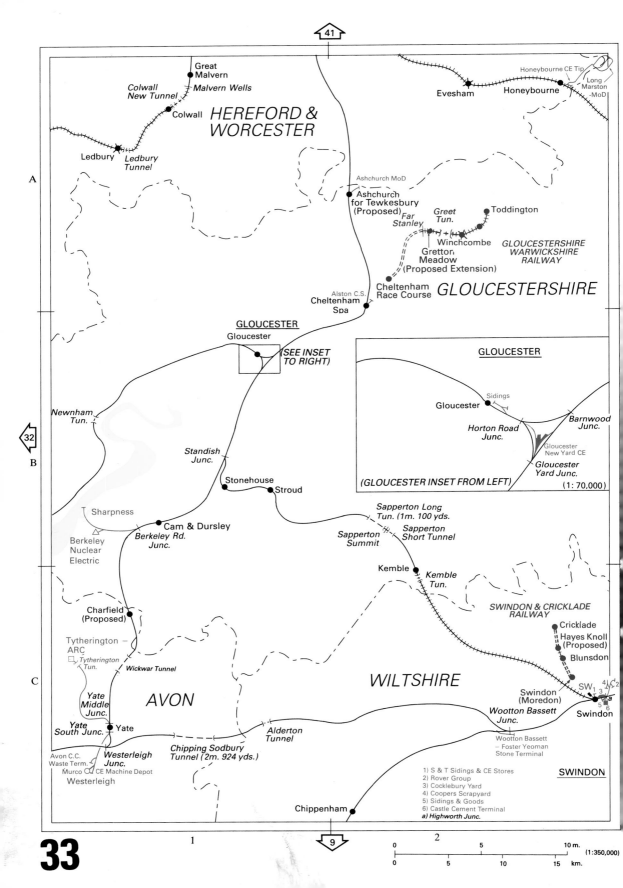

Great
Malvern

*Colwall
New Tunnel*

Malvern Wells

Colwall

HEREFORD & WORCESTER

Evesham

Honeybourne

Honeybourne CE Tip

Long
Marston
-MoD

Ledbury

*Ledbury
Tunnel*

A

Ashchurch MoD

Ashchurch
for Tewkesbury
(Proposed)

*Far
Stanley*

*Greet
Tun.*

Toddington

Winchcombe

GLOUCESTERSHIRE
WARWICKSHIRE
RAILWAY

Gretton
*Meadow
(Proposed Extension)*

Cheltenham
Race Course

GLOUCESTERSHIRE

Alston C.S.

Cheltenham
Spa

GLOUCESTER

Gloucester

*(SEE INSET
TO RIGHT)*

GLOUCESTER

Sidings

Gloucester

Barnwood
Junc.

*Horton Road
Junc.*

Gloucester
New Yard CE

*Gloucester
Yard Junc.*

(GLOUCESTER INSET FROM LEFT)

(1:70,000)

*Newnham
Tun.*

32

B

*Standish
Junc.*

Stonehouse

Stroud

Sharpness

*Sapperton Long
Tun. (1m. 100 yds.*

*Sapperton
Short Tunnel*

*Sapperton
Summit*

Cam & Dursley

*Berkeley Rd.
Junc.*

Berkeley
Nuclear
Electric

Kemble

*Kemble
Tun.*

*SWINDON & CRICKLADE
RAILWAY*

Cricklade

Hayes Knoll
(Proposed)

Blunsdon

Charfield
(Proposed)

Tytherington –
ARC

*Tytherington
Tun.*

Wickwar Tunnel

SW

4
2

1 3

Swindon
(Moredon)

*Wootton Bassett
Junc.*

Swindon

C

*Yate
Middle
Junc.*

**Yate
South Junc.**

Yate

WILTSHIRE

AVON

*Alderton
Tunnel*

Wootton Bassett
– Foster Yeoman
Stone Terminal

5
6
a

Avon C.C.
Waste Term.

Murco   CE Machine Depot

**Westerleigh
Junc.**

Westerleigh

*Chipping Sodbury
Tunnel (2m. 924 yds.)*

1) S & T Sidings & CE Stores
2) Rover Group
3) Cocklebury Yard
4) Coopers Scrapyard
5) Sidings & Goods
6) Castle Cement Terminal
a) Highworth Junc.

SWINDON

Chippenham

33

1

2

0   5   10 m.

(1:350,000)

0   5   10   15   km.

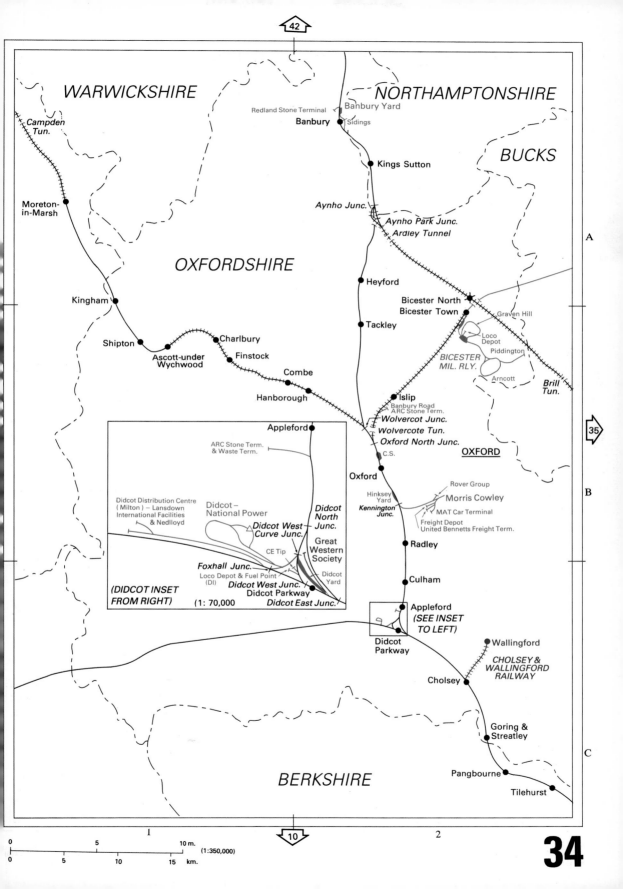

WARWICKSHIRE

NORTHAMPTONSHIRE

BUCKS

OXFORDSHIRE

Campden Tun.

Moreton-in-Marsh

Kingham

Shipton

Ascott-under Wychwood

Charlbury

Finstock

Combe

Hanborough

Appleford

Redland Stone Terminal

Banbury Yard

Banbury

Sidings

Kings Sutton

Aynho Junc.

Aynho Park Junc.
Ardley Tunnel

Heyford

Bicester North
Bicester Town

Graven Hill

Loco Depot

Piddington

BICESTER MIL. RLY.

Arncott

Brill Tun.

Tackley

Islip

Banbury Road
ARC Stone Term.

Wolvercot Junc.

Wolvercote Tun.

Oxford North Junc.

C.S.

Oxford

OXFORD

Rover Group

Morris Cowley

Hinksey Yard

Kennington Junc.

MAT Car Terminal

Freight Depot
United Bennetts Freight Term.

Radley

Culham

Appleford
(SEE INSET TO LEFT)

Didcot Parkway

Wallingford

CHOLSEY & WALLINGFORD RAILWAY

Cholsey

Goring & Streatley

Pangbourne

Tilehurst

BERKSHIRE

Didcot Inset (from right)

ARC Stone Term.
& Waste Term.

Didcot Distribution Centre
(Milton) – Lansdown
International Facilities
& Nedlloyd

Didcot –
National Power

Didcot North Junc.

Didcot West Curve Junc.

CE Tip

Great Western Society

Foxhall Junc.

Loco Depot & Fuel Point (DI)

Didcot West Junc.

Didcot Parkway

Didcot East Junc.

Didcot Yard

(DIDCOT INSET FROM LEFT)

(1: 70,000)

42

A

35

B

C

10

0   5   10 m.
(1:350,000)
0   5   10   15 km.

34

BLETCHLEY INSET

Fenny Stratford
Flyover Junc.
Denbigh Hall
South Junc.

Railway Works –
Railcare (ZN)
Transport &
Warehousing
Facilities Ltd.
Wolverton
CE & OLE
Depot
ARC Stone
Terminal
BY
C.S.
S & T Sidings Fenny
Stratford
Bletchley
Bletchley
Junc.
Stone Term.
RMC
Flyover Junc.

(1 : 90,000)
(BLETCHLEY INSET
FROM RIGHT)

BLETCHLEY

Milton
Keynes
Central

Bletchley
Fenny
Stratford

(SEE INSET TO LEFT)

(Disused)

Kempston
Hardwick

Forders Sidings
Shanks & McEwan Landfill

Elstow – Redland
Stone Terminal

Biggleswade
Plasmor
Brick
Terminal

Stewartby
Millbrook

Lidlington

Ridgmont

Woburn
Sands
Aspley Guise

Ampthill
Tuns.

BEDFORDSHIRE

Arlesey

Bow Brickhill

Flitwick

Harlington

Cambridge
Junc.
CE Plant Depot
Hitchin

A

Claydon L.N.E. Junc.
Calvert – Shanks &
McEwan Waste Terminal

Linslade Tuns.
Leighton
Buzzard

LEIGHTON BUZZARD
RLY. (2'0")

Leagrave
Limbury Rd. –
Tarmac Stone Term.
Sidings
Luton Crescent Road –
MAT Transauto Car T.
Luton
Luton Airport (Proposed)

Quainton Road*

Cheddington

GREAT WHIPSNADE RLY.
(2'6")

Harpenden

Goods & Hartwells
(Disused)
Aylesbury
C.S.

Aylesbury Diesel Depot
(AL)

Tring
Summit
Tring

HERTFORDSHIRE

34

Stoke
Mandeville

Northchurch
Tuns.

Berkhamsted

Haddenham &
Thame Parkway

Wendover

St. Albans
Abbey
St. Albans

Little
Kimble

Hemel
Hempstead
Apsley

Park St.

(SEE MAP
24)

B

Monks
Risborough
Princes
Risborough

Dutchlands
Summit

CHINNOR & PRINCES
RISBOROUGH RAILWAY
ASSOCIATION

(Disused)
Wainhill

Chinnor

Saunderton
Summit

Saunderton

Great
Missenden

Chesham
M

(MANTLES WOOD)
RTK LUL
Amersham

Chalfont
& Latimer

King's
Langley

Radlett

Chorley
Wood
Rickmansworth

Watford
Croxley
Green

Watford Junc.

BUCKINGHAMSHIRE

(READING INSET FROM BELOW)

CE
Yard
Reading
Yard
CE

Reading

Reading
New Junc.

Reading
West Junc.

RG
C.S.
Westbury
Line Junc.

Reading
Spur Junc.

Reading
West
Oxford Road Junc.

READING

Southcote
Junc.
(1 : 90,000)

High Wycombe

Beaconsfield
Seer Green

Whitehouse
Tun.

Gerrards
Cross
Denham Golf
Club

Denham

Moor
Park
M

Edgware

Stanmore
J N

Harrow-on-
the-Hill

(SEE MAP 23)

West
Ruislip
M/P
C

Rayners
Lane

(SEE MAP

SLOUGH

**GREATER
LONDON**

Uxbridge

Marlow

Cookham

Bourne End

Redland
Stone Term.

Furze Platt

Taplow
Burnham
Shell
Slough

Langley
Total

Henley-on-Thames

Shiplake

OXON. **BERKSHIRE**

Maidenhead

Langley
Iver

West
Drayton

Ealing
Bdy.

Heathrow
P

C

Wargrave

(SEE INSET
ABOVE)
Reading

Twyford

Reading West

Windsor & Eton
Central
Windsor & Eton Riverside
Sunnymeads

Datchet

Wraysbury

Feltham

(SEE MAP 19)

Richmond

11

2

15

16
(1:350,000)

0   5   10 m.

0   5   10   15   km.

Meldreth
Whittlesford
Grain Term – Myhills (Disused)

CAMBRIDGESHIRE

Duxford Ciba-Geigy
Great Chesterford

Royston

Ashwell & Morden

Littlebury Tunnel
Audley End Tunnel

Audley End

C.S.
Baldock
△ Letchworth – National Power (Disused)
Letchworth

Newport

1) Willesden Junc.
2) Finsbury Park
3) Stratford
4) Clapham Junction
5) Lewisham
6) London Bridge
7) Victoria
8) Upminster Bridge
9) Hornchurch
10) Elm Park
11) Dagenham East
12) Dagenham Heathway
13) Becontree
14) Upney
a) Tye Green Junc.
b) Coopers Junc.
c) Coopers Lane Tun.

A

Elsenham *(Summit)*

Stansted North Junc.
Stansted Mountfitchet

Peoplemover
Stansted Airport
a c b
Stansted East Junc.
Stansted South Junc.

Stevenage
Langley Junc.
Redland Stone Term.

HERTFORDSHIRE

Knebworth

Watton-at-Stone

Welwyn North Tun.
Welwyn South Tun.
Welwyn North

Molewood Tun.
Ware

Bishops Stortford
C.S.

Welwyn Garden City
Sidings

Hertford North
C.S.
Hertford East

St. Margaret's

Sawbridgeworth

Hatfield
Bayford

Rye House

Roydon

Harlow Mill

Harlow Town

Foster Yeoman Stone Terminal

(DAGENHAM INSET FROM BELOW)

Distribution Depot – Stora
C & W
Hays Distribution
Car Terminal
Ford Works

Ripple Lane Yard
Ripple Lane FLT
Dagenham Dock

Dagenham Ford Works

(1:90,000)

Ponsbourne Tun.
(1m. 924yds.)

Broxbourne

Broxbourne Junc.
Rye House Sidings – Redland
Sidings

ESSEX

North Weald
Ongar

Sidings (Disused)
Chelmsford

Welham Green

Brookmans Park
Cuffley
Cheshunt

Epping to Ongar is closed – may reopen as Ongar Railway Preservation Society

B

Potters Bar

Epping

Theydon Bois

Ingatestone

High Barnet
Cockfosters
Enfield Town

Brimsdown
Southbury

C
Debden

Chingford

C.S.
Mountnessing Junc.

Mill Hill East

P

N

Woodford
Hainault

Shenfield
Billericay

(SEE MAP 25)

C

C

Ingrave Summit
Brentwood

GREATER LONDON

UPMINSTER

(SEE MAP 26)

Hendon Central

N

(SEE MAP 21)

Romford
Harold Wood
C.S.

Railstore Dist. Dep.

West Horndon
Laindon
Basildon

Chadwell Heath
Gidea Park
LUL Depot

N

Seven Kings
Ilford
Goodmayes
OLE Depot
Emerson Pk.

2

D

3

14 13
12

10 9 8
Upminster

(Proposed High Speed Line from St Pancras to Dollands Moor)

11

1

B

Barking
(SEE INSET ABOVE)

Dagenham Dock

Ockendon

Stanford-le-Hope

C

C

North Woolwich

DL

Rainham
Chafford Hundred

Thames Haven Junc.

△
7
6

Abbey Wood
Belvedere
Erith

Purfleet
Grays

Cliffe
Brett Marine
East Tilbury

(SEE INSET P38)

Plumstead
Welling
Bexleyheath
Slade Green

Tilbury Town
Hoo Junc. Sdgs.

(SEE MAP 22)

Barnehurst

Hoo-Staff Halt*
Hoo Junc.

Falconwood
Albany Park

Ebbsfleet

D
4

5
Sidcup

Crayford
Dartford

Gravesend

Higham Tun.

Eltham
Bexley

KENT

Higham

1
0   5   10 m.
(1:350,000)
0   5   10   15 km.

2
DL DOCKLANDS
B   BAKERLOO
C   CENTRAL
O   CIRCLE
D   DISTRICT
J   JUBILEE

12

M   METROPOLITAN
M(EL) METROPOLITAN (East London)
N   NORTHERN
P   PICCADILLY
V   VICTORIA

36

37

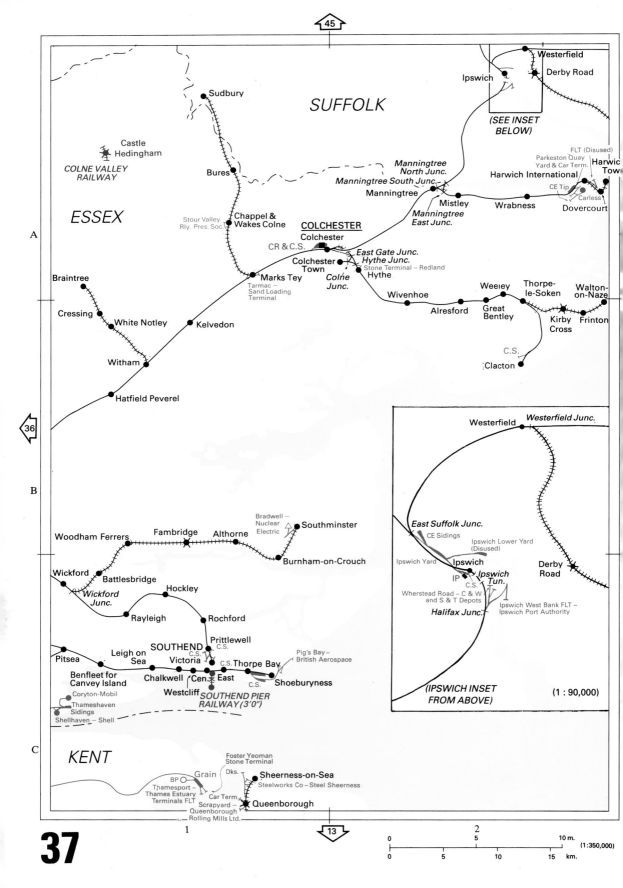

SUFFOLK

Westerfield
Derby Road
Ipswich
(SEE INSET BELOW)

Sudbury

Castle Hedingham
COLNE VALLEY RAILWAY

Bures

ESSEX

FLT (Disused)
Parkeston Quay Yard & Car Term.
Harwich Town
Manningtree North Junc.
Manningtree South Junc.
Manningtree
Mistley
Manningtree East Junc.
Harwich International
CE Tip
Carless
Dovercourt
Wrabness

Chappel & Wakes Colne
Stour Valley Rly. Pres. Soc.

COLCHESTER
Colchester
CR & C.S.
Colchester Town
East Gate Junc.
Hythe Junc.
Stone Terminal – Redland
Hythe
Colne Junc.

A

Braintree

Marks Tey
Tarmac – Sand Loading Terminal

Cressing
White Notley
Kelvedon

Wivenhoe
Alresford
Great Bentley
Weeley
Thorpe-le-Soken
Walton-on-Naze
Kirby Cross
Frinton

C.S.
Clacton

Witham

Hatfield Peverel

B

Woodham Ferrers
Fambridge
Althorne
Bradwell – Nuclear Electric
Southminster
Burnham-on-Crouch

Wickford
Battlesbridge
Hockley
Wickford Junc.
Rayleigh
Rochford

Pitsea
Leigh on Sea
Benfleet for Canvey Island
Chalkwell
SOUTHEND
Victoria
Westcliff
Cen.
East
C.S.
C.S.
Prittlewell
C.S.
Thorpe Bay
C.S.
Shoeburyness
Pig's Bay – British Aerospace

Coryton-Mobil
Thameshaven Sidings
Shellhaven – Shell
SOUTHEND PIER RAILWAY (3'0")

IPSWICH INSET

Westerfield
Westerfield Junc.

East Suffolk Junc.
CE Sidings
Ipswich Lower Yard (Disused)
Ipswich Yard
Ipswich
IP
C.S.
Ipswich Tun.
Derby Road
Wherstead Road – C & W and S & T Depots
Ipswich West Bank FLT – Ipswich Port Authority
Halifax Junc.

(IPSWICH INSET FROM ABOVE)
(1 : 90,000)

C

KENT

Foster Yeoman Stone Terminal
Grain
Dks.
Sheerness-on-Sea
Steelworks Co – Steel Sheerness
BP
Thamesport – Thames Estuary Terminals FLT
Car Term.
Scrapyard – Queenborough Rolling Mills Ltd.
Queenborough

0   2   10 m.
0   5   (1:350,000)
0   5   10   15   km.

Trimley
Felixstowe Beach Junc.
Felixstowe
Docks – Felixstowe
Dock & Railway Co.
North
FLT
Felixstowe Docks
South
FLT

**FELIXSTOWE – ZEEBRUGGE (P&O)
– HARWICH
(Orwell & Harwich Nav. Co.)**

HARWICH – *HOEK VAN HOLLAND*
INTERNATIONAL   *(Stena Line)*
PORT – *ESJBERG (Scandinavian
Seaways)*
– *GOTEBORG (Scandinavian
Seaways)*
– *HAMBURG (Scandinavian
Seaways)*

Talybont

Llanaber

Barmouth
Barmouth Viaduct

Porth
Penrhyn
Morfa Mawddach
*FAIRBOURNE
RAILWAY
(1'0¼")*
Fairbourne
Fairbourne

GWYNEDD

Llwyngwril

*TALYLLYN RAILWAY (2'3")
(Halts not shown)*

Abergynolwyn
Quarry Siding
Dolgoch Falls
Nant
Gwernol

Tonfanau

Tywyn
Wharf
Brynglas
Rhydyronen

**MACHYNLLETH RADIO
SIGNALLING CENTRE**   A

Machynlleth
Sidings

Tywyn
Tywyn Pendre

POWYS   39

MN

Aberdovey Tuns.
No. 2   No. 1
No.4
No. 3

Dovey
Junction

Aberdovey
Penhelig

Borth

DYFED

Shell
(Disused)

Aberystwyth
Glanrafon

Llanbadarn   B

Capel Bangor
Aberffrwd
Rheidol Falls

Nantyronen
Rhiwfron

Devil's
Bridge

VALE OF RHEIDOL RAILWAY (1'11½")

ESSEX

Powell
Duffryn
Oils
Purfleet

*West
Thurrock
Junc.*
Grays

Van den Berghs

West Thurrock –
Proctor & Gamble
(Disused)
Tilbury FLT

Slade
Green
Slade Green Junc.

Foster
Yeoman
Stone
Terminal

Van Ommeran
(Disused)

*(Thames Tun.
2.9 km)*

Tilbury
Grain
Terminal

Tilbury
Town   36

C.S.
SG

erry Street
Fork Junc.
Crayford Creek Junc.

**(Proposed High Speed
Line from St Pancras to
Dollands Moor)**

Proposed
Construction
Site/P.W. Depot
*Greenhithe
Tun.*

Tilbury
Northfleet
Hope FLT

Tilbury Riverside

*Crayford Spur
'A' Junc.*

Dartford
C.S.

Stone
Crossing
Greenhithe
Swanscombe
Northfleet
Gravesend West St.
*(White Horse
Ferries)*   C

Crayford
Spur 'B'
Dartford
Junc.

DARTFORD

Ebbsfleet
Gravesend

(INSET FROM MAP 36) **KENT**
(1:90,000)
Pepper Hill Tun.

0   5   10 m.   1
0   5   10   15 km.
(1:350,000)   2

38

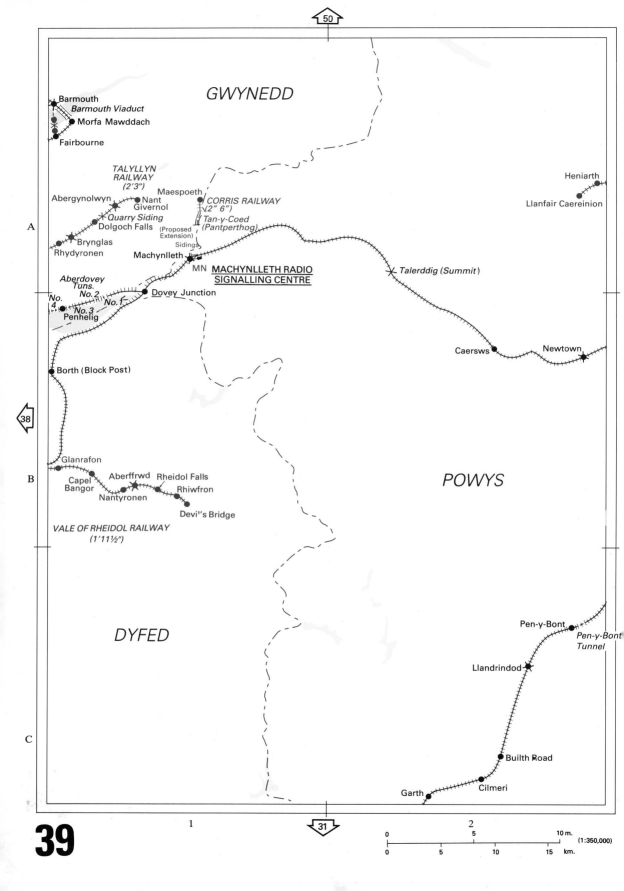

GWYNEDD

Barmouth
Barmouth Viaduct
Morfa Mawddach
Fairbourne

Heniarth

TALYLLYN RAILWAY (2'3")

Maespoeth

Llanfair Caereinion

Abergynolwyn
Nant Givernol
CORRIS RAILWAY (2" 6")

Quarry Siding
Dolgoch Falls
Tan-y-Coed (Pantperthog)

A

Brynglas
Rhydyronen

(Proposed Extension)
Sidings

Machynlleth
MN
MACHYNLLETH RADIO SIGNALLING CENTRE

Talerddig (Summit)

Aberdovey Tuns. No. 2
No. 4   No. 3   No. 1
Penhelig

Dovey Junction

Caersws
Newtown

Borth (Block Post)

POWYS

Glanrafon

B

Capel Bangor
Aberffrwd
Rheidol Falls
Rhiwfron
Nantyronen
Devi''s Bridge

VALE OF RHEIDOL RAILWAY (1'11½")

Pen-y-Bont
Pen-y-Bont Tunnel

DYFED

Llandrindod

C

Builth Road

Garth
Cilmeri

39

2

0   5   10 m.
(1:350,000)

0   5   10   15   km.

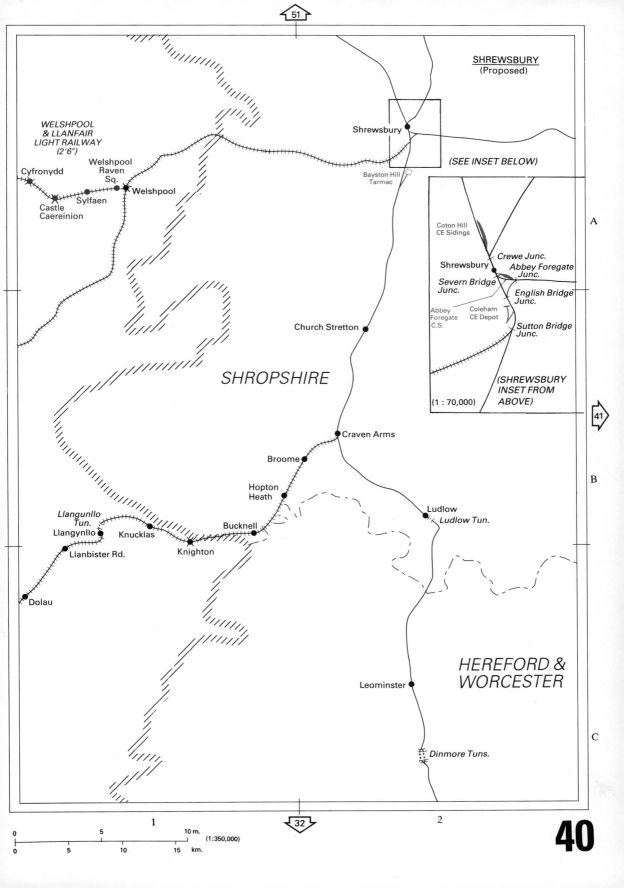

SHREWSBURY
(Proposed)

WELSHPOOL
& LLANFAIR
LIGHT RAILWAY
(2'6")

Cyfronydd

Welshpool
Raven
Sq.

Sylfaen

Welshpool

Castle
Caereinion

Shrewsbury

Bayston Hill
Tarmac

(SEE INSET BELOW)

A

Coton Hill
CE Sidings

Crewe Junc.

Shrewsbury

*Abbey Foregate
Junc.*

*Severn Bridge
Junc.*

*English Bridge
Junc.*

Abbey
Foregate
C.S.

Coleham
CE Depot

*Sutton Bridge
Junc.*

(1 : 70,000)

*(SHREWSBURY
INSET FROM
ABOVE)*

41

SHROPSHIRE

Church Stretton

Craven Arms

B

Broome

Hopton
Heath

Ludlow
Ludlow Tun.

*Llangunllo
Tun.*

Llangynllo

Knucklas

Bucknell

Llanbister Rd.

Knighton

Dolau

HEREFORD &
WORCESTER

Leominster

C

Dinmore Tuns.

1

10 m.

(1:350,000)

0   5

0   5   10   15   km.

2

40

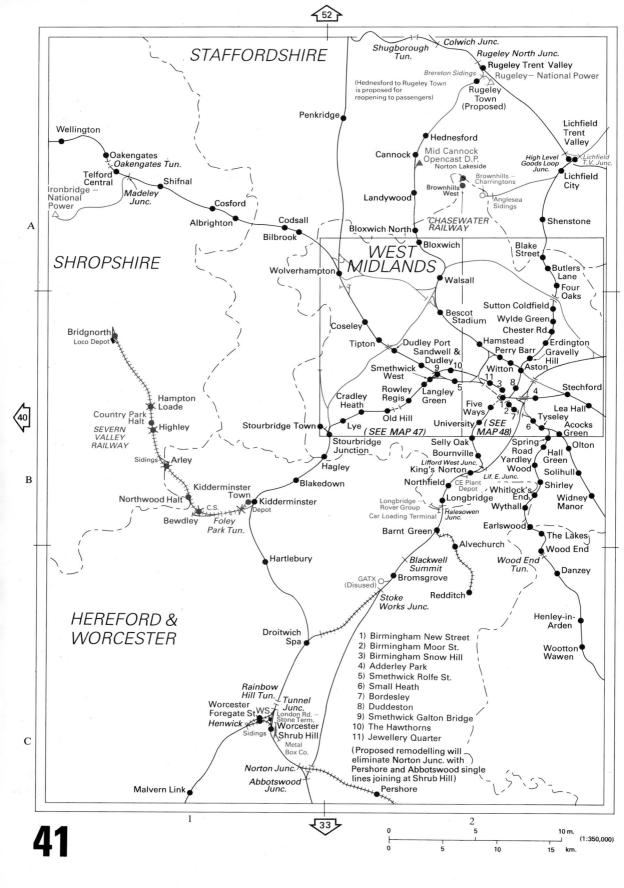

STAFFORDSHIRE

Shugborough Tun.
Colwich Junc.
Rugeley North Junc.
Brereton Sidings
Rugeley Trent Valley
Rugeley— National Power
(Hednesford to Rugeley Town is proposed for reopening to passengers)
Rugeley Town (Proposed)

Penkridge

Hednesford

Cannock

Mid Cannock Opencast D.P.
Norton Lakeside

Wellington

Oakengates
Oakengates Tun.
Telford Central
Shifnal

Madeley Junc.

Ironbridge— National Power

Cosford

Albrighton

Codsall

Bilbrook

Bloxwich North

SHROPSHIRE

Landywood

Brownhills— Charringtons
Brownhills West
Anglesea Sidings

CHASEWATER RAILWAY

Lichfield Trent Valley
High Level Goods Loop Junc.
Lichfield T.V. Junc.
Lichfield City

Shenstone

A

Wolverhampton

WEST MIDLANDS

Bloxwich
Blake Street
Butlers Lane
Four Oaks

Walsall

Bescot Stadium

Sutton Coldfield
Wylde Green
Chester Rd

Coseley

Tipton

Dudley Port
Sandwell & Dudley

Hamstead
Perry Barr

Erdington
Gravelly Hill

Bridgnorth
Loco Depot

Smethwick West
9
10
Witton
11
3
8
Aston
Stechford

Cradley Heath

Rowley Regis
Langley Green
5
4

Hampton Loade

Country Park Halt

Highley

SEVERN VALLEY RAILWAY

Five Ways
1
2
6
Lea Hall
Tyseley
Acocks Green

Stourbridge Town

Lye

Old Hill

University

(SEE MAP 47)

(SEE MAP 48)

40

Sidings

Arley

Stourbridge Junction

Selly Oak
Bournville

Olton

Hagley

Spring Road
Yardley Wood

Hall Green
Solihull

Kidderminster Town

Blakedown

King's Norton
Lifford West Junc.
Lif. E. Junc.

Shirley

B

Northwood Halt

C.S.

Kidderminster
Depot

Northfield

CE Plant Depot
Whitlock's End

Widney Manor

Bewdley
Foley Park Tun.

Longbridge Rover Group
Car Loading Terminal
Halesowen Junc.

Longbridge

Wythall

Earlswood

Hartlebury

Barnt Green

Alvechurch

The Lakes
Wood End

Blackwell Summit
Bromsgrove

Wood End Tun.

Danzey

HEREFORD & WORCESTER

GATX (Disused)

Stoke Works Junc.

Redditch

Henley-in-Arden

Droitwich Spa

1) Birmingham New Street
2) Birmingham Moor St.
3) Birmingham Snow Hill
4) Adderley Park
5) Smethwick Rolfe St.
6) Small Heath
7) Bordesley
8) Duddeston
9) Smethwick Galton Bridge
10) The Hawthorns
11) Jewellery Quarter

Wootton Wawen

Rainbow Hill Tun.
Tunnel Junc.
Worcester Foregate St
WS
Henwick
London Rd.— Stone Term.
Worcester Shrub Hill
Sidings
Metal Box Co.

(Proposed remodelling will eliminate Norton Junc. with Pershore and Abbotswood single lines joining at Shrub Hill)

C

Norton Junc.
Abbotswood Junc.

Malvern Link

Pershore

2

0   5   10 m.
0   5   10   15 km.
(1:350,000)

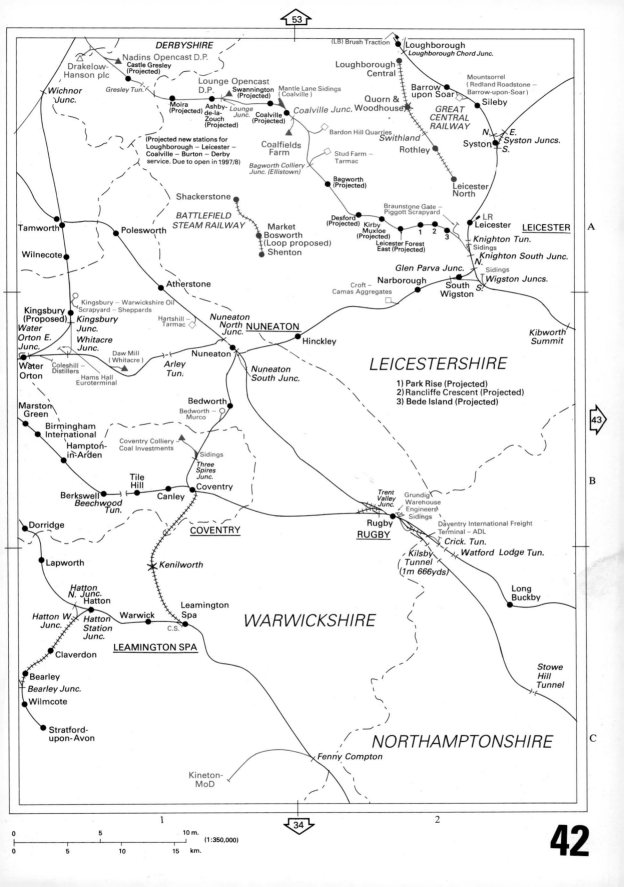

DERBYSHIRE

Nadins Opencast D.P.

Drakelow- Hanson plc

Castle Gresley (Projected)

(LB) Brush Traction

Loughborough

Loughborough Chord Junc.

Loughborough Central

Mountsorrel (Redland Roadstone – Barrow-upon-Soar)

Wichnor Junc.

Gresley Tun.

Lounge Opencast D.P.

Swannington (Projected)

Mantle Lane Sidings (Coalville)

Barrow upon Soar

Sileby

Moira (Projected)

Ashby- de-la- Zouch (Projected)

Lounge Junc.

Coalville (Projected)

Coalville Junc.

Quorn & Woodhouse

GREAT CENTRAL RAILWAY

Bardon Hill Quarries

Swithland

Coalfields Farm

Stud Farm – Tarmac

Rothley

N. E.
Syston Juncs.
Syston S.

(Projected new stations for Loughborough – Leicester – Coalville – Burton – Derby service. Due to open in 1997/8)

Bagworth Colliery Junc. (Ellistown)

Bagworth (Projected)

Leicester North

Shackerstone

BATTLEFIELD STEAM RAILWAY

Desford (Projected)

Braunstone Gate – Piggott Scrapyard

Kirby Muxloe (Projected)

Tamworth

Polesworth

Market Bosworth (Loop proposed)

Leicester Forest East (Projected)

1 2 3

LR Leicester

LEICESTER A

Shenton

Knighton Tun.

Wilnecote

Sidings

Knighton South Junc.

N.

Atherstone

Glen Parva Junc.

Sidings

Wigston Juncs. S.

Kingsbury (Proposed)

Kingsbury – Warwickshire Oil Scrapyard – Sheppards

Nuneaton North Junc.

Narborough

South Wigston

Water Orton E. Junc.

Kingsbury Junc.

Hartshill – Tarmac

Croft – Camas Aggregates

Whitacre Junc.

NUNEATON

Hinckley

Kibworth Summit

Water Orton

Coleshill Distillers

Daw Mill (Whitacre)

Nuneaton

LEICESTERSHIRE

Hams Hall Euroterminal

Arley Tun.

Nuneaton South Junc.

1) Park Rise (Projected)
2) Rancliffe Crescent (Projected)
3) Bede Island (Projected)

Marston Green

Bedworth

Birmingham International

Bedworth – Murco

Hampton- in-Arden

Coventry Colliery Coal Investments

Sidings

B

Tile Hill

Three Spires Junc.

Berkswell

Beechwood Tun.

Canley

Coventry

Trent Valley Junc.

Grundig Warehouse Engineers Sidings

Dorridge

COVENTRY

Rugby

RUGBY

Daventry International Freight Terminal – ADL

Crick. Tun.

Lapworth

Kenilworth

Kilsby Tunnel (1m 666yds)

Watford Lodge Tun.

Hatton N. Junc.

Hatton

Leamington Spa

Long Buckby

Hatton W. Junc.

Hatton Station Junc.

Warwick

C.S.

WARWICKSHIRE

Claverdon

LEAMINGTON SPA

Bearley

Stowe Hill Tunnel

Bearley Junc.

Wilmcote

Stratford- upon-Avon

NORTHAMPTONSHIRE C

Fenny Compton

Kineton- MoD

1

10 m.

2

(1:350,000)

0 5 10 15 km.

42

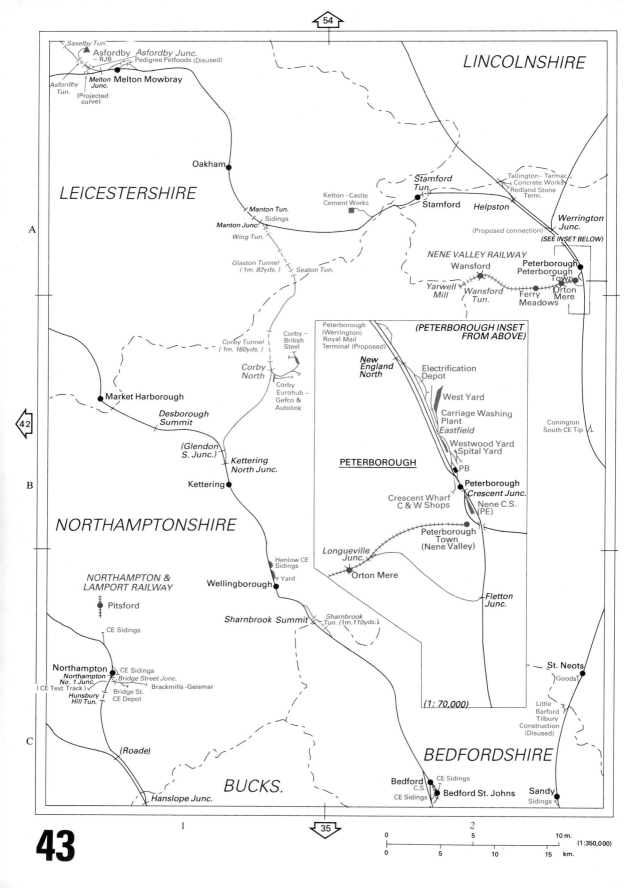

LINCOLNSHIRE

Saxelby Tun.
Asfordby *Asfordby Junc.*
– RJB
Pedigree Petfoods (Disused)
Asfordby
Tun.
Melton Junc. Melton Mowbray
(Projected curve)

LEICESTERSHIRE

Oakham

Manton Tun.
Sidings
Manton Junc!
Wing Tun.

Ketton - Castle
Cement Works

Stamford
Tun.
Stamford
Helpston

Tallington – Tarmac.
Concrete Works
Redland Stone
Term.

*Werrington
Junc.*
(Proposed connection)
(SEE INSET BELOW)

A

Glaston Tunnel
(1m. 82yds.)
Seaton Tun.

NENE VALLEY RAILWAY
Wansford
*Yarwell
Mill*
*Wansford
Tun.*
Ferry
Meadows
Peterborough
Peterborough
Town
Orton
Mere

Corby Tunnel
(1m. 160yds.)
Corby –
British Steel

*Corby
North*

Corby
Eurohub –
Gefco &
Autolink

Peterborough
(Werrington)
Royal Mail
Terminal (Proposed)

*(PETERBOROUGH INSET
FROM ABOVE)*

*New
England
North*

Electrification
Depot

42

Market Harborough

*Desborough
Summit*

West Yard

Carriage Washing
Plant
Eastfield

Westwood Yard
Spital Yard

Conington
South CE Tip

*(Glendon
S. Junc.)*
*Kettering
North Junc.*

PETERBOROUGH

PB

B

Kettering

Peterborough
Crescent Junc.

Nene C.S.
(PE)

NORTHAMPTONSHIRE

Crescent Wharf
C & W Shops

Peterborough
Town
(Nene Valley)

Henlow CE
Sidings
Y Yard

*Longueville
Junc.*
Orton Mere

NORTHAMPTON &
LAMPORT RAILWAY

Pitsford

Wellingborough

*Fletton
Junc.*

CE Sidings

Sharnbrook Summit
*Sharnbrook
Tun. (1m.110yds.)*

St. Neots

GoodsT

Northampton
*Northampton
No. 1 Junc.*
(CE Test Track)
*Hunsbury
Hill Tun.*

CE Sidings
Bridge Street Junc.
Brackmills -Geismar

Bridge St.
CE Depot

(1: 70,000)

Little
Barford
Tilbury
Construction
(Disused)

C

(Roade)

BUCKS.

Bedford
C.S.
CE Sidings
Bedford St. Johns

BEDFORDSHIRE

Sandy
Sidings

Hanslope Junc.

1

2

0   5   10 m.
(1:350,000)
0   5   10   15   km.

43

CE Sidings

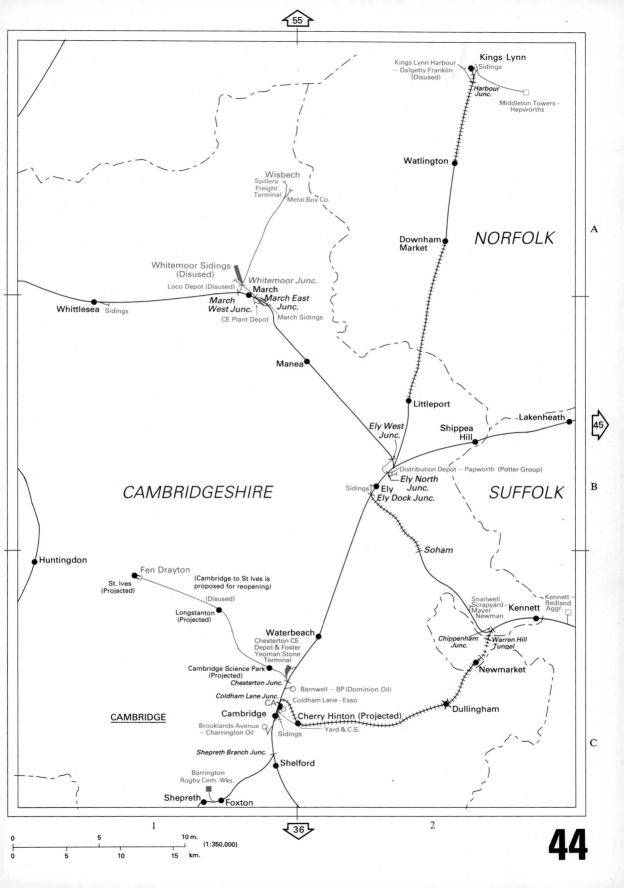

Kings Lynn Harbour
– Dalgetty Franklin
(Disused)

Kings Lynn
Sidings

Harbour Junc.

Middleton Towers -
Hepworths

Watlington

Wisbech
Spillers
Freight
Terminal
Metal Box Co.

NORFOLK

A

Downham
Market

Whitemoor Sidings
(Disused)
Loco Depot (Disused)
Whitemoor Junc.
March
*March East
Junc.*
*March
West Junc.*
CE Plant Depot
March Sidings

Whittlesea
Sidings

Manea

Littleport

Lakenheath

*Ely West
Junc.*

Shippea
Hill

CAMBRIDGESHIRE

Distribution Depot – Papworth (Potter Group)
*Ely North
Junc.*
Sidings
Ely
Ely Dock Junc.

SUFFOLK

B

Soham

Huntingdon

Fen Drayton
St. Ives
(Projected)
(Cambridge to St Ives is
proposed for reopening)
(Disused)

Longstanton
(Projected)

Snailwell
Scrapyard
Mayer
Newman

Kennett

Kennett –
Redland
Aggr.

*Chippenham
Junc.*

Waterbeach
Chesterton CE
Depot & Foster
Yeoman Stone
Terminal

*Warren Hill
Tunnel*

Cambridge Science Park
(Projected)
Chesterton Junc.

Newmarket

Barnwell – BP (Dominion Oil)

Coldham Lane Junc.
Coldham Lane - Esso

CAMBRIDGE

CA
Cambridge

Cherry Hinton (Projected)
Dullingham

Brooklands Avenue
– Charrington Oil
Sidings
Yard & C.S.

C

Shepreth Branch Junc.

Shelford

Barrington
Rugby Cem. Wks.

Shepreth
Foxton

1

2

0   5   10 m.
(1:350,000)
0   5   10   15 km.

45

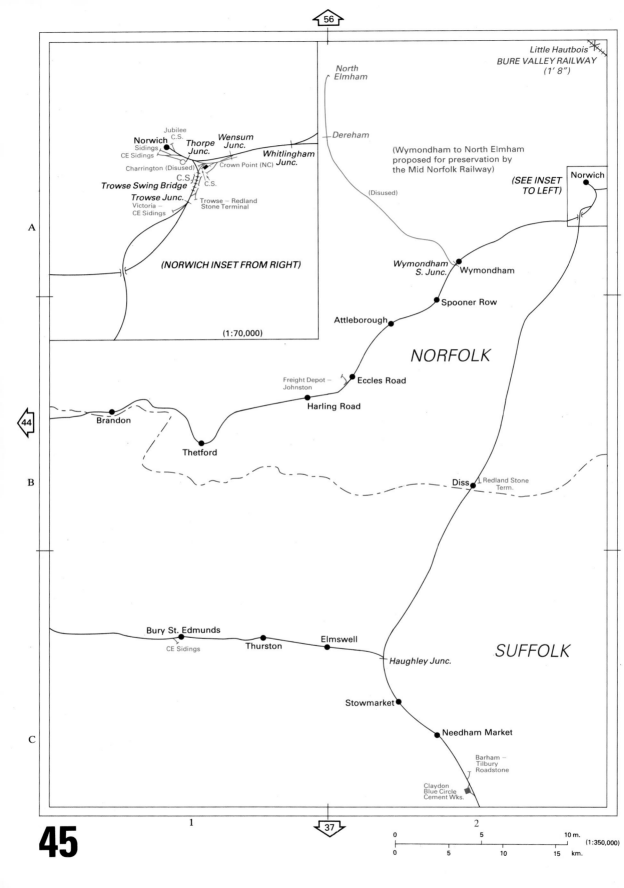

Little Hautbois
BURE VALLEY RAILWAY
(1' 8")

North
Elmham

Dereham

Norwich

(Wymondham to North Elmham
proposed for preservation by
the Mid Norfolk Railway)

*(SEE INSET
TO LEFT)*

Jubilee
C.S.
Sidings
CE Sidings
Norwich
*Thorpe
Junc.*
*Wensum
Junc.*
Charrington (Disused)
Crown Point (NC)
*Whitlingham
Junc.*
C.S.
C.S.
Trowse Swing Bridge
Trowse Junc.
Trowse – Redland
Stone Terminal
Victoria –
CE Sidings

(NORWICH INSET FROM RIGHT)

(Disused)

*Wymondham
S. Junc.*
Wymondham

Spooner Row

Attleborough

NORFOLK

(1:70,000)

Freight Depot –
Johnston
Eccles Road

Harling Road

Brandon

Thetford

Diss
Redland Stone
Term.

Bury St. Edmunds
CE Sidings
Thurston
Elmswell
Haughley Junc.

SUFFOLK

Stowmarket

Needham Market

Barham –
Tilbury
Roadstone

Claydon
Blue Circle
Cement Wks.

A

44

B

C

45

1

2

0   5   10 m.
(1:350,000)
0   5   10   15 km.

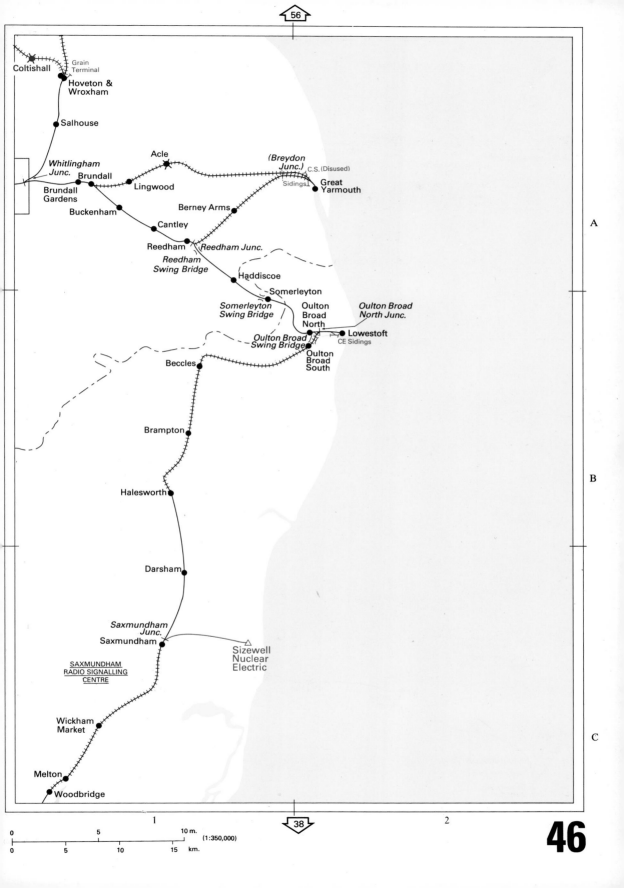

Coltishall
Grain Terminal
Hoveton & Wroxham
Salhouse
Whitlingham Junc.
Acle
Brundall
(Breydon Junc.)
C.S. (Disused)
Brundall Gardens
Lingwood
Sidings
Great Yarmouth
Buckenham
Berney Arms
Cantley
Reedham
Reedham Junc.
Reedham Swing Bridge
Haddiscoe
Somerleyton
Somerleyton Swing Bridge
Oulton Broad North
Oulton Broad North Junc.
Oulton Broad Swing Bridge
Lowestoft
CE Sidings
Oulton Broad South
Beccles
Brampton
Halesworth
Darsham
Saxmundham Junc.
Saxmundham
Sizewell Nuclear Electric
SAXMUNDHAM RADIO SIGNALLING CENTRE
Wickham Market
Melton
Woodbridge

A

B

C

1

2

0   5   10 m.
(1:350,000)
0   5   10   15   km.

46

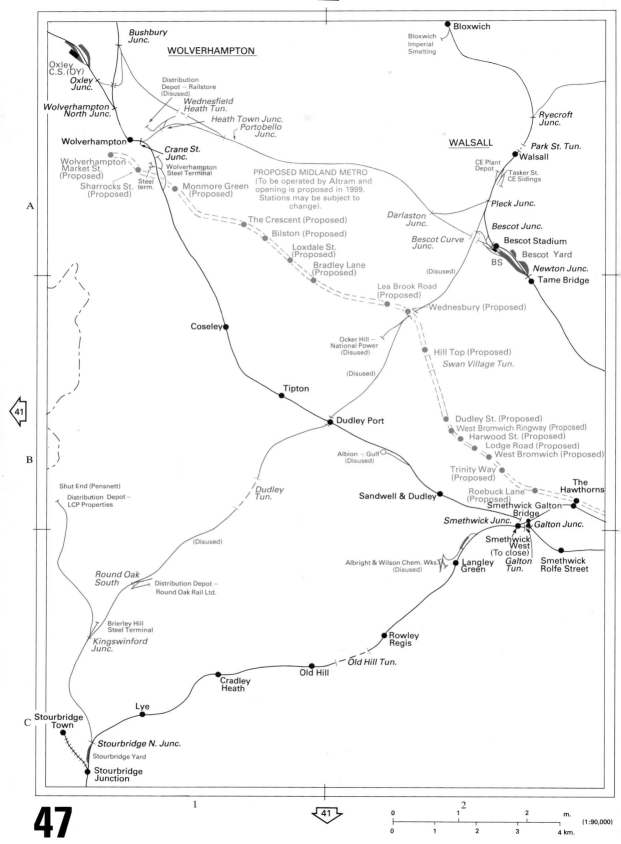

Bloxwich

Bloxwich
Imperial
Smelting

Bushbury
Junc.

WOLVERHAMPTON

Oxley
C.S.(OY)

Oxley
Junc.

Distribution
Depot – Railstore
(Disused)

Wednesfield
Heath Tun.

Ryecroft
Junc.

Wolverhampton
North Junc.

Heath Town Junc.
Portobello
Junc.

WALSALL

Park St. Tun.

Wolverhampton

Walsall

Crane St.
Junc.

CE Plant
Depot

Tasker St.
CE Sidings

Wolverhampton
Market St.
(Proposed)

Wolverhampton
Steel Terminal

PROPOSED MIDLAND METRO
(To be operated by Altram and
opening is proposed in 1999.
Stations may be subject to
change).

Pleck Junc.

Sharrocks St.
(Proposed)

Steel
term.

Monmore Green
(Proposed)

Darlaston
Junc.

Bescot Junc.

The Crescent (Proposed)

Bescot Curve
Junc.

Bescot Stadium

A

Bilston (Proposed)

Bescot Yard

Loxdale St.
(Proposed)

BS

Newton Junc.

Bradley Lane
(Proposed)

(Disused)

Tame Bridge

Lea Brook Road
(Proposed)

Wednesbury (Proposed)

Coseley

Ocker Hill –
National Power
(Disused)

Hill Top (Proposed)

Swan Village Tun.

(Disused)

Tipton

Dudley St. (Proposed)

Dudley Port

West Bromwich Ringway (Proposed)

Harwood St. (Proposed)

Albion – Gulf
(Disused)

Lodge Road (Proposed)

West Bromwich (Proposed)

B

Trinity Way
(Proposed)

The Hawthorns

Shut End (Pennsett)

Dudley
Tun.

Sandwell & Dudley

Roebuck Lane
(Proposed)

Distribution Depot –
LCP Properties

Smethwick Galton
Bridge

Smethwick Junc.

Galton Junc.

(Disused)

Smethwick
West
(To close)

Galton
Tun.

Smethwick
Rolfe Street

Round Oak
South

Distribution Depot –
Round Oak Rail Ltd.

Albright & Wilson Chem. Wks.
(Disused)

Langley
Green

Brierley Hill
Steel Terminal

Kingswinford
Junc.

Rowley
Regis

Old Hill Tun.

Cradley
Heath

Old Hill

Lye

Stourbridge
Town

C

Stourbridge N. Junc.

Stourbridge Yard

Stourbridge
Junction

1

41

2

0   1   2   m.

0   1   2   3   4 km.

(1:90,000)

41

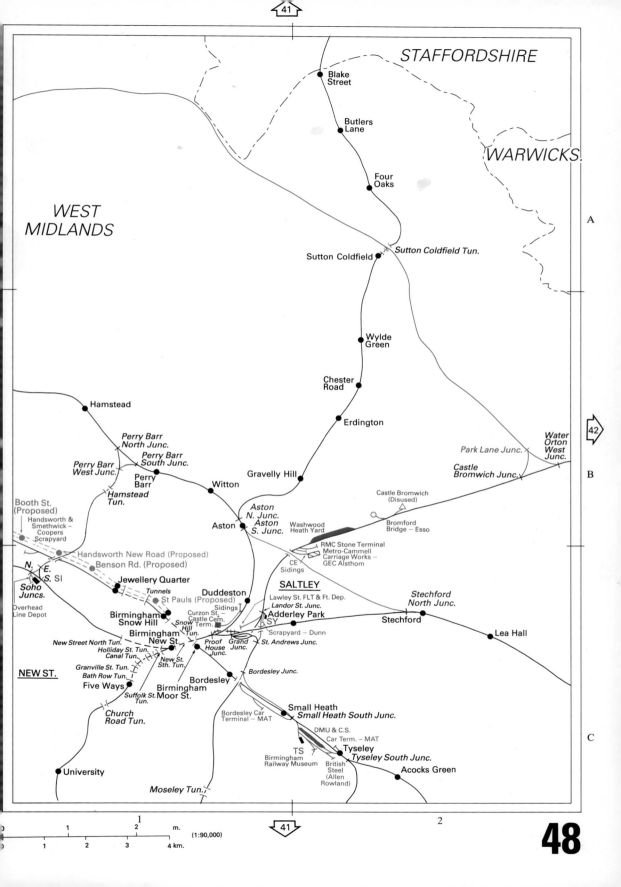

STAFFORDSHIRE

WARWICKS.

Blake
Street

Butlers
Lane

Four
Oaks

A

Sutton Coldfield Tun.

Sutton Coldfield

WEST
MIDLANDS

Wylde
Green

Chester
Road

Erdington

Hamstead

42

Water
Orton
West
Junc.

*Perry Barr
North Junc.*

*Perry Barr
South Junc.*

Park Lane Junc.

*Perry Barr
West Junc.*

Perry
Barr

*Castle
Bromwich Junc.*

B

Witton

Gravelly Hill

*Hamstead
Tun.*

Booth St.
(Proposed)

Handsworth &
Smethwick –
Coopers
Scrapyard

*Aston
N. Junc.
Aston
S. Junc.*

Aston

Washwood
Heath Yard

Castle Bromwich
(Disused)

Bromford
Bridge – Esso

RMC Stone Terminal
Metro-Cammell
Carriage Works –
GEC Alsthom

Handsworth New Road (Proposed)
Benson Rd. (Proposed)

N. E.
S. SI

CE
Sidings

*Soho
Juncs.*

Jewellery Quarter

SALTLEY

Overhead
Line Depot

Tunnels

St Pauls (Proposed)

Duddeston

*Stechford
North Junc.*

Lawley St. FLT & Ft. Dep.
Landor St. Junc.

Sidings

Adderley Park

Stechford

Birmingham
Snow Hill

Curzon St. –
Castle Cem.
*Snow
Hill Tun.*

SY

Lea Hall

New Street North Tun.

Birmingham
New St.

Scrapyard – Dunn
St. Andrews Junc.

*Holliday St. Tun.
Canal Tun.*

*Proof
House
Junc.*

*Grand
Junc.*

NEW ST.

*New St.
Sth. Tun.*

*New St.
Sth. Tun.*

*Granville St. Tun.
Bath Row Tun.*

Bordesley

Bordesley Junc.

Five Ways

*Suffolk St.
Tun.*

Birmingham
Moor St.

Small Heath
Small Heath South Junc.

*Church
Road Tun.*

Bordesley Car
Terminal – MAT

DMU & C.S.
Car Term. – MAT

C

TS

Tyseley
Tyseley South Junc.

University

Birmingham
Railway Museum

British
Steel
(Allen
Rowland)

Acocks Green

Moseley Tun.

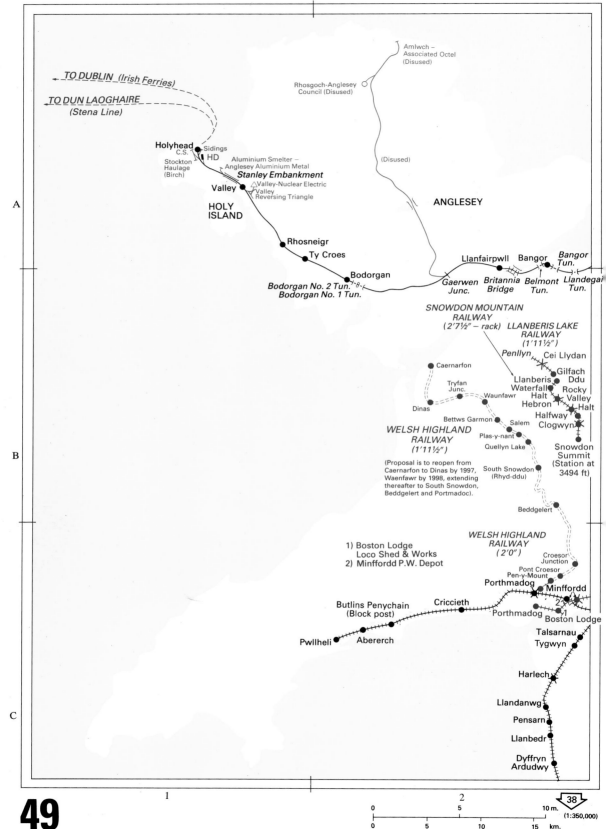

TO DUBLIN (Irish Ferries)

TO DUN LAOGHAIRE
(Stena Line)

Amlwch –
Associated Octel
(Disused)

Rhosgoch-Anglesey
Council (Disused)

(Disused)

ANGLESEY

Holyhead
C.S.   Sidings
HD
Stockton
Haulage   Aluminium Smelter –
(Birch)   Anglesey Aluminium Metal
Stanley Embankment
Valley   Valley-Nuclear Electric
        Valley
        Reversing Triangle
HOLY
ISLAND

A

Rhosneigr
Ty Croes
Bodorgan
Bodorgan No. 2 Tun.
Bodorgan No. 1 Tun.

Llanfairpwll   Bangor   Bangor
        Tun.
Gaerwen   Britannia   Belmont   Llandegai
Junc.   Bridge   Tun.   Tun.

SNOWDON MOUNTAIN
RAILWAY
(2'7½" – rack)   LLANBERIS LAKE
        RAILWAY
        (1'11½")
Penllyn   Cei Llydan
        Gilfach
Caernarfon   Llanberis   Ddu
        Waterfall   Rocky
Tryfan   Halt   Valley
Junc.   Hebron   Halt
Waunfawr   Halfway
Dinas   Clogwyn
Bettws Garmon   Salem
WELSH HIGHLAND   Plas-y-nant
RAILWAY   Quellyn Lake   Snowdon
(1'11½")   Summit
        (Station at
(Proposal is to reopen from   South Snowdon   3494 ft)
Caernarfon to Dinas by 1997,   (Rhyd-ddu)
Waenfawr by 1998, extending
thereafter to South Snowdon,
Beddgelert and Portmadoc).
        Beddgelert

B

WELSH HIGHLAND
RAILWAY
(2'0")
        Croesor
1) Boston Lodge   Junction
   Loco Shed & Works   Pont Croesor
2) Minffordd P.W. Depot   Pen-y-Mount
        Porthmadog   Minffordd
Butlins Penychain   Criccieth   2
(Block post)   1
        Porthmadog
        Boston Lodge
Pwllheli   Abererch   Talsarnau
        Tygwyn

        Harlech

C   Llandanwg
        Pensarn
        Llanbedr
        Dyffryn
        Ardudwy

49

1   2   10 m.
        (1:350,000)
0   5
        38
0   5   10   15   km.

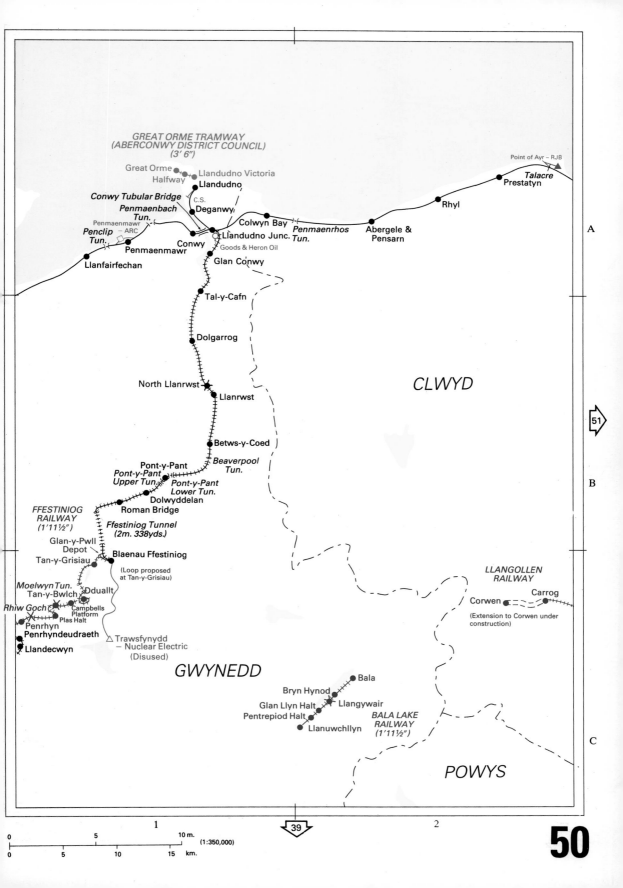

GREAT ORME TRAMWAY
(ABERCONWY DISTRICT COUNCIL)
(3' 6")

Great Orme • Llandudno Victoria
Halfway •
Llandudno

Conwy Tubular Bridge
C.S.
Deganwy
Penmaenbach
Tun.
Penmaenmawr – ARC
Colwyn Bay
Penclip
Tun.
Conwy
Penmaenrhos
Tun.
Abergele &
Pensarn
Llandudno Junc.
Goods & Heron Oil
Llanfairfechan
Penmaenmawr
Glan Conwy

Point of Ayr – RJB
Talacre
Prestatyn
Rhyl

Tal-y-Cafn

Dolgarrog

CLWYD

North Llanrwst
Llanrwst

51

Betws-y-Coed

Pont-y-Pant
Pont-y-Pant *Beaverpool*
Upper Tun. *Tun.*
Pont-y-Pant
Lower Tun.
Dolwyddelan
Roman Bridge

B

FFESTINIOG
RAILWAY
(1' 11½")

Ffestiniog Tunnel
(2m. 338yds.)
Glan-y-Pwll
Depot
Blaenau Ffestiniog
Tan-y-Grisiau
(Loop proposed
at Tan-y-Grisiau)

LLANGOLLEN
RAILWAY

Moelwyn Tun.
Tan-y-Bwlch
Dduallt
Corwen
Carrog
Rhiw Goch
Campbells
Platform
Plas Halt
Penrhyn
Penrhyndeudraeth
△ Trawsfynydd
– Nuclear Electric
(Disused)
Llandecwyn

(Extension to Corwen under
construction)

GWYNEDD

Bala
Bryn Hynod
Glan Llyn Halt
Llangywair
Pentrepiod Halt
BALA LAKE
RAILWAY
(1' 11½")
Llanuwchllyn

C

POWYS

1
2
39

0   5   10 m.
(1:350,000)
0   5   10   15   km.

50

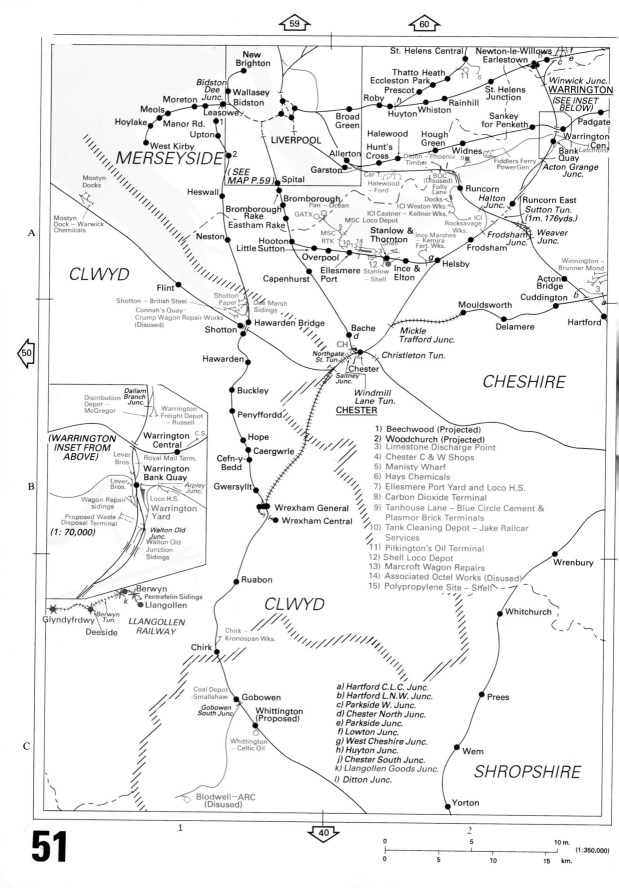

MERSEYSIDE

New Brighton
Wallasey
Bidston
Bidston Dee Junc.
Moreton
Leasowe
Meols
Manor Rd.
Hoylake
Upton
West Kirby
Broad Green
LIVERPOOL

St. Helens Central
Newton-le-Willows
Earlestown
Winwick Junc.
Thatto Heath
Eccleston Park
Prescot
St. Helens Junction
WARRINGTON
(SEE INSET BELOW)
Roby
Rainhill
Huyton
Whiston
Sankey for Penketh
Padgate
Halewood
Hough Green
Widnes
Warrington Cen.
Hunt's Cross
Allerton
Ditton
Phoenix
Latchford
Bank Quay
Garston
Car T.
Halewood – Ford
Fiddlers Ferry PowerGen
Acton Grange Junc.

Mostyn Docks
Mostyn Dock – Warwick Chemicals

CLWYD

Heswall
Spital
(SEE MAP P.59)
Bromborough
Pan – Ocean
GATX
ICI Weston Wks.
Runcorn
Halton Junc.
Runcorn East
Sutton Tun.
(1m. 176yds.)
Bromborough Rake
Eastham Rake
ICI Castner – Kellner Wks.
MSC Loco Depot
Rocksavage Wks.
Frodsham Junc.
Weaver Junc.
Neston
MSC RTK
Stanlow & Thornton
Ince Marshes – Kemira Fert. Wks.
Frodsham
Hooton
Little Sutton
Overpool
Ellesmere Port
Stanlow – Shell
Ince & Elton
Helsby
Capenhurst
Shell
Winnington – Brunner Mond
Acton Bridge
Cuddington
Hartford

Flint
Shotton – British Steel
Connah's Quay – Crump Wagon Repair Works (Disused)
Shotton Paper
Dee Marsh Sidings
Hawarden Bridge
Bache
Mickle Trafford Junc.
Mouldsworth
Delamere
Shotton
CH
Northgate St. Tun.
Chester
Christleton Tun.

CHESHIRE

Hawarden
Saltney Junc.
Windmill Lane Tun.
CHESTER

Buckley

Penyffordd
Hope
Caergwrle
Cefn-y-Bedd
Gwersyllt
Wrexham General
Wrexham Central

1) Beechwood (Projected)
2) Woodchurch (Projected)
3) Limestone Discharge Point
4) Chester C & W Shops
5) Manisty Wharf
6) Hays Chemicals
7) Ellesmere Port Yard and Loco H.S.
8) Carbon Dioxide Terminal
9) Tanhouse Lane – Blue Circle Cement & Plasmor Brick Terminals
10) Tank Cleaning Depot – Jake Railcar Services
11) Pilkington's Oil Terminal
12) Shell Loco Depot
13) Marcroft Wagon Repairs
14) Associated Octel Works (Disused)
15) Polypropylene Site – Shell

Wrenbury

Ruabon

CLWYD

Berwyn
Pentrefelin Sidings
Llangollen
Berwyn Tun.
Glyndyfrdwy
Deeside
LLANGOLLEN RAILWAY

Whitchurch

Chirk – Kronospan Wks.

Coal Depot – Smallshaw
Gobowen
Gobowen South Junc.
Chirk
Whittington (Proposed)
Whittington – Celtic Oil

Prees

a) Hartford C.L.C. Junc.
b) Hartford L.N.W. Junc.
c) Parkside W. Junc.
d) Chester North Junc.
e) Parkside Junc.
f) Lowton Junc.
g) West Cheshire Junc.
h) Huyton Junc.
j) Chester South Junc.
k) Llangollen Goods Junc.
l) Ditton Junc.

Wem

SHROPSHIRE

Blodwell – ARC (Disused)

Yorton

0   5   10 m.
(1:350,000)
0   5   10   15   km.

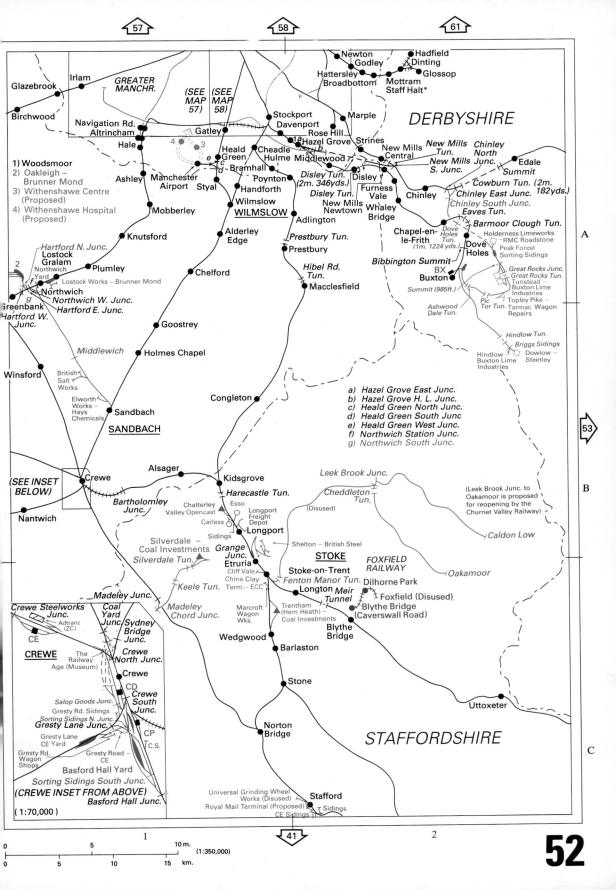

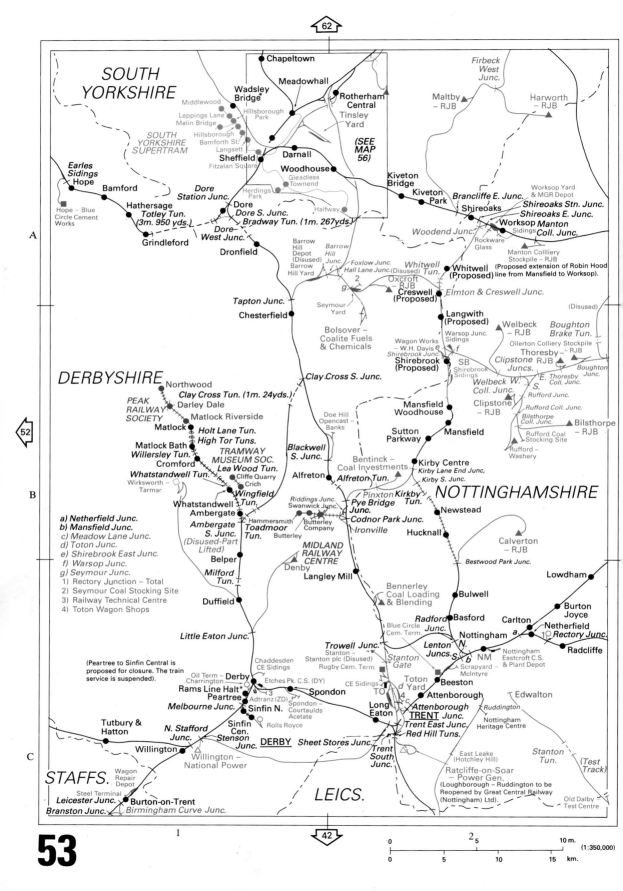

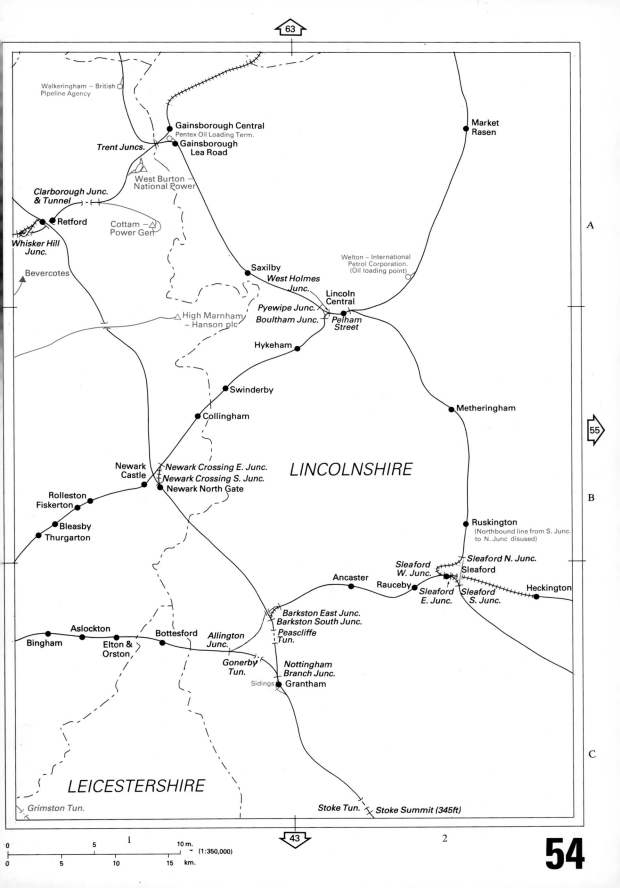

Walkeringham – British
Pipeline Agency

Gainsborough Central
Pentex Oil Loading Term.
Trent Juncs.
Gainsborough
Lea Road

Market
Rasen

West Burton –
National Power

*Clarborough Junc.
& Tunnel*

Retford

Cottam –
Power Gen

*Whisker Hill
Junc.*

Bevercotes

Welton – International
Petrol Corporation.
(Oil loading point)

Saxilby
*West Holmes
Junc.*

Lincoln
Central
Pyewipe Junc.
Boultham Junc.
*Pelham
Street*

△ High Marnham
– Hanson plc

Hykeham

Swinderby

Metheringham

Collingham

LINCOLNSHIRE

Newark
Castle
Newark Crossing E. Junc.
Newark Crossing S. Junc.
Newark North Gate

Rolleston
Fiskerton

Ruskington
(Northbound line from S. Junc.
to N. Junc disused)

Bleasby
Thurgarton

B

Sleaford N. Junc.
*Sleaford
W. Junc.*
Sleaford
Ancaster
Rauceby
Heckington
*Sleaford
E. Junc.*
*Sleaford
S. Junc.*

Aslockton
Bingham
Elton &
Orston

Bottesford
*Allington
Junc.*

Barkston East Junc.
Barkston South Junc.
*Peascliffe
Tun.*

*Gonerby
Tun.*
*Nottingham
Branch Junc.*
Sidings
Grantham

LEICESTERSHIRE

Grimston Tun.

Stoke Tun. *Stoke Summit (345ft)*

A

55

C

0   5   1   10 m.
― (1:350,000)
0   5   10   15   km.

2

54

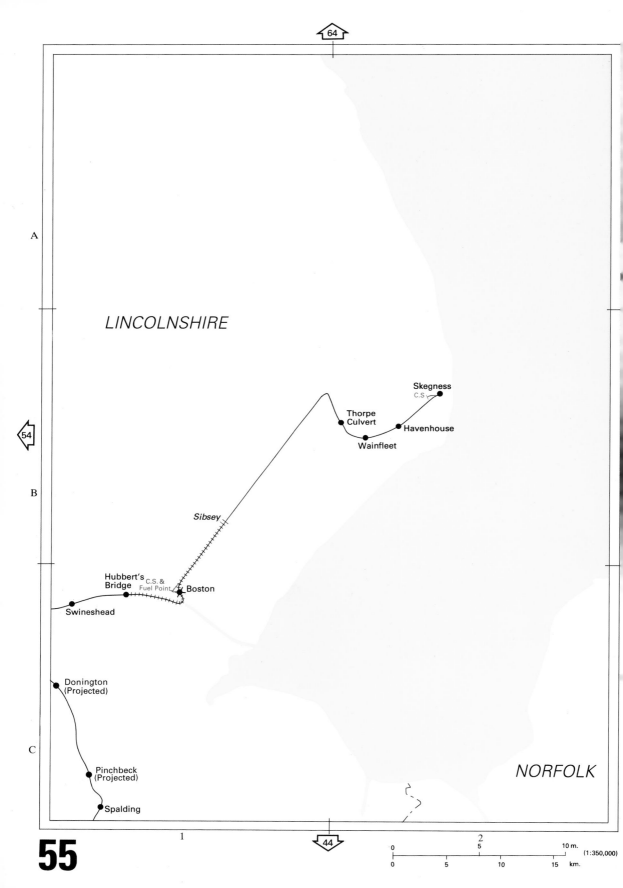

LINCOLNSHIRE

A

54

Skegness
C.S

Thorpe
Culvert
Havenhouse
Wainfleet

B

Sibsey

Hubbert's
Bridge
C.S. &
Fuel Point
Boston

Swineshead

Donington
(Projected)

C

Pinchbeck
(Projected)

Spalding

NORFOLK

55

0   2 5   10 m.
     (1:350,000)
0   5   10   15   km.

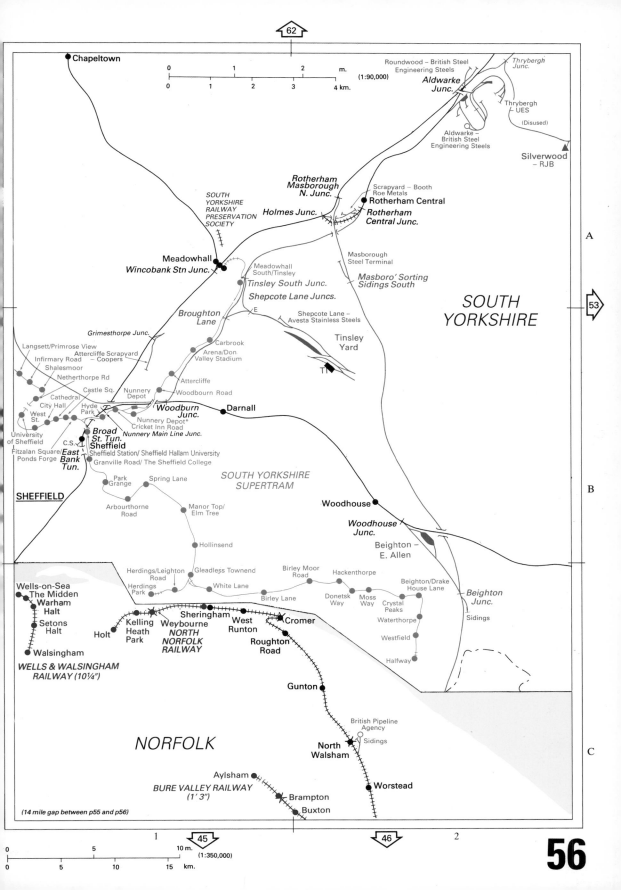

Chapeltown

0   1   2   m.
0   1   2   3   4 km.   (1:90,000)

Roundwood – British Steel
Engineering Steels
Aldwarke
Junc.

Thrybergh
Junc.

Thrybergh
– UES

Aldwarke –
British Steel
Engineering Steels

(Disused)

Silverwood
– RJB

Rotherham
Masborough
N. Junc.

Scrapyard – Booth
Roe Metals

Rotherham Central

Holmes Junc.

Rotherham
Central Junc.

SOUTH
YORKSHIRE
RAILWAY
PRESERVATION
SOCIETY

Meadowhall
Wincobank Stn Junc.

Meadowhall
South/Tinsley

Tinsley South Junc.

Shepcote Lane Juncs.

Masborough
Steel Terminal

Masboro' Sorting
Sidings South

SOUTH
YORKSHIRE

Broughton
Lane

Grimesthorpe Junc.

E

Shepcote Lane –
Avesta Stainless Steels

Tinsley Yard

Langsett/Primrose View
Infirmary Road
Shalesmoor
Netherthorpe Rd

Attercliffe Scrapyard
– Coopers

Carbrook

Arena/Don
Valley Stadium

TI

Castle Sq.   Nunnery
Depot

Cathedral
City Hall
Hyde
Park

West
St.

University
of Sheffield

C.S.

Fitzalan Square/
Ponds Forge

Broad
St. Tun.

East
Bank
Tun.

SHEFFIELD

Attercliffe

Woodbourn Road

Nunnery
Depot*

Cricket Inn Road

Nunnery Main Line Junc.

Woodburn
Junc.

Darnall

Sheffield

Sheffield Station/ Sheffield Hallam University
Granville Road/ The Sheffield College

SOUTH YORKSHIRE
SUPERTRAM

Park
Grange

Spring Lane

Arbourthorne
Road

Manor Top/
Elm Tree

Woodhouse

Woodhouse
Junc.

Beighton –
E. Allen

Hollinsend

Gleadless Townend

Herdings/Leighton
Road

Herdings
Park

White Lane

Birley Lane

Birley Moor
Road

Hackenthorpe

Donetsk
Way

Moss
Way

Crystal
Peaks

Beighton/Drake
House Lane

Waterthorpe

Westfield

Halfway

Beighton
Junc.

Sidings

Wells-on-Sea
The Midden
Warham
Halt
Setons
Halt
Walsingham

WELLS & WALSINGHAM
RAILWAY (10¼")

Holt

Kelling
Heath
Park

Sheringham

Weybourne

NORTH
NORFOLK
RAILWAY

West
Runton

Cromer

Roughton
Road

Gunton

NORFOLK

North
Walsham

British Pipeline
Agency

Sidings

Aylsham

BURE VALLEY RAILWAY
(1' 3")

Brampton

Buxton

Worstead

(14 mile gap between p55 and p56)

0   5   10 m.
0   5   10   15 km.   (1:350,000)

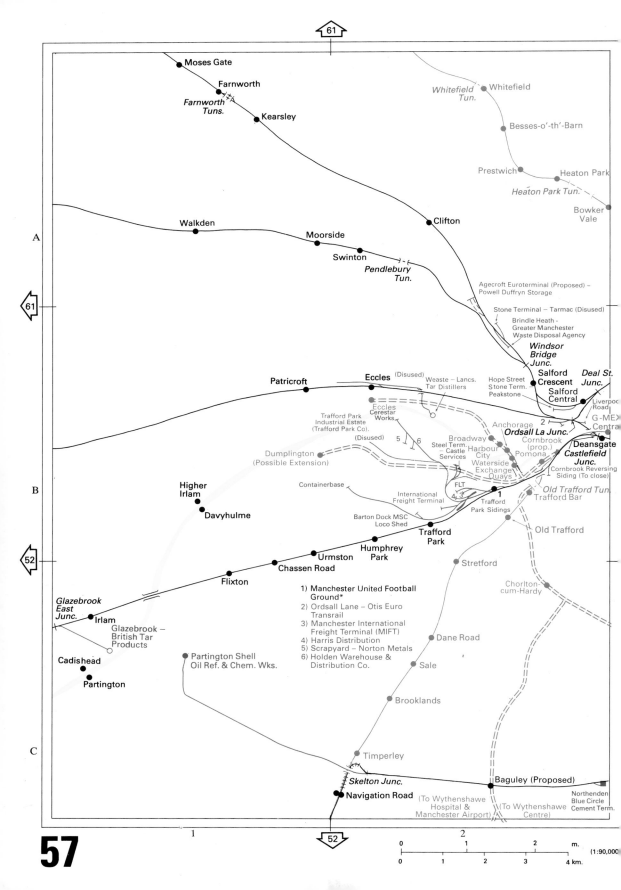

Moses Gate

Farnworth

Farnworth Tuns.

Kearsley

Whitefield Tun. Whitefield

Besses-o'-th'-Barn

Prestwich Heaton Park

Heaton Park Tun.

Bowker Vale

Walkden

Moorside

Swinton

Pendlebury Tun.

Clifton

A

Agecroft Euroterminal (Proposed) –
Powell Duffryn Storage

Stone Terminal – Tarmac (Disused)

Brindle Heath -
Greater Manchester
Waste Disposal Agency

*Windsor
Bridge
Junc.*

Patricroft

Eccles (Disused)

Weaste – Lancs.
Tar Distillers

Hope Street
Stone Term.

Peakstone

Salford
Crescent

Salford
Central

*Deal St.
Junc.*

Liverpool
Road

G-MEX
Central

Trafford Park
Industrial Estate
(Trafford Park Co.)

*Eccles
Cerestar
Works*

(Disused)

Anchorage

Ordsall La Junc.

2

Cornbrook
(prop.)

Deansgate

*Castlefield
Junc.*

Dumplington
(Possible Extension)

5 6

Broadway

Steel Term.
– Castle
Services

Harbour
City

Pomona

Cornbrook Reversing
Siding (To close)

Containerbase

Waterside
Exchange
Quays

FLT

4 3

Old Trafford Tun.

Trafford Bar

B

Higher
Irlam

Davyhulme

International
Freight Terminal

Barton Dock MSC
Loco Shed

Trafford
Park

1 Trafford
Park Sidings

Old Trafford

Humphrey
Park

Stretford

52

Urmston

Chassen Road

Chorlton-
cum-Hardy

Flixton

1) Manchester United Football
  Ground*
2) Ordsall Lane – Otis Euro
  Transrail
3) Manchester International
  Freight Terminal (MIFT)
4) Harris Distribution
5) Scrapyard – Norton Metals
6) Holden Warehouse &
  Distribution Co.

Dane Road

*Glazebrook
East
Junc.*

Irlam

Glazebrook –
British Tar
Products

Sale

Cadishead

Partington Shell
Oil Ref. & Chem. Wks.

Brooklands

Partington

C

Timperley

Baguley (Proposed)

Skelton Junc.

Navigation Road

(To Wythenshawe
Hospital &
Manchester Airport)

(To Wythenshawe
Centre)

Northenden
Blue Circle
Cement Term.

57

1

2

0 1 2 m.

0 1 2 3 4 km.

(1:90,000)

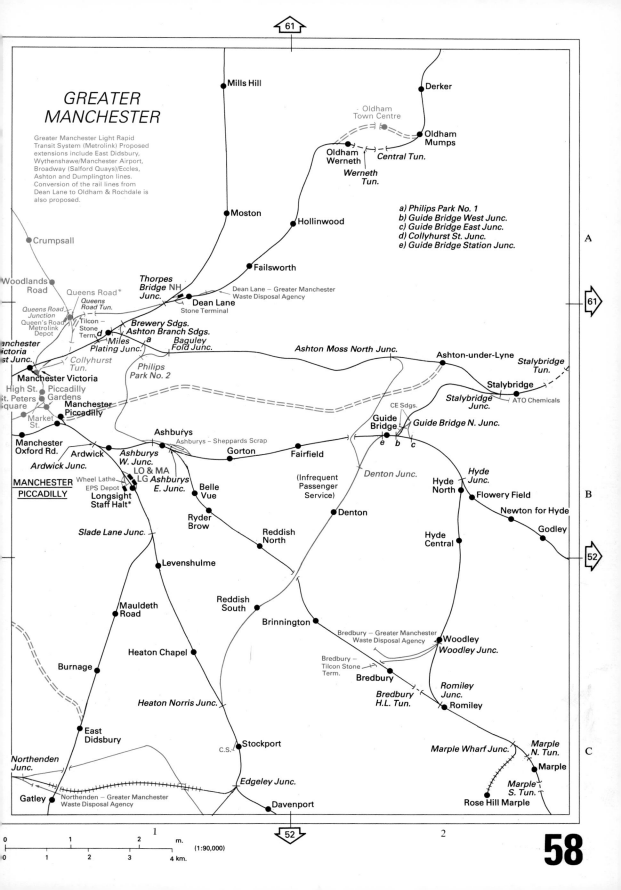

GREATER MANCHESTER

Greater Manchester Light Rapid
Transit System (Metrolink) Proposed
extensions include East Didsbury,
Wythenshawe/Manchester Airport,
Broadway (Salford Quays)/Eccles,
Ashton and Dumplington lines.
Conversion of the rail lines from
Dean Lane to Oldham & Rochdale is
also proposed.

a) Philips Park No. 1
b) Guide Bridge West Junc.
c) Guide Bridge East Junc.
d) Collyhurst St. Junc.
e) Guide Bridge Station Junc.

A

61

Mills Hill

Derker

Oldham
Town Centre

Oldham
Mumps

Moston

Hollinwood

Oldham
Werneth

Central Tun.

*Werneth
Tun.*

Crumpsall

Failsworth

Woodlands
Road

*Thorpes
Bridge NH
Junc.*

Dean Lane — Greater Manchester
Waste Disposal Agency

Queens Road*

*Queens
Road Tun.*

Dean Lane
Stone Terminal

*Queens Road
Junction*

Queen's Road
Metrolink
Depot

*Tilcon —
Stone
Term.*

Brewery Sdgs.
Ashton Branch Sdgs.

*Miles
Plating Junc.*

*Baguley
Fold Junc.*

Ashton Moss North Junc.

Ashton-under-Lyne

*Stalybridge
Tun.*

Manchester
Victoria
st Junc.

d

a

*Collyhurst
Tun.*

*Philips
Park No. 2*

Stalybridge

Manchester Victoria

*Stalybridge
Junc.*

ATO Chemicals

High St.
St. Peters
Square

Piccadilly
Gardens

CE Sdgs.

Guide
Bridge

Guide Bridge N. Junc.

**Manchester
Piccadilly**

Market
St.

Ashburys

e   b   c

**Manchester
Oxford Rd.**

Ardwick

Ashburys – Sheppards Scrap

Gorton

Fairfield

Ardwick Junc.

*Ashburys
W. Junc.*

Denton Junc.

*Hyde
Junc.*

B

UNDERLINE MANCHESTER
PICCADILLY

Wheel Lathe
EPS Depot

LO & MA
LG *Ashburys
E. Junc.*

**Belle
Vue**

(Infrequent
Passenger
Service)

Hyde
North

Flowery Field

**Longsight
Staff Halt***

**Ryder
Brow**

Denton

Newton for Hyde

Slade Lane Junc.

**Reddish
North**

Hyde
Central

Godley

Levenshulme

52

**Mauldeth
Road**

**Reddish
South**

Heaton Chapel

Brinnington

Bredbury – Greater Manchester
Waste Disposal Agency

Woodley

Burnage

Woodley Junc.

Bredbury –
Tilcon Stone
Term.

*Romiley
Junc.*

Heaton Norris Junc.

Bredbury

*Bredbury
H.L. Tun.*

Romiley

**East
Didsbury**

C.S.

Stockport

Marple Wharf Junc.

*Marple
N. Tun.*

C

*Northenden
Junc.*

Edgeley Junc.

Marple

Gatley

Northenden – Greater Manchester
Waste Disposal Agency

Davenport

*Marple
S. Tun.*

Rose Hill Marple

0   1   2
m.
(1:90,000)

0   1   2   3   4 km.

1

2

MERSEYSIDE

Hall Road
HR

Blundellsands
& Crosby

Old Roan

Kirkby

Waterloo

Excursion
Platform*

Aintree

Fazakerley Junc.

Seaforth &
Litherland

(Disused)

Fazakerley

TO DOUGLAS (Isle of Man
Steam Packet Seaways)

Seaforth FLT
& Cawood Coal
Export Terminal

Orrell
Park

Seaforth
Grain Term.
Allied Mills
(Disused)

Walton

Rice Lane

Walton Junc.

Gladstone Dock
– Powergen

Bootle
New Strand

MDHC

Bootle
Oriel Rd.

Kirkdale No. 1 Tun.

Kirkdale No. 2 Tun.

RTK

Kirkdale

m

Spellow Tun.

b

k

Westminster Rd. Tun.

Bank Hall

Kirkdale EMU Depot

New Brighton

Sandhills Junc.

Wallasey Grove Rd.

Sandhills

Wallasey Village

MERSEYRAIL

Vauxhall
(Projected)

1) Pacific Road Depot
2) Egerton Bridge
a) *Derby Square Junc.*
b) *Bootle Junc.*
c) *Paradise Junc.*
d) *Mann Island Junc.*
e) *Canning St. Junc.*
f) *Bootle Branch Junc.*
g) *Picton Road Junc.*
h) *Hamilton Sq. Junc.*
j) *Picko No. 2 Tun.*
k) *Oriel Road Tun.*
l) *Bury Street Tun.*
m) *Alexandra Dock Tun.*
n) *Haymarket Tun.*
p) *Canning St. N.*

*Bidston
E. Junc.*

RTK

MDHC

*(M.P.T.E.
FERRIES)*

Moorfields

Lime St.

EDGE HILL

Seacombe

Russell St. Tun.

Tuebrook
CE Sidings

j

Broad Green

BD

BIRKENHEAD
TRAMWAY

Pier Head

LIVERPOOL

c

Edge
Hill

Birkenhead
North

(Disused)

d

a

Central

f

Sidings

JAMES ST.

James St.

*Mount
Pleasant
Tun.*

CE
Shop

g

Birkenhead
Park

MDHC

p

Mersey Tun.

*Overbury St.
Tun.*

*Crown
St. Tun.*

Spekeland
Road Goods

Conway Park (Proposed
for opening in 1997)

RTK

2

1

Woodside

h

e

Gullet
Sidings

Downhill
C.S.(LL)

Wavertree Junc.

Birkenhead
Hamilton
Square

Birkenhead
Central

n

*St. James
Tuns.*

Depot

Brunswick Park
(Projected)

*Hinderton
Field Tun.*

Green Lane

Mossley Hill

Dingle Tun.

St. Michaels

Rock Ferry

St. Michaels Tun.

West
Allerton

*Rock Ferry
S. Junc.*

*Fulwood
Tun.*

Woodchurch
(Projected)

Aigburth

Hunts Cross
West Junc.

Bebington

Cressington

Allerton

AN

Garston

*Speke
Junc.*

Garston FLT

*Garston
Junc.*

Port Sunlight

Garston Coal
Terminal – ABP
(Disused)

Speke
Yard

Spital

Car Terminal –
– Axial

A

B

C

51

51

60

1

2

59

0   1   2   m.

0   1   2   3   4 km.

(1:90,000)

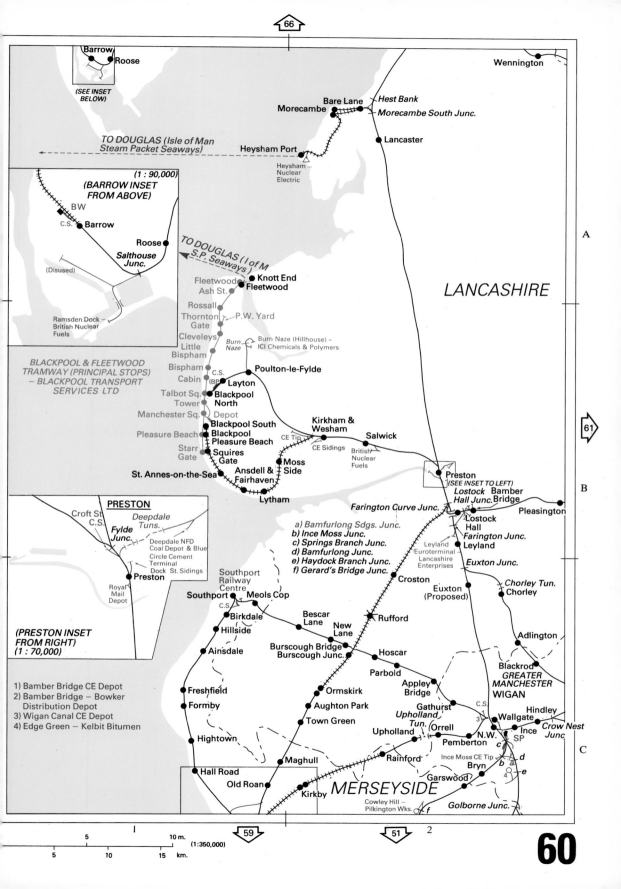

Barrow
Roose
(SEE INSET BELOW)

Wennington

Bare Lane   *Hest Bank*
Morecambe   *Morecambe South Junc.*

Lancaster

TO DOUGLAS (Isle of Man Steam Packet Seaways)

Heysham Port

Heysham Nuclear Electric

(1 : 90,000)
(BARROW INSET FROM ABOVE)

BW
C.S.   Barrow

Roose
Salthouse Junc.

(Disused)

Ramsden Dock – British Nuclear Fuels

TO DOUGLAS (I of M S.P. Seaways)

Fleetwood Ash St.
Knott End
Fleetwood

Rossall
Thornton Gate   P.W. Yard
Cleveleys
Little Bispham
Burn Naze (Hillhouse) – ICI Chemicals & Polymers
Burn Naze

Bispham
Cabin   C.S. (BP)
Layton
Poulton-le-Fylde

BLACKPOOL & FLEETWOOD TRAMWAY (PRINCIPAL STOPS) – BLACKPOOL TRANSPORT SERVICES LTD

Talbot Sq.
Tower   Blackpool North
Manchester Sq.   Depot
Blackpool South
Pleasure Beach   Blackpool Pleasure Beach
Squires Gate
Starr Gate

LANCASHIRE

Kirkham & Wesham
Salwick
CE Tip
CE Sidings
British Nuclear Fuels

Moss Side
Ansdell & Fairhaven
St. Annes-on-the-Sea
Lytham

Preston
(SEE INSET TO LEFT)

Lostock Bamber
Hall Junc. Bridge

Pleasington

PRESTON
Deepdale Tuns.
Croft St C.S.
Fylde Junc.
Deepdale NFD Coal Depot & Blue Circle Cement Terminal
Dock St. Sidings
Royal Mail Depot
Preston

a) Bamfurlong Sdgs. Junc.
b) Ince Moss Junc.
c) Springs Branch Junc.
d) Bamfurlong Junc.
e) Haydock Branch Junc.
f) Gerard's Bridge Junc.

Faringant Curve Junc.
Lostock Hall
Farington Junc.
Leyland
Leyland Euroterminal
Lancashire Enterprises
Euxton Junc.

(PRESTON INSET FROM RIGHT)
(1 : 70,000)

1) Bamber Bridge CE Depot
2) Bamber Bridge – Bowker Distribution Depot
3) Wigan Canal CE Depot
4) Edge Green – Kelbit Bitumen

Southport Railway Centre
Meols Cop
Southport
C.S.
Birkdale
Hillside
Ainsdale

Bescar Lane
New Lane
Burscough Bridge
Burscough Junc.

Croston
Euxton (Proposed)

Chorley Tun.
Chorley

Rufford
Hoscar
Parbold

Adlington

Blackrod
GREATER MANCHESTER
WIGAN

Freshfield
Formby

Ormskirk
Aughton Park
Town Green

Appley Bridge
Gathurst
Upholland Tun.
Orrell
Pemberton

C.S.
Wallgate
Hindley
N.W.
Ince
SP
Crow Nest Junc.

Hightown

Upholland
Rainford

Ince Moss CE Tip
Bryn

c
d
b a
e
4

Maghull

Garswood

Hall Road
Old Roan
Kirkby

MERSEYSIDE

Cowley Hill – Pilkington Wks.
f
Golborne Junc.

5   10 m.
(1:350,000)
5   10   15   km.

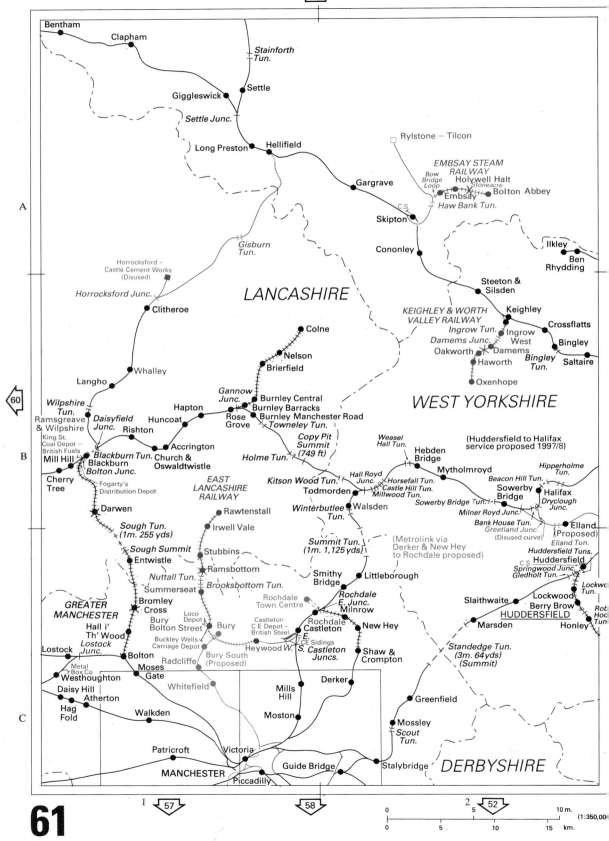

Bentham

Clapham

Stainforth Tun.

Settle

Giggleswick

Settle Junc.

Long Preston

Hellifield

Gargrave

☐ Rylstone – Tilcon

EMBSAY STEAM RAILWAY

Bow Bridge Loop Holywell Halt

Stoneacre

Embsay ✕ Bolton Abbey

C.S. *Haw Bank Tun.*

Skipton

A

Cononley

Ilkley

Ben Rhydding

Steeton & Silsden

KEIGHLEY & WORTH VALLEY RAILWAY

Keighley

Ingrow Tun. Ingrow West

Crossflatts

LANCASHIRE

Colne

Nelson

Brierfield

Damems Junc. Damems

Bingley

Bingley Tun.

Saltaire

Oakworth

Haworth

Oxenhope

WEST YORKSHIRE

Whalley

Langho

Wilpshire Tun.

Ramsgreave & Wilpshire

Daisyfield Junc.

Rishton

Hapton

Huncoat

Gannow Junc.

Burnley Central

Burnley Barracks

Rose Grove

Burnley Manchester Road

Towneley Tun.

Copy Pit Summit (749 ft)

Holme Tun.

Weasel Hall Tun.

Hebden Bridge

Mytholmroyd

(Huddersfield to Halifax service proposed 1997/8)

Hipperholme Tun.

60

King St. Coal Depot – British Fuels

Mill Hill

Blackburn Tun.

Church & Oswaldtwistle

Accrington

Blackburn Bolton Junc.

Fogarty's Distribution Depot

B

Cherry Tree

Darwen

EAST LANCASHIRE RAILWAY

Kitson Wood Tun.

Todmorden

Hall Royd Junc.

Horsefall Tun.

Beacon Hill Tun.

Millwood Tun.

Castle Hill Tun.

Sowerby Bridge

Halifax

Sowerby Bridge Tun. *Dryclough Junc.*

Milner Royd Junc.

Bank House Tun.

Greetland Junc. Elland

(Disused curve) (Proposed)

Elland Tun.

Huddersfield Tuns.

HUDDERSFIELD

Springwood Junc.

Gledholt Tun.

Lockw...

Lockwood Tun.

Rawtenstall

Irwell Vale

Sough Tun. (1m. 255 yds)

Sough Summit

Entwistle

Nuttall Tun.

Stubbins

Ramsbottom

Brooksbottom Tun.

Smithy Bridge

Littleborough

Summit Tun. (1m. 1,125 yds)

Winterbutlee Tun.

Walsden

(Metrolink via Derker & New Hey to Rochdale proposed)

Slaithwaite

Lockwood

Berry Brow

GREATER MANCHESTER

Bromley Cross

Summerseat

Loco Depot

Bury Bolton Street

Bury

Rochdale E. Junc.

Milnrow

Rochdale Town Centre

New Hey

Rochdale E.

Marsden

Honley

Rob Hod Tun.

Hall i' Th' Wood

Lostock Junc.

Buckley Wells Carriage Depot

Castleton C E Depot – British Steel

Heywood

Castleton

C E Sidings

W. & S. Castleton Juncs.

Shaw & Crompton

Standedge Tun. (3m. 64yds) (Summit)

Lostock

Bolton

Moses Gate

Radcliffe

Bury South (Proposed)

Metal Box Co

Westhoughton

Whitefield

Mills Hill

Derker

Greenfield

Daisy Hill

Atherton

Walkden

Moston

Mossley

Scout Tun.

C

Hag Fold

Patricroft

Victoria

Guide Bridge

Stalybridge

DERBYSHIRE

MANCHESTER

Piccadilly

61

1 ▽ 57

▽ 58

2 ▽ 52

Horrocksford – Castle Cement Works (Disused)

Horrocksford Junc.

Clitheroe

Gisburn Tun.

0   5   10 m.

0   5   10   15   km.

(1:350,00

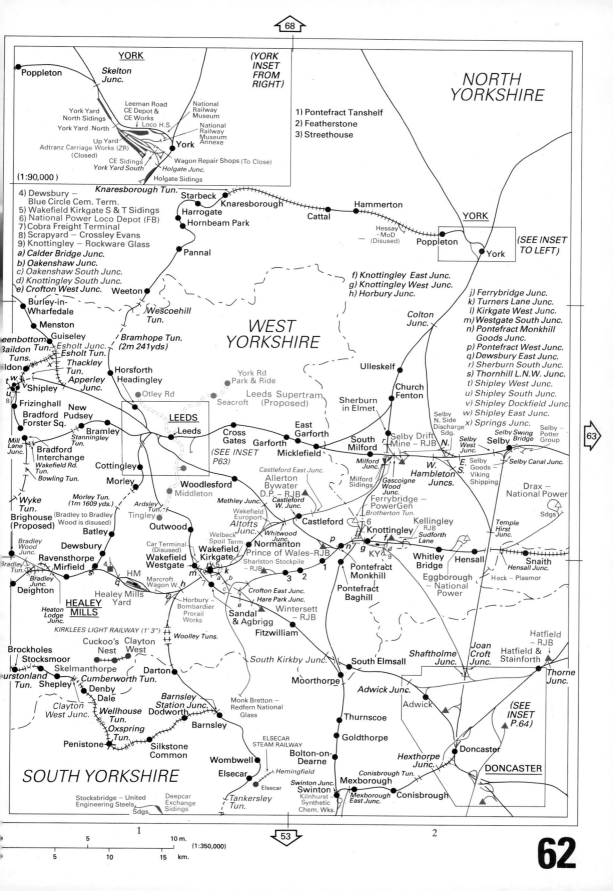

YORK
(YORK INSET FROM RIGHT)

Poppleton
Skelton Junc.

York Yard North Sidings
York Yard North
Up Yard
Adtranz Carriage Works (ZR) (Closed)
York Yard South

Leeman Road CE Depot & CE Works
Loco H.S.
National Railway Museum
National Railway Museum Annexe
York
CE Sidings
Wagon Repair Shops (To Close)
Holgate Junc.
Holgate Sidings

(1:90,000)

1) Pontefract Tanshelf
2) Featherstone
3) Streethouse

4) Dewsbury – Blue Circle Cem. Term.
5) Wakefield Kirkgate S & T Sidings
6) National Power Loco Depot (FB)
7) Cobra Freight Terminal
8) Scrapyard – Crossley Evans
9) Knottingley – Rockware Glass
a) Calder Bridge Junc.
b) Oakenshaw Junc.
c) Oakenshaw South Junc.
d) Knottingley South Junc.
e) Crofton West Junc.

f) Knottingley East Junc.
g) Knottingley West Junc.
h) Horbury Junc.

j) Ferrybridge Junc.
k) Turners Lane Junc.
l) Kirkgate West Junc.
m) Westgate South Junc.
n) Pontefract Monkhill Goods Junc.
p) Pontefract West Junc.
q) Dewsbury East Junc.
r) Sherburn South Junc.
s) Thornhill L.N.W. Junc.
t) Shipley West Junc.
u) Shipley South Junc.
v) Shipley Dockfield Junc.
w) Shipley East Junc.
x) Springs Junc.

NORTH YORKSHIRE

WEST YORKSHIRE

SOUTH YORKSHIRE

DONCASTER

YORK
(SEE INSET TO LEFT)

Knaresborough Tun.
Starbeck
Knaresborough
Hammerton
Harrogate
Hornbeam Park
Cattal
Hessay – MoD (Disused)
Poppleton
York

Pannal
Weeton
Colton Junc.

Burley-in-Wharfedale
Wescoehill Tun.
Menston
Guiseley
Greenbottom Tun.
Baildon Tun.
Bramhope Tun. (2m 241yds)
Esholt Junc.
Esholt Tun.
Thackley Tun.
Apperley Junc.
Horsforth
Headingley
Ulleskelf
Sherburn in Elmet
Church Fenton
Shipley
Frizinghall
New Pudsey
York Rd Park & Ride
Seacroft
Leeds Supertram (Proposed)
Bradford Forster Sq.
Bramley
Stanningley Tun.
LEEDS
Leeds
Cross Gates
East Garforth
Selby N. Side Discharge Sdg.
Selby Swing Bridge
Selby – Potter Group
Mill Lane Junc.
Bradford Interchange
Wakefield Rd. Tun.
Bowling Tun.
Cottingley
Morley
Garforth
Micklefield
South Milford
Selby Drift Mine – RJB N.
Selby West Junc.
Selby
Selby Goods Viking Shipping
Selby Canal Junc.
Wyke Tun.
Brighouse (Proposed)
Morley Tun. (1m 1609 yds.)
Ardsley Tun.
Tingley
Woodlesford
Middleton
Methley Junc.
Allerton Bywater
Castleford East Junc.
Milford Junc.
Milford Sidings
Gascoigne Wood Junc.
W. Hambleton Juncs.
E. S.
Selby Goods
Drax – National Power
Sdgs
Batley
Bradley Wood Junc.
Dewsbury
Ravensthorpe
Mirfield
Deighton
Outwood
Car Terminal (Disused)
Wakefield Westgate
Altofts Junc.
Welbeck Spoil Term.
Whitwood Junc.
Castleford W. Junc.
Wakefield Europort
Castleford
Ferrybridge – PowerGen
Brotherton Tun.
Knottingley
Kellingley RJB
Sudforth Lane
Temple Hirst Junc.
Bradley Tun.
HM
Bramley
Wakefield Kirkgate
Normanton
Prince of Wales – RJB
Sharlston Stockpile – RJB
Pontefract Monkhill
Whitley Bridge
Hensall
Snaith
Hensall Junc.
Healey Mills Yard
KIRKLEES LIGHT RAILWAY (1' 3")
Heaton Lodge Junc.
Horbury – Bombardier Prorail Works
Marcroft Wagon W.
Sandal & Agbrigg
Crofton East Junc.
Hare Park Junc.
Wintersett – RJB
Pontefract Baghill
Eggborough – National Power
Heck – Plasmor
Brockholes
Stocksmoor
Cuckoo's Nest
Clayton West
Woolley Tuns.
Fitzwilliam
Shaftholme Junc.
Joan Croft Junc.
Hatfield – RJB
Hatfield & Stainforth
Thorne Junc.
Thurstonland Tun.
Shepley
Skelmanthorpe
Cumberworth Tun.
Darton
South Kirkby Junc.
South Elmsall
Moorthorpe
Adwick Junc.
Adwick
(SEE INSET P.64)
Denby Dale
Clayton West Junc.
Wellhouse Tun.
Oxspring Tun.
Barnsley Station Junc.
Dodworth
Monk Bretton – Redfern National Glass
Thurnscoe
Goldthorpe
Hexthorpe Junc.
Doncaster
Penistone
Silkstone Common
Barnsley
ELSECAR STEAM RAILWAY
Bolton-on-Dearne
Wombwell
Elsecar
Hemingfield
Elsecar
Swinton Junc.
Conisbrough Tun.
Mexborough
Conisbrough
Stocksbridge – United Engineering Steels Sdgs.
Deepcar Exchange Sidings
Tankersley Tun.
Swinton
Kilnhurst Synthetic Chem. Wks.
Mexborough East Junc.

63

1
5
10 m.
5
10
15 km.
(1:350,000)
2

62

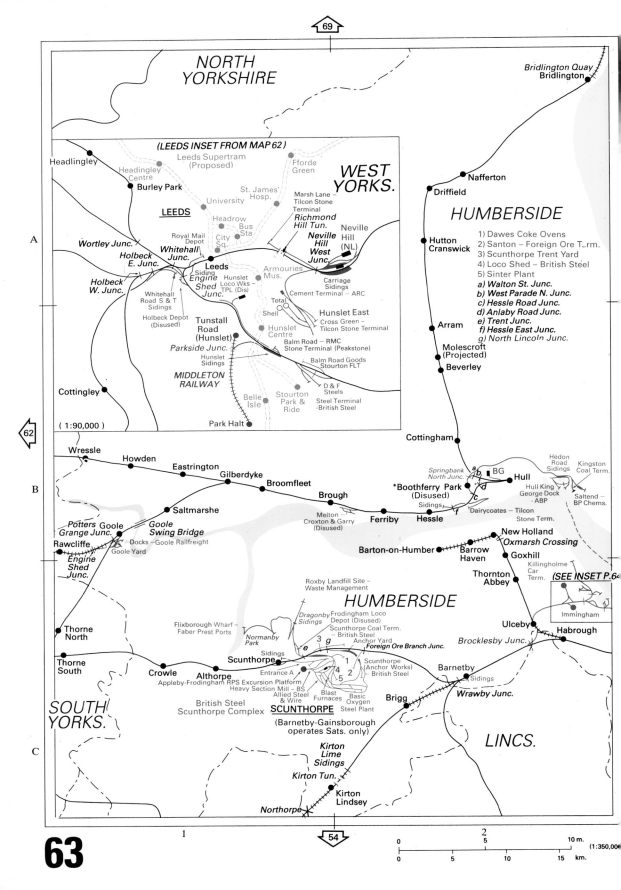

NORTH
YORKSHIRE

WEST
YORKS.

Bridlington Quay
Bridlington

Headlingley

(LEEDS INSET FROM MAP 62)

Leeds Supertram
(Proposed)

Headingley
Centre

Fforde
Green

Nafferton

Burley Park

Driffield

University

St. James'
Hosp.

HUMBERSIDE

LEEDS

Headrow
Bus
Sta.

Marsh Lane
Tilcon Stone
Terminal
Richmond
Hill Tun.

1) Dawes Coke Ovens
2) Santon – Foreign Ore Term.
3) Scunthorpe Trent Yard
4) Loco Shed – British Steel
5) Sinter Plant
a) Walton St. Junc.
b) West Parade N. Junc.
c) Hessle Road Junc.
d) Anlaby Road Junc.
e) Trent Junc.
f) Hessle East Junc.
g) North Lincoln Junc.

A

Wortley Junc.

Royal Mail
Depot

City
Sq.

Whitehall
Junc.

Holbeck
E. Junc.

Neville
Hill
(NL)

Neville
Hill
West
Junc.

Hutton
Cranswick

Siding
Engine
Shed

Leeds

Hunslet
Loco Wks –
TPL (Dis)

Armouries
Mus.

Holbeck
W. Junc.

Carriage
Sidings

Whitehall
Road S & T
Sidings

Cement Terminal – ARC

Arram

Total
Shell

Hunslet East

Molescroft
(Projected)

Holbeck Depot
(Disused)

Tunstall
Road
(Hunslet)

Hunslet
Centre

Cross Green –
Tilcon Stone Terminal

Beverley

Parkside Junc.

Balm Road – RMC
Stone Terminal (Peakstone)

Hunslet
Sidings

MIDDLETON
RAILWAY

Balm Road Goods
Stourton FLT

Cottingley

Belle
Isle

D & F
Steels

Cottingham

Stourton
Park &
Ride

Steel Terminal
–British Steel

(1:90,000)

Park Halt

Wressle

Springbank
North Junc.

a
b

BG

Hedon
Road
Sidings

Kingston
Coal Term.

Howden

Eastrington

Hull

B

Gilberdyke

d

Broomfleet

*Boothferry Park
(Disused)

c

Hull King
George Dock
– ABP

Saltend –
BP Chems.

Brough

Saltmarshe

Melton
Croxton & Garry
(Disused)

Sidings

f

Ferriby

Hessle

*Dairycoates – Tilcon
Stone Term.*

Potters
Grange Junc.

Goole

Goole
Swing Bridge

Rawcliffe

Docks –Goole Railfreight

Barton-on-Humber

Barrow
Haven

New Holland
Oxmarsh Crossing

Goxhill

Engine
Shed
Junc.

Goole Yard

Thornton
Abbey

Killingholme
Car
Term.

(SEE INSET P.64

Roxby Landfill Site –
Waste Management

HUMBERSIDE

Ulceby

Habrough

Thorne
North

Dragonby
Sidings

Frodingham Loco
Depot (Disused)
Scunthorpe Coal Term.
– British Steel
Anchor Yard

Immingham

Flixborough Wharf –
Faber Prest Ports

Normanby
Park

3

g

Brocklesby Junc.

Thorne
South

Crowle

Althorpe

e

Foreign Ore Branch Junc.

Sidings

Scunthorpe

1

Scunthorpe
(Anchor Works)
– British Steel

Barnetby

Sidings

Entrance A

4

Appleby-Frodingham RPS Excursion Platform
Heavy Section Mill – BS
Allied Steel
& Wire

5

2

SOUTH
YORKS.

Blast
Furnaces

Basic
Oxygen
Steel Plant

Brigg

Wrawby Junc.

British Steel
Scunthorpe Complex

SCUNTHORPE

(Barnetby-Gainsborough
operates Sats. only)

LINCS.

C

Kirton
Lime
Sidings

Kirton Tun.

Kirton
Lindsey

Northorpe

2
5

10 m.

(1:350,00

0

5

10

15

km.

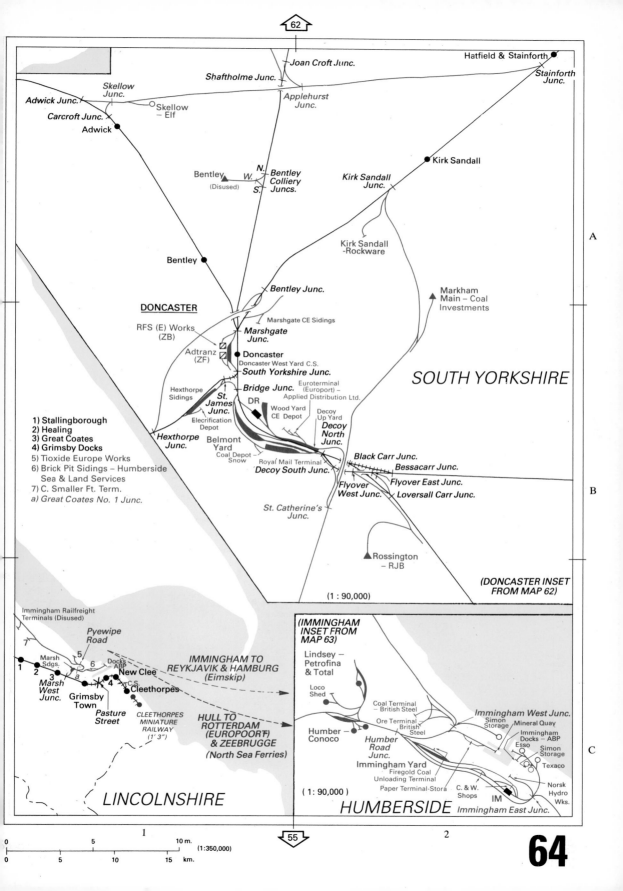

Joan Croft Junc.

Hatfield & Stainforth

Shaftholme Junc.

Stainforth Junc.

Adwick Junc.

Skellow Junc.

Applehurst Junc.

Skellow – Elf

Carcroft Junc.

Adwick

Kirk Sandall

Bentley (Disused)

N.

W.

Bentley Colliery Juncs.

S.

Kirk Sandall Junc.

A

Kirk Sandall -Rockware

Bentley

Bentley Junc.

Markham Main – Coal Investments

DONCASTER

Marshgate CE Sidings

RFS (E) Works (ZB)

Marshgate Junc.

SOUTH YORKSHIRE

Adtranz (ZF)

Doncaster

Doncaster West Yard C.S.

South Yorkshire Junc.

Hexthorpe Sidings

Bridge Junc.

Euroterminal (Europort) – Applied Distribution Ltd.

St. James Junc.

DR

Wood Yard CE Depot

Decoy Up Yard

Electrification Depot

Decoy North Junc.

1) Stallingborough
2) Healing
3) Great Coates
4) Grimsby Docks
5) Tioxide Europe Works
6) Brick Pit Sidings – Humberside Sea & Land Services
7) C. Smaller Ft. Term.
a) Great Coates No. 1 Junc.

Hexthorpe Junc.

Belmont Yard

Coal Depot Snow

Royal Mail Terminal

Decoy South Junc.

Black Carr Junc.

Bessacarr Junc.

Flyover West Junc.

Flyover East Junc.

Loversall Carr Junc.

B

St. Catherine's Junc.

Rossington – RJB

(1 : 90,000)

(DONCASTER INSET FROM MAP 62)

Immingham Railfreight Terminals (Disused)

Pyewipe Road

7

(IMMINGHAM INSET FROM MAP 63)

Lindsey – Petrofina & Total

5

Marsh Sdgs.

6

Docks ABP

IMMINGHAM TO REYKJAVIK & HAMBURG (Eimskip)

Loco Shed

Coal Terminal – British Steel

Immingham West Junc.

1

2

3

a

4

New Clee

C.S.

Simon Storage

Mineral Quay

Marsh West Junc.

Grimsby Town

Cleethorpes

Ore Terminal British Steel

Immingham Docks – ABP

Esso

Pasture Street

CLEETHORPES MINIATURE RAILWAY (1' 3")

HULL TO ROTTERDAM (EUROPOORT) & ZEEBRUGGE (North Sea Ferries)

Humber Conoco

Humber Road Junc.

Immingham Yard

Firegold Coal Unloading Terminal

Simon Storage

Texaco

Paper Terminal-Stora

C. & W. Shops

Norsk Hydro Wks.

C

LINCOLNSHIRE

(1 : 90,000)

HUMBERSIDE

IM

Immingham East Junc.

0   5   10 m.   (1:350,000)

0   5   10   15   km.

1

2

64

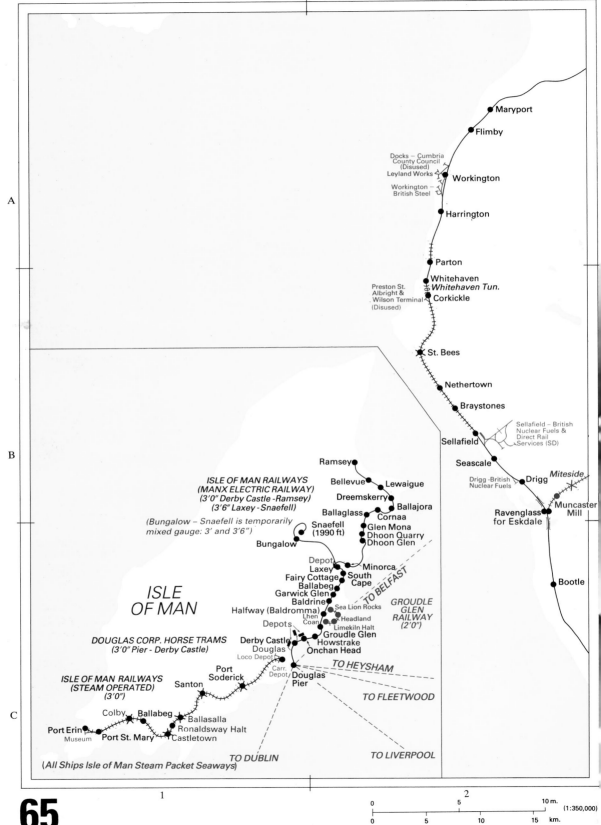

Maryport

Flimby

Docks – Cumbria
County Council
(Disused)
Leyland Works

Workington

Workington –
British Steel

Harrington

Parton

Whitehaven
Whitehaven Tun.

Preston St.
Albright &
Wilson Terminal
(Disused)

Corkickle

St. Bees

Nethertown

Braystones

Sellafield – British
Nuclear Fuels &
Direct Rail
Services (SD)

Sellafield

Seascale

Drigg – British
Nuclear Fuels

Drigg

Miteside

Muncaster
Mill

Ravenglass
for Eskdale

Bootle

Ramsey

Bellevue

Lewaigue

Dreemskerry

*ISLE OF MAN RAILWAYS
(MANX ELECTRIC RAILWAY)
(3'0" Derby Castle -Ramsey)
(3'6" Laxey - Snaefell)*

Ballajora

Ballaglass

Cornaa

*(Bungalow – Snaefell is temporarily
mixed gauge: 3' and 3'6")*

Glen Mona

Snaefell
(1990 ft)

Dhoon Quarry

Dhoon Glen

Bungalow

Minorca

Depot

Laxey

South
Cape

TO BELFAST

Fairy Cottage

*GROUDLE
GLEN
RAILWAY
(2'0")*

Ballabeg

Garwick Glen

Baldrine

Halfway (Baldromma)

Sea Lion Rocks

Lhen
Coan

Headland

Limekiln Halt

Depots

*ISLE
OF MAN*

Derby Castle

Groudle Glen

Douglas

Howstrake

*DOUGLAS CORP. HORSE TRAMS
(3'0" Pier - Derby Castle)*

Onchan Head

Loco Depot

Carr.
Depot

TO HEYSHAM

Port
Soderick

Douglas
Pier

*ISLE OF MAN RAILWAYS
(STEAM OPERATED)
(3'0")*

Santon

TO FLEETWOOD

Colby

Ballabeg

Ballasalla

Ronaldsway Halt

Port Erin

Museum

Port St. Mary

Castletown

TO DUBLIN

TO LIVERPOOL

(All Ships Isle of Man Steam Packet Seaways)

A

B

C

1

2

0   5   10 m.

(1:350,000)

0   5   10   15   km.

65

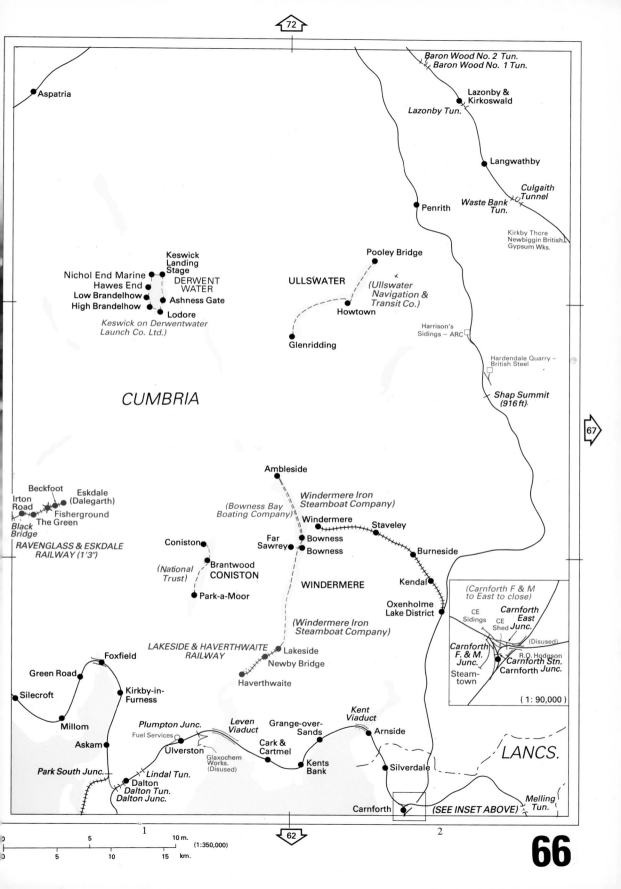

Aspatria

Baron Wood No. 2 Tun.
Baron Wood No. 1 Tun.

Lazonby &
Kirkoswald

Lazonby Tun.

Langwathby

*Culgaith
Tunnel*

Penrith

*Waste Bank
Tun.*

Kirkby Thore
Newbiggin British
Gypsum Wks.

Keswick
Landing
Stage
Nichol End Marine
Hawes End   DERWENT
Low Brandelhow   WATER
High Brandelhow   Ashness Gate
                   Lodore
*Keswick on Derwentwater
Launch Co. Ltd.)*

Pooley Bridge

ULLSWATER

*(Ullswater
Navigation &
Transit Co.)*

Howtown

Harrison's
Sidings – ARC

Glenridding

*Hardendale Quarry –
British Steel*

CUMBRIA

*Shap Summit
(916 ft.)*

Ambleside

*Windermere Iron
Steamboat Company)*

Beckfoot   Eskdale
             (Dalegarth)
Irton
Road   Fisherground
Black   The Green
Bridge

*(Bowness Bay
Boating Company)*

Windermere

Staveley

*RAVENGLASS & ESKDALE
RAILWAY (1'3")*

Coniston

Far
Sawrey   Bowness
          Bowness

Burneside

*(National
Trust)*   Brantwood
             CONISTON

WINDERMERE

Kendal

Park-a-Moor

Oxenholme
Lake District

*(Windermere Iron
Steamboat Company)*

*(Carnforth F & M
to East to close)*

CE
Sidings   *Carnforth
           East
CE   Junc.*
Shed
           (Disused)

*Carnforth
F. & M.
Junc.*   R.O. Hodgson
           Carnforth Stn.
           Carnforth **Junc.**
Steam-
town

*LAKESIDE & HAVERTHWAITE
RAILWAY*

Lakeside
Newby Bridge

Haverthwaite

(1: 90,000)

Foxfield

Green Road

Kirkby-in-
Furness

*Kent
Viaduct*

Silecroft

*Leven
Viaduct*   Grange-over-
             Sands   Arnside

Plumpton Junc.
Fuel Services

Millom   Cark &
             Cartmel

LANCS.

Askam   Ulverston
             *Glaxochem
             Works.
             (Disused)*   Kents
                            Bank   Silverdale

Park South Junc.   *Lindal Tun.*
                          Dalton
                          Dalton Tun.
                          Dalton Junc.

Carnforth   *(SEE INSET ABOVE)*   *Melling
                                      Tun.*

Eastgate

(Disused)

CUMBRIA

DURHAM

A

Appleby

(Disused)

*Helm
Tunnel*

Warcop

Crosby Garrett Tunnel

66

Kirkby Stephen

Birkett Tun.

B

Ais Gill Summit (1167 ft)

Shotlock Hill Tun.

Moorcock Tun.

Garsdale

Redmire
– MoD

Rise Hill Tun.

Dent

*Blea Moor Tun.
(1m 869 yds)*

Blea Moor

Ribblehead

ARC
(Disused)

C

Horton-in-Ribblesdale

0
2
5
10 m.
(1:350,000)

0
5
10
15
km.

67

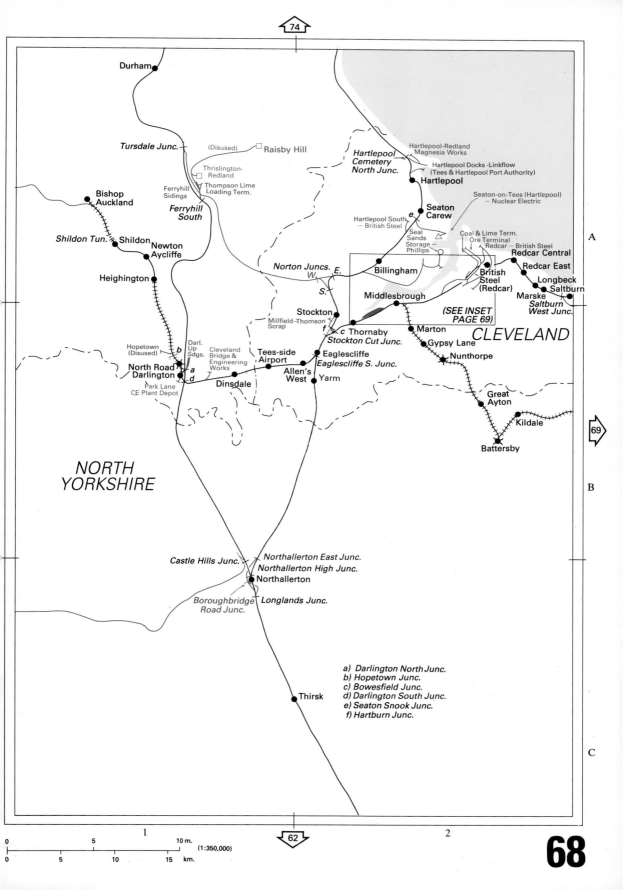

Durham

Tursdale Junc.

(Disused) □ Raisby Hill

Thrislington–
Redland
Ferryhill
Sidings
□ Thompson Lime
Loading Term.

Hartlepool-Redland
Magnesia Works

Hartlepool
Cemetery
North Junc.

Hartlepool Docks -Linkflow
(Tees & Hartlepool Port Authority)

Hartlepool

Bishop
Auckland

Ferryhill
South

Seaton-on-Tees (Hartlepool)
– Nuclear Electric

Shildon Tun. Shildon

Newton
Aycliffe

e
Seaton
Carew

Heighington

Hartlepool South
– British Steel

Seal
Sands
Storage –
Phillips

Coal & Lime Term.
Ore Terminal
Redcar – British Steel

Redcar Central

Norton Juncs. E.
W.

Billingham

British
Steel
(Redcar)

Redcar East

Longbeck
Saltburn

S.

Middlesbrough

Marske
Saltburn
West Junc.

Stockton

Millfield–Thomson
Scrap

f
c Thornaby
Stockton Cut Junc.

(SEE INSET
PAGE 69)

CLEVELAND

Marton

Hopetown
(Disused)
b

Darl.
Up
Sdgs.

Cleveland
Bridge &
Engineering
Works

Tees-side
Airport

Eaglescliffe
Eaglescliffe S. Junc.

Gypsy Lane

Nunthorpe

North Road
Darlington

a
d

Allen's
West

Yarm

Park Lane
CE Plant Depot

Dinsdale

Great
Ayton

Kildale

NORTH
YORKSHIRE

Battersby

69

B

Castle Hills Junc.

Northallerton East Junc.
Northallerton High Junc.
Northallerton

Boroughbridge
Road Junc.
Longlands Junc.

a) Darlington North Junc.
b) Hopetown Junc.
c) Bowesfield Junc.
d) Darlington South Junc.
e) Seaton Snook Junc.
f) Hartburn Junc.

Thirsk

C

1
0   5   10 m.
(1:350,000)
0   5   10   15   km.

2

68

CLEVELAND

Billingham

Seal Sands Junc.

Simon Storage

Monsanto Sidings Junc.
Seal Sands
BASF Chemicals

Tees Dock – Cleveland Potash

Shell Ore Term.
Junc.

Redcar
Junc.

3

British Steel (Redcar)

Belasis Lane Loco Shed

Billingham Junc.

Tees Dock

Tees Dock Exchange Sidings

Coal Term.

Haverton Hill East Grid

Port Clarence – Phillips
Middlesbrough Wharf – Dawson

Export Terminal – British Steel

3

Wilton – ICI Chemicals & Polymers

ICI Haverton Hill (Billingham)

Ayrton Store – Dawson

Port Clarence Sidings

Beam Mill Junc.

Loco Depot – ICI

Cobra Freight Term.

Middlesbrough

C.S.

South Bank

2
1
4
4
4

Hot Metal Wagon Repair Shops

4 4 4

Wilton – FLT & Euroterminal

Thornaby

Tees Yard

Middlesbrough Goods

Guisborough Junc.

1) Loco Depot – British Steel
2) Lackenby Grids (Exchange Sidings)
3) 'Hot metal' Railway
4) Teeside Works – British Steel

Thornaby East Junc.

Wagon Storage

Newport East Junc.

A

TE

C. & W. Shops

(TEES-SIDE INSET FROM P.68)

(1 : 90,000)

Skinningrove – British Steel

Boulby – Cleveland Potash

Crag Hall

Grinkle Tun.

Commondale

Castleton Moor

Danby

Lealholm

Whitby

Ruswarp

Sleights

Glaisdale Egton Grosmont

Grosmont Tun.

B

Goathland

NORTH YORKSHIRE MOORS RAILWAY

Newtondale Halt

NORTH YORKSHIRE

Scalby Mills

NORTH BAY RAILWAY (1' 8")

Beach

Peasholm Park

Levisham

Turntable

Scarborough

Pickering

Seamer West Junc.

Seamer

C

Filey

Hunmanby

Malton

HUMBERSIDE

Bempton

69

0   5   10 m.

(1:350,000)

0   5   10   15   km.

1   2

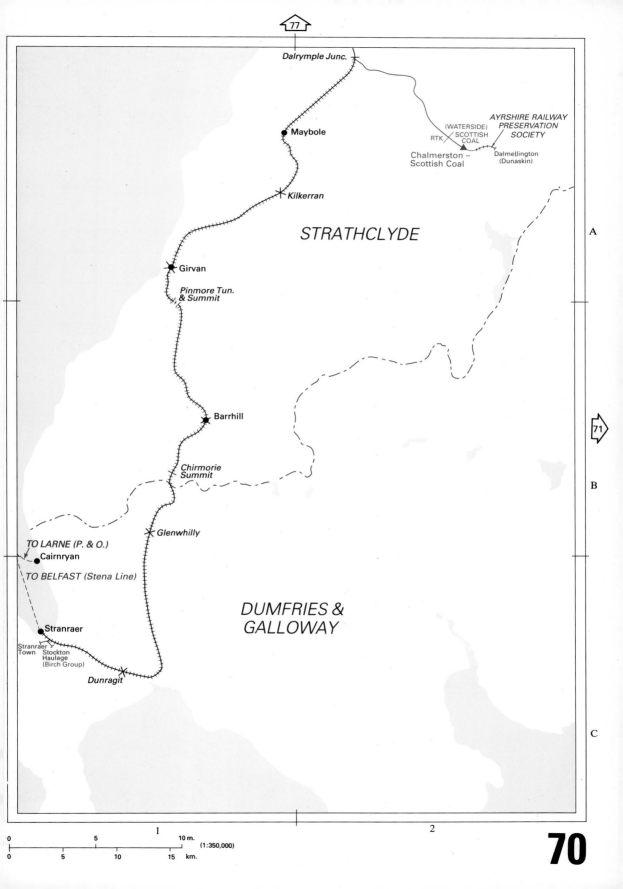

Dalrymple Junc.

● Maybole

(WATERSIDE)
SCOTTISH
RTK COAL

*AYRSHIRE RAILWAY
PRESERVATION
SOCIETY*

Chalmerston –
Scottish Coal

Dalmellington
(Dunaskin)

Kilkerran

STRATHCLYDE

A

● Girvan

*Pinmore Tun.
& Summit*

71

● Barrhill

*Chirmorie
Summit*

B

Glenwhilly

TO LARNE (P. & O.)
● Cairnryan

TO BELFAST (Stena Line)

DUMFRIES &
GALLOWAY

● Stranraer

Stranraer
Town

Stockton
Haulage
(Birch Group)

Dunragit

C

0   5   10 m.
                              (1:350,000)
0   5   10   15   km.

70

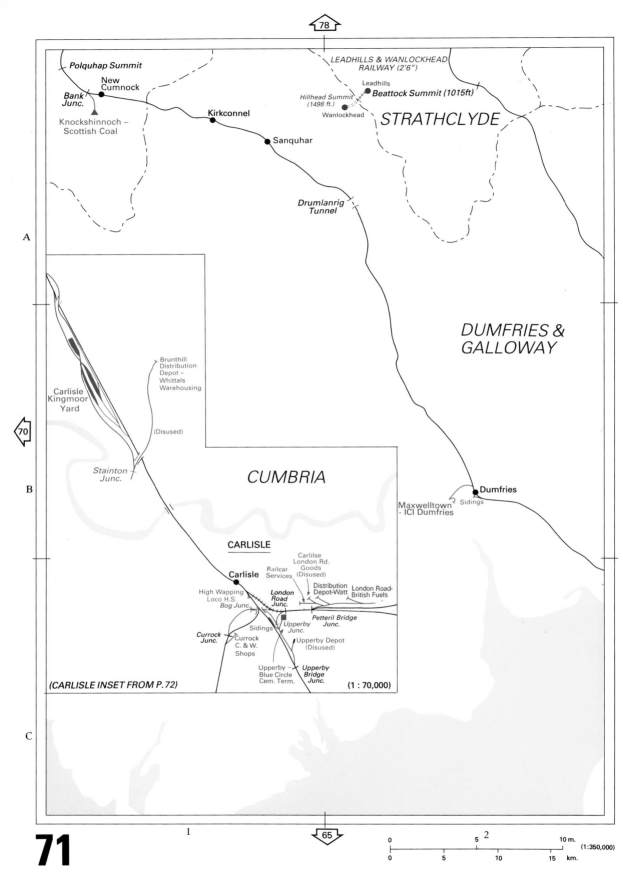

Polquhap Summit

New
Cumnock

Bank
Junc.

Knockshinnoch –
Scottish Coal

Kirkconnel

Sanquhar

LEADHILLS & WANLOCKHEAD
RAILWAY (2'6")

Hillhead Summit
(1498 ft.)

Leadhills

Wanlockhead

Beattock Summit (1015ft)

STRATHCLYDE

Drumlanrig
Tunnel

A

DUMFRIES &
GALLOWAY

Carlisle
Kingmoor
Yard

Brunthill
Distribution
Depot –
Whittals
Warehousing

(Disused)

70

Stainton
Junc.

CUMBRIA

B

Maxwelltown
- ICI Dumfries

Sidings

Dumfries

CARLISLE

Carlilse
London Rd.
Goods
(Disused)

Carlisle

Railcar
Services

High Wapping
Loco H.S.
Bog Junc.

London
Road
Junc.

Distribution
Depot-Watt

London Road-
British Fuels

Petteril Bridge
Junc.

Currock
Junc.

Sidings

Currock
C. & W.
Shops

Upperby
Junc.

Upperby Depot
(Disused)

Upperby –
Blue Circle
Cem. Term.

Upperby
Bridge
Junc.

(CARLISLE INSET FROM P. 72)

(1 : 70,000)

C

1

2

0   5   10 m.

(1:350,000)

0   5   10   15   km.

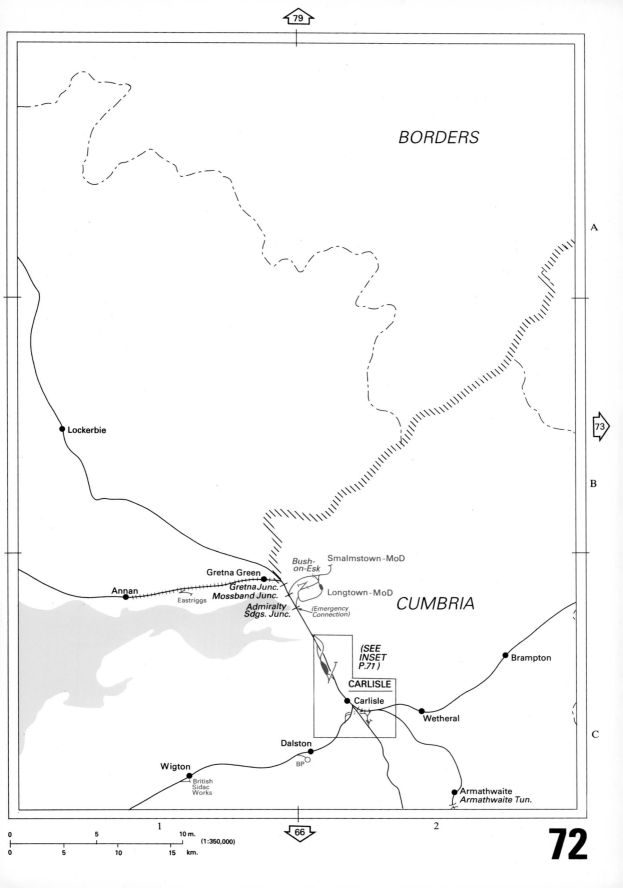

BORDERS

73

● Lockerbie

A

B

Smalmstown-MoD

Bush-on-Esk

Gretna Green

Gretna Junc.
Mossband Junc.

Longtown-MoD

● Annan

Eastriggs

Admiralty
Sdgs. Junc.

(Emergency
Connection)

CUMBRIA

*(SEE
INSET
P.71)*

● Brampton

CARLISLE

● Carlisle

● Wetheral

Dalston ●

BP

Wigton ●

C

British
Sidac
Works

● Armathwaite
Armathwaite Tun.

1

2

0   5   10 m.

(1:350,000)

0   5   10   15   km.

72

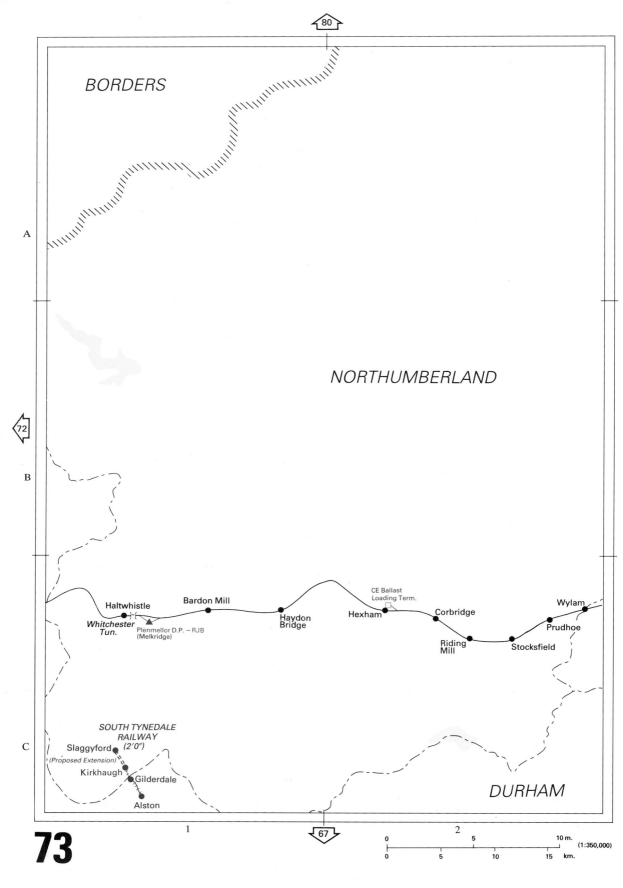

BORDERS

NORTHUMBERLAND

A

B

CE Ballast
Loading Term.

Wylam

Haltwhistle   Bardon Mill   Hexham   Corbridge   Prudhoe

Whitchester
Tun.   Plenmellor D.P. – RJB   Haydon   Riding   Stocksfield
          (Melkridge)   Bridge   Mill

SOUTH TYNEDALE
RAILWAY
(2'0")

C   Slaggyford

(Proposed Extension)

Kirkhaugh

          Gilderdale

          Alston

DURHAM

73

1   2   10 m.   (1:350,000)

0   5   10   15   km.

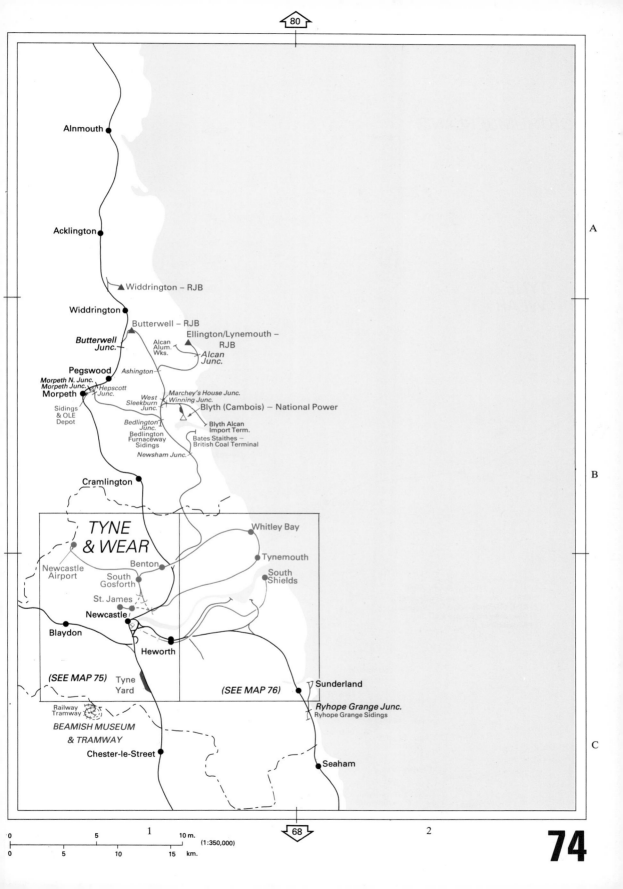

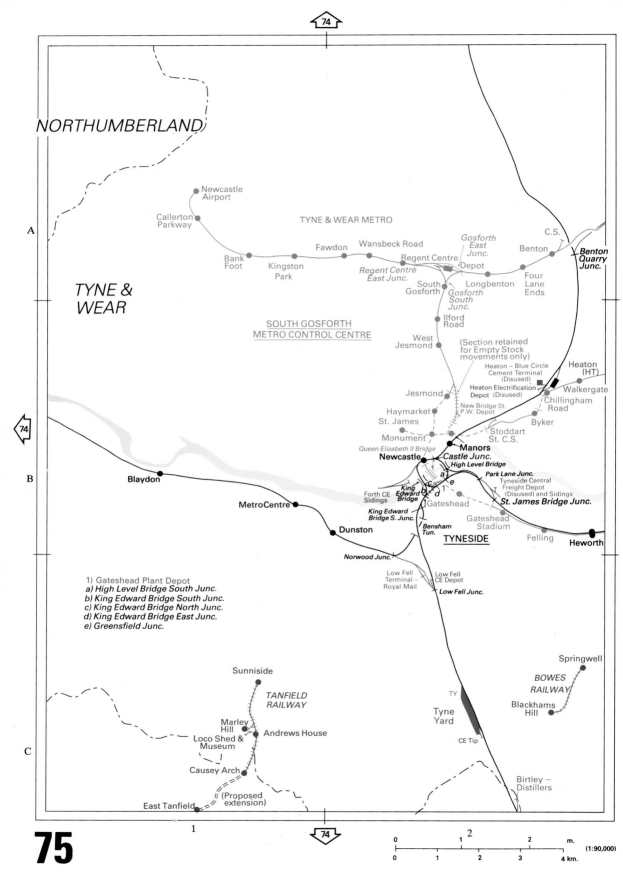

NORTHUMBERLAND

TYNE & WEAR

Newcastle Airport

Callerton Parkway

TYNE & WEAR METRO

Fawdon

Wansbeck Road

Gosforth East Junc.

C.S.

Benton

Benton Quarry Junc.

Bank Foot

Kingston Park

Regent Centre

Depot

Longbenton

Four Lane Ends

Regent Centre East Junc.

South Gosforth

Gosforth South Junc.

SOUTH GOSFORTH METRO CONTROL CENTRE

Ilford Road

West Jesmond

(Section retained for Empty Stock movements only)

Heaton – Blue Circle Cement Terminal (Disused)

Heaton (HT)

Heaton Electrification Depot (Disused)

Walkergate

Jesmond

New Bridge St. P.W. Depot

Chillingham Road

Byker

Haymarket St. James

Monument

Stoddart St. C.S.

Queen Elizabeth II Bridge

Manors

Newcastle

Castle Junc.

High Level Bridge

a

Park Lane Junc.

Tyneside Central Freight Depot (Disused) and Sidings

St. James Bridge Junc.

Blaydon

c

b

e

Forth CE Sidings

King Edward Bridge

d

MetroCentre

King Edward Bridge S. Junc.

Gateshead

Gateshead Stadium

Felling

Heworth

Dunston

Bensham Tun.

TYNESIDE

Norwood Junc.

1) Gateshead Plant Depot
a) *High Level Bridge South Junc.*
b) *King Edward Bridge South Junc.*
c) *King Edward Bridge North Junc.*
d) *King Edward Bridge East Junc.*
e) *Greensfield Junc.*

Low Fell Terminal – Royal Mail

Low Fell CE Depot

Low Fell Junc.

Springwell

Sunniside

TANFIELD RAILWAY

TY

BOWES RAILWAY

Marley Hill

Loco Shed & Museum

Andrews House

Tyne Yard

Blackhams Hill

Causey Arch

CE Tip

East Tanfield

(Proposed extension)

Birtley – Distillers

1

2

0		1		2		m.

(1:90,000)

0	1	2	3	4 km.

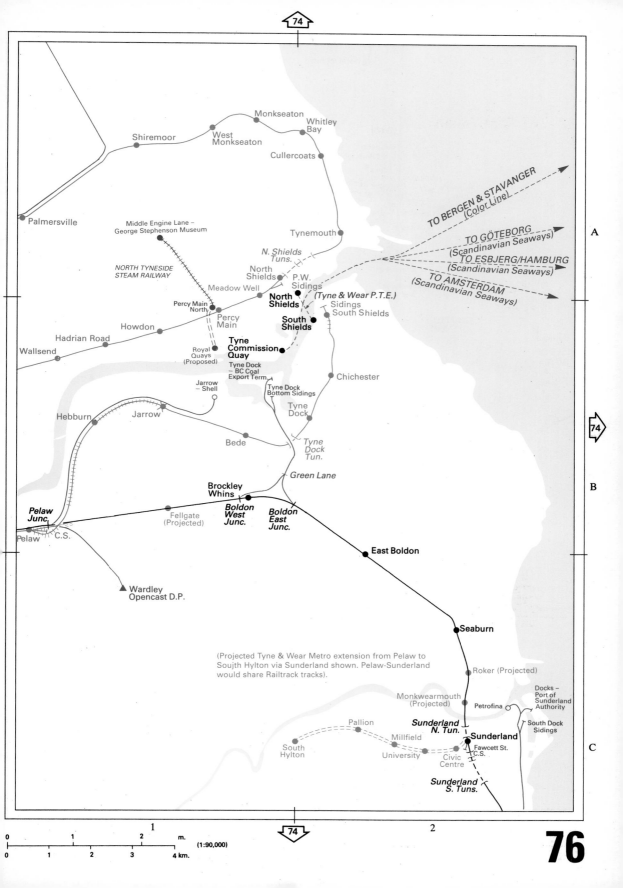

Monkseaton

Whitley Bay

Shiremoor

West Monkseaton

Cullercoats

Palmersville

Tynemouth

Middle Engine Lane – George Stephenson Museum

TO BERGEN & STAVANGER (Color Line)

A

TO GÖTEBORG (Scandinavian Seaways)

TO ESBJERG/HAMBURG (Scandinavian Seaways)

TO AMSTERDAM (Scandinavian Seaways)

N. Shields Tuns.

North Shields

NORTH TYNESIDE STEAM RAILWAY

Meadow Well

P.W. Sidings

(Tyne & Wear P.T.E.)

North Shields

Percy Main North

Percy Main

Sidings South Shields

South Shields

Howdon

Hadrian Road

Wallsend

Royal Quays (Proposed)

Tyne Commission Quay

Tyne Dock – BC Coal Export Term.

Chichester

Jarrow – Shell

Tyne Dock Bottom Sidings

Hebburn

Jarrow

Tyne Dock

Bede

Tyne Dock Tun.

Green Lane

B

Brockley Whins

Boldon West Junc.

Boldon East Junc.

Pelaw Junc.

Fellgate (Projected)

Pelaw

C.S.

East Boldon

▲ Wardley Opencast D.P.

Seaburn

(Projected Tyne & Wear Metro extension from Pelaw to Soujth Hylton via Sunderland shown. Pelaw-Sunderland would share Railtrack tracks).

Roker (Projected)

Monkwearmouth (Projected)

Petrofina

Docks – Port of Sunderland Authority

South Dock Sidings

Pallion

Millfield

Sunderland N. Tun.

Sunderland

South Hylton

University

Civic Centre

Fawcett St. C.S.

C

Sunderland S. Tuns.

0   1   m.

0   1   2   3   4 km.

(1:90,000)

1

2

76

Garelochhead

Luss

(Loch Lomond Marina Co.)

LOCH LOMOND

Helensburgh Upper
(Block Post)

Balloch Pier
Balloch

Helensburgh Central
Kilcreggan

Craigendoran
Craigendoran Junc.

Alexandria

Cardross

Renton

(Cal-Mac)
(Western Ferries)

(Clyde Marine)

Hunter's Quay
Gourock
Fort Matilda

Greenock West
Greenock Central
Cartsdyke

Dalreoch Tuns.

Dalreoch

Dumbarton Cen.

(SEE MAP 81)

Dunoon

(Cal-Mac)

IBM Halt

Bogston

James Watt Dock
(Disused)

Woodhall

Dumbarton East
Bowling

Milngavie

COWAL

McInroy's Point

Branchton
Whinhill

Port Glasgow

No.2 Tun.

Bishopton
No.1 Tun.

Dalmuir

Singer

Yoker

Langbank

Dunrod

Inverkip
Inverkip Tun.

British Aerospace
(Disused)

Bishopton

Wemyss Bay

a) Ladyburn Junc.
b) Wemyss Bay Junc.
c) Newton St. Tun.
   (1m 351 yds)
d) Cartsburn Tun.
e) Ann St. Tun.
f) Wellpark Tun.

Paisley Gilmour St.

Johnstone
Milliken Park

Paisley Canal

Rothesay

ISLE OF BUTE

Barrhead

Neilston

Cumbrae Slip
Largs

Lochwinnoch

ISLE OF GT. CUMBRAE
Millport

MoD

Fairlie Tun.

Fairlie

Lugton – Clegg

Lugton

(Cal-Mac)

Fairlie High – Scottish Nuclear

Giffen – MoD

Glengarnock

Dunlop

Hunterston BSC Ore Reduction Plant
(Disused)

Hunterston Ore Terminal (Disused)

Dairy – Roche Products

Swinlees

Dalry

Stewarton

West Kilbride

Holm Junc.

Ardrossan South Beach
Dubbs Junc.

Sdgs.

Kilwinning

Byrehill Junc.

STRATHCLYDE

Ardrossan Harbour

(Cal-Mac)
TO BRODICK (ARRAN)

Ardrossan Town
Saltcoats

ICI Ardeer
(Disused)

ICI Snodgrass

Bogside Junc.

Kilmaurs

J. Walker Distillery

Kilmarnock

TO DOUGLAS (I. OF MAN) (Cal-Mac)
I. of Man Steam Packet Co.)

Stevenston

Irvine

CE Works & CE Sidings

Kay Park Junc.

CE Depot

CE Works

Shewalton CE Tip

Riccarton – BP

Barleith – J. Walker Distillery

Falkland Junc.

Falkland Yard
Ayr Harbour Junc.

Newton-on-Ayr

Newton Junc.

Irvine – Caledonian Paper

Locomotive Works
Hunslet – Barclay (ZK)

Ayr Harbour & Coal Terminal.

AY

Barassie

Meadowhead
Barassie Junc.

Troon

Barassie CE Sidings

(Reversing Spur)

Mossgiel Tun.

Mauchline Junc.

Ayr

Townhead C.S.

Prestwick – BP

Prestwick International Airport

Prestwick Town

Annbank Junc.

Newton-on-Ayr

(SEE INSET TO LEFT)

Ayr

Auchinleck

Killoch Washery

(1 : 90,000)

(AYR INSET FROM RIGHT)

77

1

2

0   5   10 m.
(1:350,000)

0   5   10   15   km.

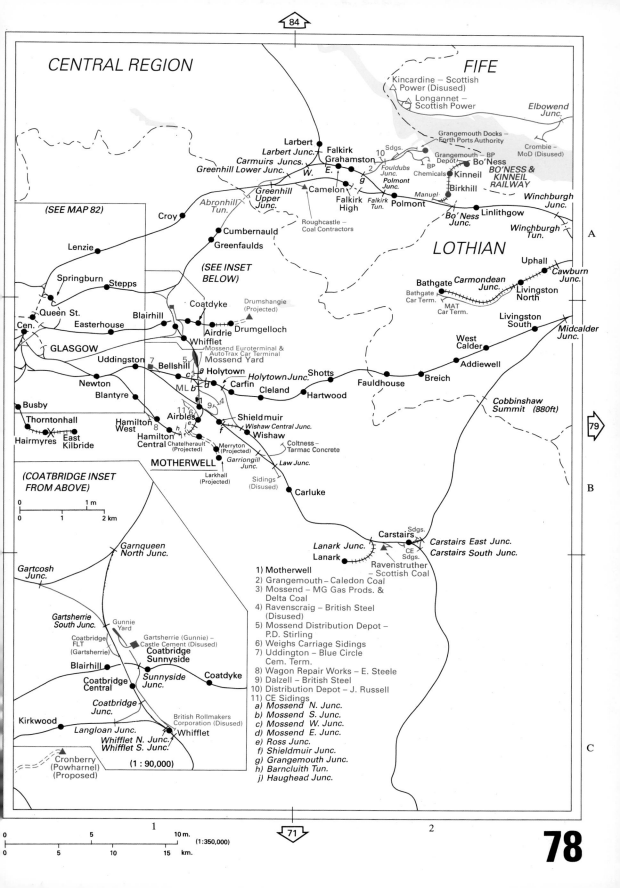

CENTRAL REGION

FIFE

Kincardine – Scottish Power (Disused)
Longannet – Scottish Power

Elbowend Junc.

Larbert
Larbert Junc.
Carmuirs Juncs.
Greenhill Lower Junc.
Greenhill Upper Junc.

Falkirk
Grahamston

Sdgs.
10
Fouldubs Junc.
2
W. E.
g
Polmont Junc.
Camelon
Falkirk High
Falkirk Tun.
Polmont

Grangemouth Docks – Forth Ports Authority
Grangemouth – BP Depot
BP Chemicals
Kinneil
Birkhill
Manuel

Bo'Ness
BO'NESS & KINNEIL RAILWAY

Crombie – MoD (Disused)

Winchburgh Junc.

Abronhill Tun.

Roughcastle – Coal Contractors

Bo'Ness Junc.
Linlithgow

Winchburgh Tun.

A

Croy

Cumbernauld
Greenfaulds

LOTHIAN

(SEE MAP 82)

Lenzie

Springburn
Stepps

(SEE INSET BELOW)

Coatdyke

Drumshangie (Projected)

Uphall
Cawburn Junc.

Bathgate
Carmondean Junc.
Bathgate Car Term.
MAT Car Term.

Livingston North

Livingston South

Midcalder Junc.

Queen St.
Cen.
Easterhouse

Blairhill

Airdrie
Drumgelloch
Whifflet
Mossend Euroterminal & AutoTrax Car Terminal
Mossend Yard

West Calder

Addiewell

GLASGOW

Uddingston
7
Bellshill
5
c a
b
ML
d
Holytown
Carfin
Holytown Junc.
Cleland
Shotts
Hartwood
Fauldhouse
Breich

Cobbinshaw Summit (880ft)

Newton
Blantyre

Busby
Thorntonhall
Hairmyres
East Kilbride

Hamilton West
8
11 6
9 4
Airbles
i e
h
f
Shieldmuir
Wishaw Central Junc.
Wishaw
Coltness – Tarmac Concrete

79

Hamilton Central
Chatelherault (Projected)
Merryton (Projected)
Garriongill Junc.
Law Junc.

MOTHERWELL

Larkhall (Projected)

Sidings (Disused)

Carluke

B

(COATBRIDGE INSET FROM ABOVE)

0   1 m
0   1   2 km

Carstairs
Sdgs.
Lanark Junc.
Lanark
CE Sdgs.
Carstairs East Junc.
Carstairs South Junc.
Ravenstruther – Scottish Coal

1) Motherwell
2) Grangemouth – Caledon Coal
3) Mossend – MG Gas Prods. & Delta Coal
4) Ravenscraig – British Steel (Disused)
5) Mossend Distribution Depot – P.D. Stirling
6) Weighs Carriage Sidings
7) Uddington – Blue Circle Cem. Term.
8) Wagon Repair Works – E. Steele
9) Dalzell – British Steel
10) Distribution Depot – J. Russell
11) CE Sidings
a) Mossend N. Junc.
b) Mossend S. Junc.
c) Mossend W. Junc.
d) Mossend E. Junc.
e) Ross Junc.
f) Shieldmuir Junc.
g) Grangemouth Junc.
h) Barncluith Tun.
j) Haughead Junc.

Garnqueen North Junc.

Gartcosh Junc.

Gartsherrie South Junc.
Gunnie Yard
Coatbridge FLT (Gartsherrie)
Gartsherrie (Gunnie) – Castle Cement (Disused)
Coatbridge Sunnyside

Blairhill
Coatbridge Central
Sunnyside Junc.
Coatdyke
Coatbridge Junc.

Kirkwood
Langloan Junc.
Whifflet N. Junc.
Whifflet S. Junc.
Whifflet
British Rollmakers Corporation (Disused)

Cronberry (Powharnel) (Proposed)

(1 : 90,000)

C

1
0   5   10 m.
0   5   10   15 km.
(1:350,000)

71

2

78

84

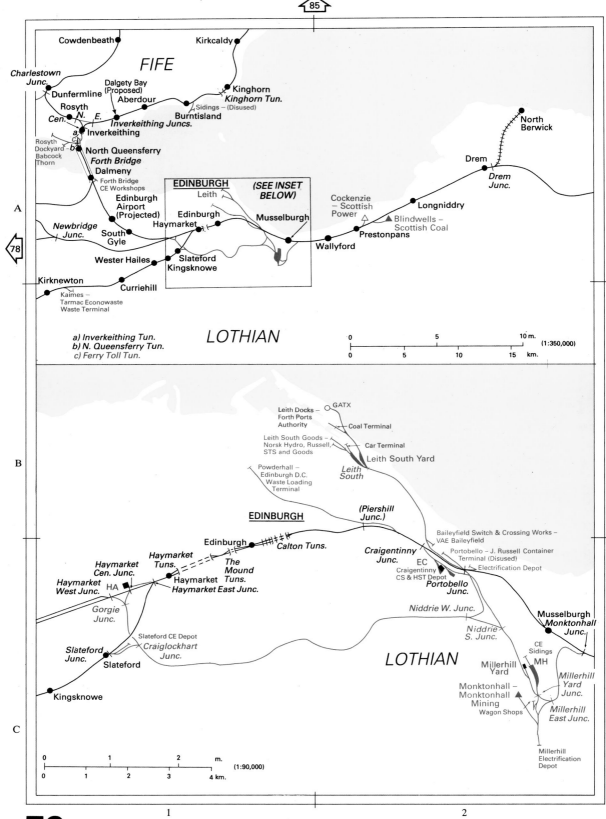

Cowdenbeath

Kirkcaldy

FIFE

Charlestown Junc.

Dunfermline

Dalgety Bay (Proposed)

Aberdour

Kinghorn

Kinghorn Tun.

Rosyth
Cen. N. E.

a)

c)

Inverkeithing

Inverkeithing Juncs.

Burntisland

Sidings – (Disused)

North Berwick

Rosyth Dockyard
Babcock
Thorn

b)

North Queensferry

Forth Bridge

Dalmeny

Forth Bridge
CE Workshops

Drem

Drem Junc.

Edinburgh
Airport
(Projected)

EDINBURGH

Leith

(SEE INSET
BELOW)

Cockenzie – Scottish Power

Longniddry

A

Edinburgh

Haymarket

Musselburgh

Blindwells –
Scottish Coal

Prestonpans

Newbridge Junc.

South Gyle

Wallyford

78

Wester Hailes

Slateford
Kingsknowe

Kirknewton

Curriehill

Kaimes –
Tarmac Econowaste
Waste Terminal

a) Inverkeithing Tun.
b) N. Queensferry Tun.
c) Ferry Toll Tun.

LOTHIAN

0		5		10 m.

(1:350,000)

0	5	10	15

km.

Leith Docks –
Forth Ports
Authority

GATX

Coal Terminal

Leith South Goods –
Norsk Hydro, Russell,
STS and Goods

Car Terminal

Leith South Yard

B

Leith
South

Powderhall –
Edinburgh D.C.
Waste Loading
Terminal

EDINBURGH

(Piershill Junc.)

Baileyfield Switch & Crossing Works –
VAE Baileyfield

Edinburgh

Calton Tuns.

Portobello – J. Russell Container
Terminal (Disused)

Craigentinny Junc.

EC

Electrification Depot

*Haymarket
Tuns.*

Craigentinny
CS & HST Depot

Portobello

*Haymarket
Cen. Junc.*

The
Mound
Tuns.

Haymarket

Portobello Junc.

*Haymarket
West Junc.*

HA

Haymarket East Junc.

Musselburgh
*Monktonhall
Junc.*

*Gorgie
Junc.*

Niddrie W. Junc.

*Niddrie
S. Junc.*

LOTHIAN

CE
Sidings

MH

*Millerhill
Yard
Junc.*

Slateford CE Depot

*Craiglockhart
Junc.*

*Slateford
Junc.*

Slateford

Millerhill
Yard

Monktonhall –
Monktonhall
Mining

Wagon Shops

*Millerhill
East Junc.*

C

Kingsknowe

Millerhill
Electrification
Depot

0		1		2		m.

(1:90,000)

0	1	2	3	4 km.

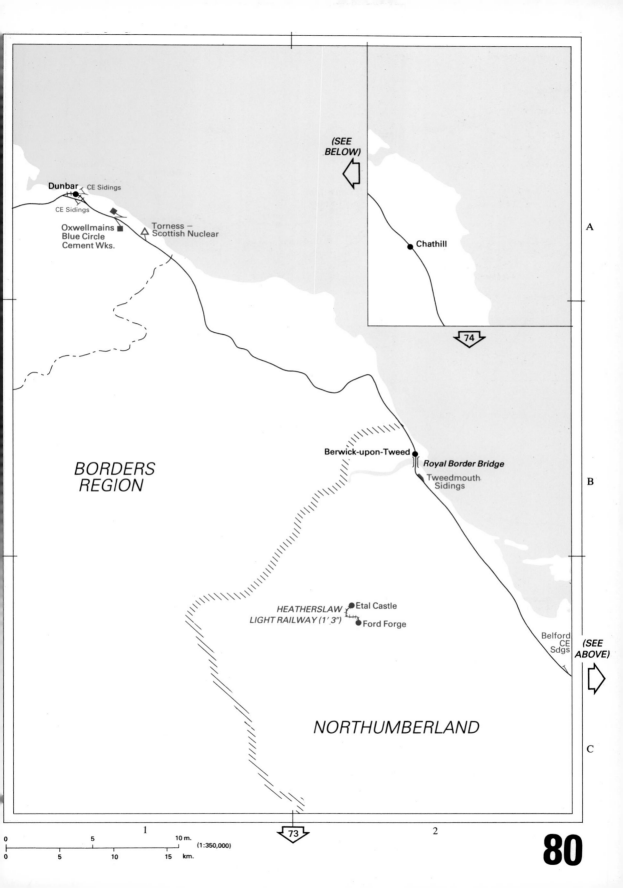

(SEE BELOW)

Dunbar   CE Sidings

CE Sidings

Oxwellmains
Blue Circle
Cement Wks.

Torness —
Scottish Nuclear

Chathill

74

BORDERS
REGION

Berwick-upon-Tweed   *Royal Border Bridge*

Tweedmouth
Sidings

HEATHERSLAW   Etal Castle
LIGHT RAILWAY (1' 3")   Ford Forge

Belford
CE
Sdgs

(SEE ABOVE)

NORTHUMBERLAND

1   10 m.

0   5   (1:350,000)

0   5   10   15   km.

73

2

80

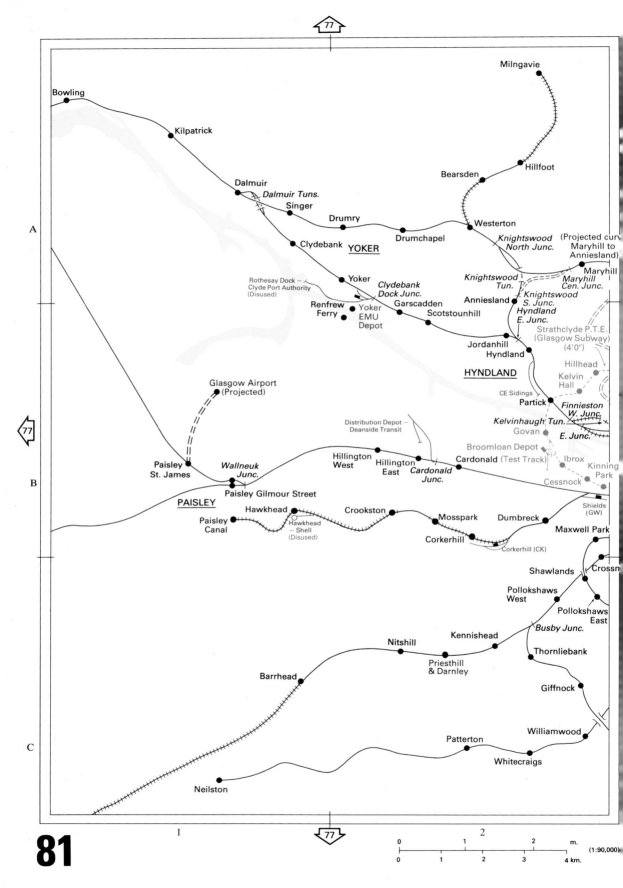

Milngavie

Bowling

Kilpatrick

Hillfoot

Bearsden

Dalmuir

Dalmuir Tuns.

Singer

Drumry

Westerton

A

Drumchapel

Knightswood North Junc.

(Projected cur
Maryhill to
Anniesland)

Clydebank

YOKER

Maryhill

Knightswood Tun.

Maryhill Cen. Junc.

Rothesay Dock –
Clyde Port Authority
(Disused)

Yoker

Clydebank Dock Junc.

Anniesland

Knightswood S. Junc.

Hyndland E. Junc.

Renfrew
Ferry

Yoker
EMU
Depot

Garscadden

Scotstounhill

Strathclyde P.T.E.
(Glasgow Subway)
(4'0")

Jordanhill

Hillhead

Hyndland

HYNDLAND

Kelvin
Hall

CE Sidings

Partick

Finnieston W. Junc.

Glasgow Airport
(Projected)

Kelvinhaugh Tun.

Govan

E. Junc.

Distribution Depot –
Deanside Transit

Broomloan Depot
(Test Track)

Ibrox

Cardonald

Kinning
Park

Hillington
West

Hillington
East

Cardonald Junc.

Cessnock

Paisley
St. James

Wallneuk Junc.

B

Paisley Gilmour Street

Shields
(GW)

PAISLEY

Hawkhead

Crookston

Mosspark

Dumbreck

Maxwell Park

Paisley
Canal

Hawkhead
– Shell
(Disused)

Corkerhill

Corkerhill (CK)

Crossn

Shawlands

Pollokshaws
West

Pollokshaws
East

Kennishead

Busby Junc.

Nitshill

Thornliebank

Barrhead

Priesthill
& Darnley

Giffnock

Williamwood

C

Patterton

Whitecraigs

Neilston

I

81

2

0   1   2   m.

0   1   2   3   4 km.

(1:90,000)

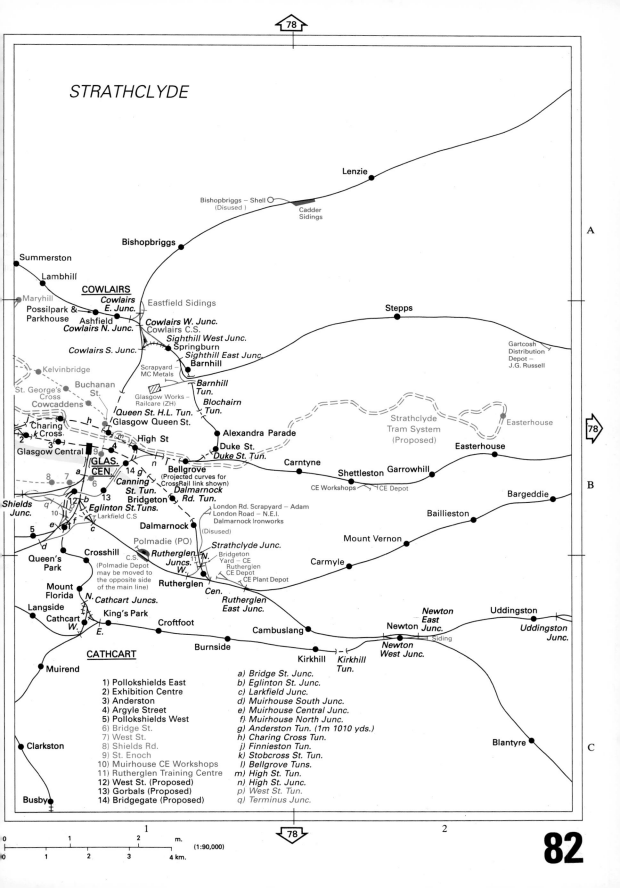

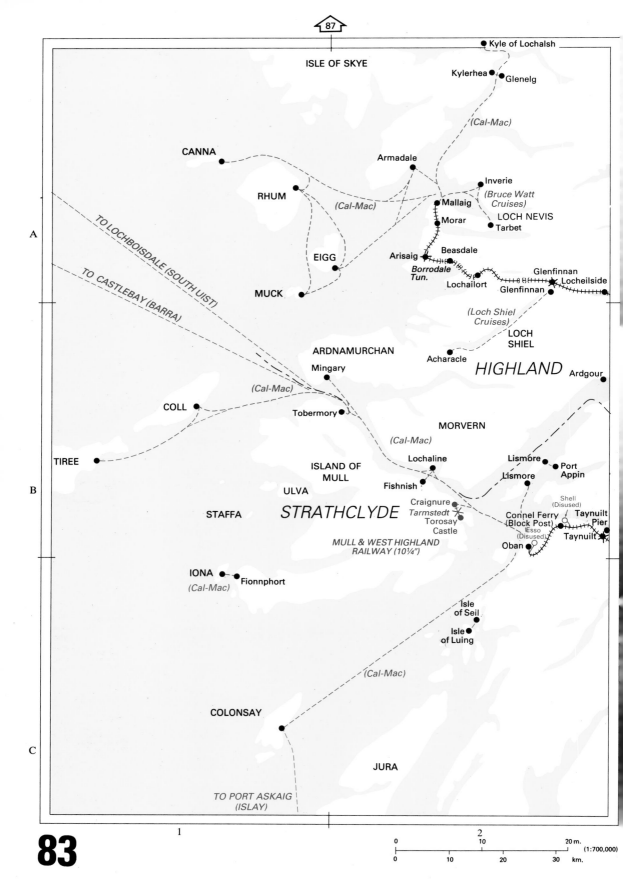

ISLE OF SKYE

Kyle of Lochalsh

Kylerhea
Glenelg

(Cal-Mac)

CANNA

Armadale

Inverie

RHUM

(Cal-Mac)

(Bruce Watt Cruises)

Mallaig

LOCH NEVIS

Morar

Tarbet

EIGG

Arisaig
Beasdale

Borrodale Tun.

Lochailort

Glenfinnan
Locheilside

MUCK

Glenfinnan

A

TO LOCHBOISDALE (SOUTH UIST)

TO CASTLEBAY (BARRA)

(Loch Shiel Cruises)

LOCH SHIEL

ARDNAMURCHAN

Acharacle

HIGHLAND

Ardgour

Mingary

(Cal-Mac)

COLL

MORVERN

Lismore

Port Appin

Tobermory

(Cal-Mac)

Lochaline

Lismore

Shell (Disused)

B

TIREE

ISLAND OF MULL

Taynuilt Pier

ULVA

Fishnish

Craignure
Tarmstedt
Torosay Castle

Connel Ferry (Block Post)

STAFFA

STRATHCLYDE

Esso (Disused)

Taynuilt

MULL & WEST HIGHLAND RAILWAY (10¼")

Oban

IONA
Fionnphort

(Cal-Mac)

Isle of Seil

Isle of Luing

(Cal-Mac)

COLONSAY

C

JURA

TO PORT ASKAIG (ISLAY)

83

1

2
10

20 m.

(1:700,000)

0   10   20   30   km.

Slochd
Slochd Summit (1315ft)
Sidings
Carrbridge
Grantown-on-Spey
(Proposed Extension)
Broomhill
Boat of Garten
STRATHSPEY RAILWAY

AVIEMORE

HIGHLAND

Aviemore
Aviemore (Speyside)

Kincraig

Kingussie
Newtonmore

A

GRAMPIAN

BANAVIE RADIO SIGNALLING CENTRE

Dalwhinnie

Annat (Corpach Paper Mill)– Arjo Wiggins
Spean Bridge
Roy Bridge (Block Post)
Loch Eil Outward Bound
Banavie (Block Post)
Tulloch
Fersit Tun.
FW
Mallaig Junc. Yard & Goods
Lochaber – British Alcan Aluminium
Corpach
West Highland Oil (Disused)
Fort William
Fort William Junc.

Druimuachdar Summit (1484ft)

Blair Atholl
Killiecrankie Tun.

Corrour Summit (1350ft)
Corrour

Pitlochry

Corran

Cruach Snow Shed
Rannoch

TAYSIDE

LOCH ETIVE
Lochetivehead (D. Kennedy)

Bridge of Orchy

Gortan

Inver Tun.
Dunkeld & Birnam
Kingswood Tun.

B

Dail
Armaddy
Inverliver
Craig
Glennoe
Loch Awe
Falls of Cruachan (Seasonal service)
Dalmally

Tyndrum Summit (840ft)
Upper Tyndrum
Fillan (Block Post)
West Highland County March Summit (1024ft)

Tyndrum Lower
Lower Crianlarich (Block Post)
Crianlarich

STRATHCLYDE

Ardlui

Stronachlachar
Inversnaid
LOCH KATRINE
Trossachs Pier
(Strathclyde Water Dept.)

Gleneagles

(Stirling to Alloa is proposed for reopening to passenger traffic)

Arrochar & Tarbet
Timber Loading Terminal
Tarbet
MoD
Glen Douglas
LOCH LOMOND
Rowardennan
(Loch Lomond Marina Co.)

Whistlefield Summit

CENTRAL

Kippenross Tun.
Dunblane
Causewayhead (Proposed)
Bridge of Allan
Cambus (Proposed)
(Disused)
Stirling
Sidings
Alloa (Proposed)

Garelochhead
Luss

Helensburgh Upper
Helensburgh Central
Balloch Pier
Balloch

FIFE

C

Larbert

85

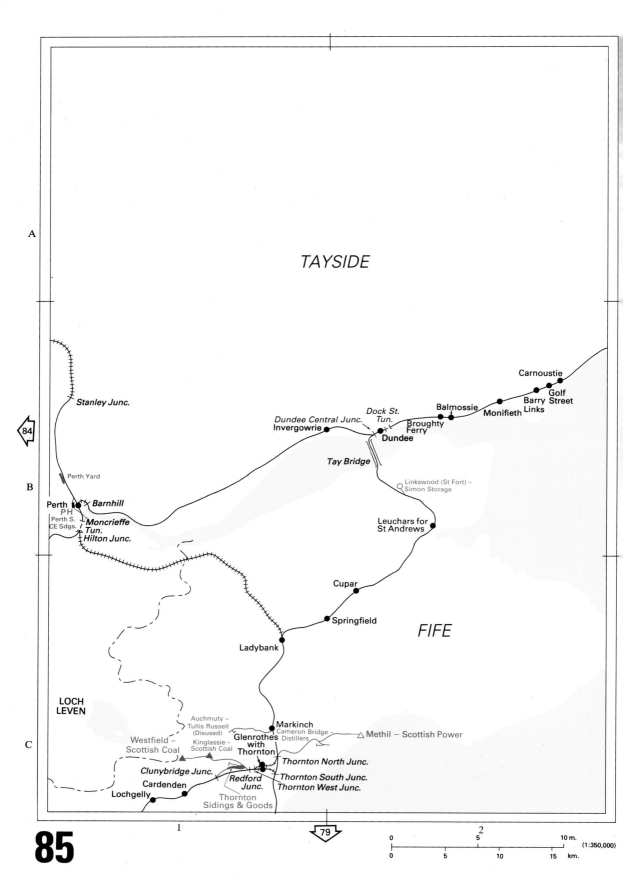

TAYSIDE

Stanley Junc.

Perth Yard

Perth
PH
Perth S.
CE Sdgs.
Barnhill
Moncrieffe
Tun.
Hilton Junc.

Dundee Central Junc.
Invergowrie
Dock St.
Tun.
Broughty
Ferry
Dundee

Balmossie
Monifieth

Carnoustie
Golf
Street
Barry
Links

Tay Bridge

Linkswood (St Fort) –
Simon Storage

Leuchars for
St Andrews

Cupar

Springfield

FIFE

Ladybank

LOCH
LEVEN

Auchmuty –
Tullis Russell
(Disused)
Markinch
Cameron Bridge
Distillers
Methil – Scottish Power
Westfield –
Scottish Coal
Kinglassie –
Scottish Coal
Glenrothes
with
Thornton
Thornton North Junc.
Clunybridge Junc.
Cardenden
Redford
Junc.
Thornton South Junc.
Thornton West Junc.
Lochgelly
Thornton
Sidings & Goods

A

B

C

84

85

1

79

2
5

10 m.

(1:350,000)

0

0

5

10

15

km.

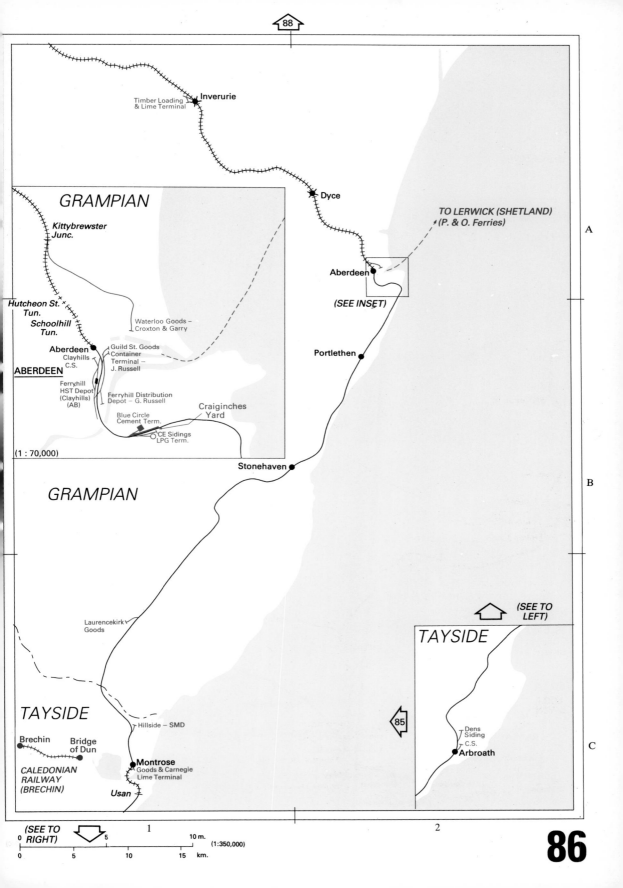

Inverurie

Timber Loading
& Lime Terminal

Dyce

TO LERWICK (SHETLAND)
(P. & O. Ferries)

Aberdeen

(SEE INSET)

A

GRAMPIAN

*Kittybrewster
Junc.*

*Hutcheon St.
Tun.*
*Schoolhill
Tun.*

Waterloo Goods –
Croxton & Garry

Aberdeen
Clayhills
C.S.

Guild St. Goods
Container
Terminal –
J. Russell

ABERDEEN

Ferryhill
HST Depot
(Clayhills)
(AB)

Ferryhill Distribution
Depot – G. Russell

Craiginches
Yard

Blue Circle
Cement Term.

CE Sidings
LPG Term.

(1 : 70,000)

Portlethen

GRAMPIAN

B

Stonehaven

Laurencekirk
Goods

(SEE TO
LEFT)

TAYSIDE

85

TAYSIDE

Hillside – SMD

Brechin

Bridge
of Dun

Dens
Siding
C.S.
Arbroath

C

*CALEDONIAN
RAILWAY
(BRECHIN)*

Montrose
Goods & Carnegie
Lime Terminal

Usan

(SEE TO
RIGHT)

0   5

1

10 m.

(1:350,000)

0   5   10   15   km.

2

86

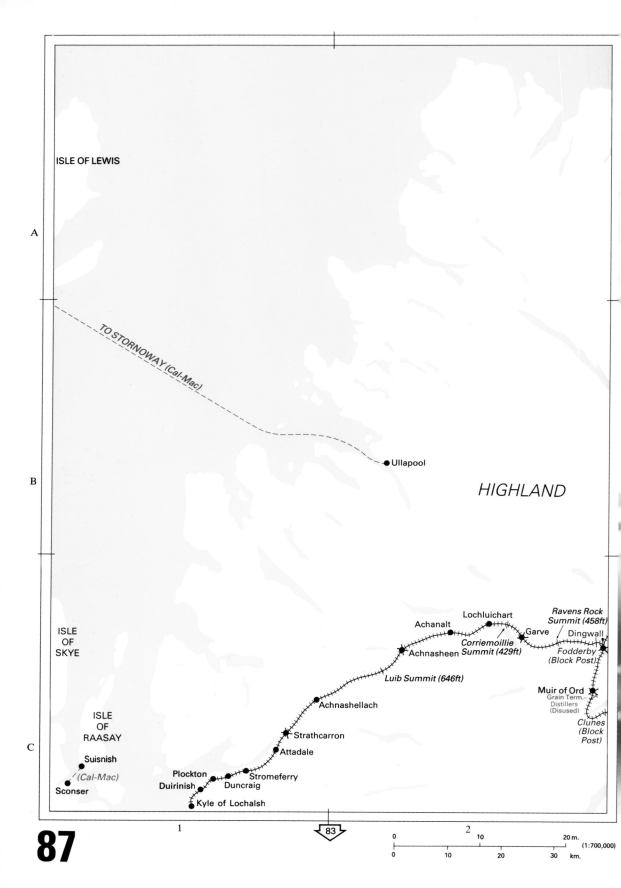

ISLE OF LEWIS

A

TO STORNOWAY (Cal-Mac)

● Ullapool

HIGHLAND

B

ISLE
OF
SKYE

Lochluichart

Ravens Rock
Summit (458ft)

Achanalt

Garve

Dingwall

Corriemoillie
Summit (429ft)

Fodderby
(Block Post)

Achnasheen

ISLE
OF
RAASAY

Luib Summit (646ft)

Muir of Ord
Grain Term.–
Distillers
(Disused)

Achnashellach

Clunes
(Block
Post)

Suisnish

Strathcarron

(Cal-Mac)

Attadale

Sconser

C

Plockton

Stromeferry

Duirinish

Duncraig

Kyle of Lochalsh

87

1

83

0   10   20 m.
(1:700,000)
0   10   20   30 km.

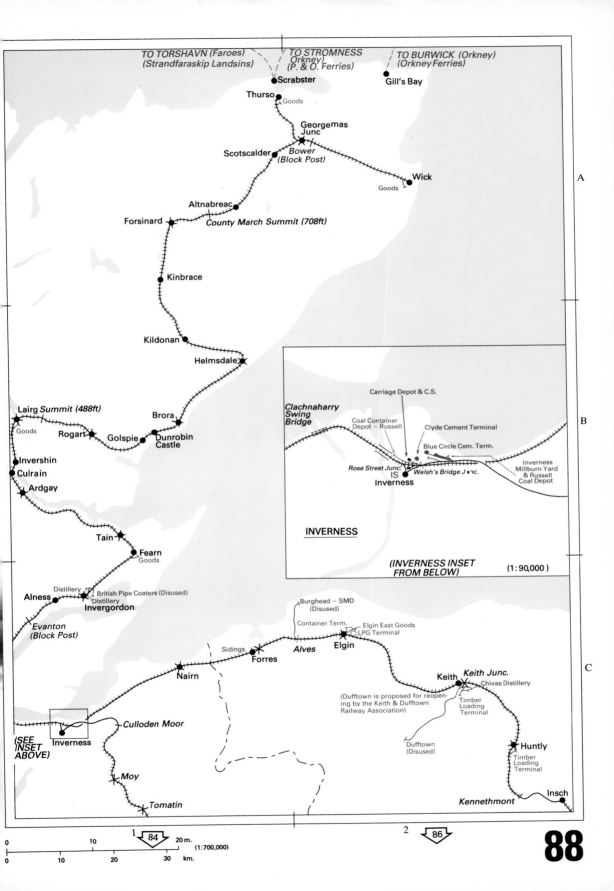

TO TORSHAVN (Faroes)
(Strandfaraskip Landsins)

TO STROMNESS
Orkney
(P. & O. Ferries)

TO BURWICK (Orkney)
(Orkney Ferries)

Scrabster

Gill's Bay

Thurso
Goods

Georgemas
Junc

Scotscalder   Bower
(Block Post)

Wick
Goods

A

Altnabreac

Forsinard   *County March Summit (708ft)*

Kinbrace

Kildonan

Helmsdale

Lairg *Summit (488ft)*

Goods
Rogart

Brora

Golspie

Dunrobin
Castle

Invershin
Culrain

Ardgay

Tain

Fearn
Goods

Distillery   British Pipe Coaters (Disused)
Alness   Distillery
             Invergordon

Evanton
(Block Post)

CLACHNAHARRY SWING BRIDGE / INVERNESS INSET

*Clachnaharry
Swing
Bridge*

Carriage Depot & C.S.

Coal Container
Depot – Russell

Clyde Cement Terminal

Blue Circle Cem. Term.

Rose Street Junc.
IS
Inverness

Welsh's Bridge Junc.

Inverness
Millburn Yard
& Russell
Coal Depot

B

INVERNESS

*(INVERNESS INSET
FROM BELOW)*   (1 : 90,000)

Burghead – SMD
(Disused)

Container Term.   Elgin East Goods
                      LPG Terminal

Sidings
Forres   *Alves*   Elgin

Keith   *Keith Junc.*
        Chivas Distillery

Nairn

(Dufftown is proposed for reopening by the Keith & Dufftown
Railway Association)

Timber
Loading
Terminal

C

*Dufftown
(Disused)*

Culloden Moor

**(SEE
INSET
ABOVE)**

Inverness

Huntly
Timber
Loading
Terminal

Moy

Tomatin

Kennethmont   Insch

0   10   20 m.
1 [84] (1:700,000)

0   10   20   30 km.

2 [86]

88

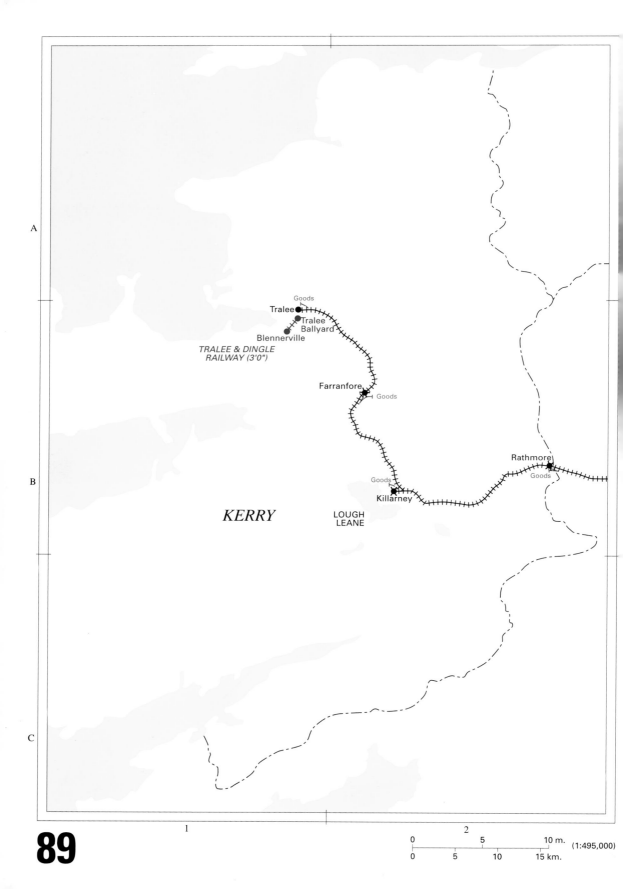

A

Goods
Tralee ●
● Tralee
Ballyard
Blennerville ●

*TRALEE & DINGLE
RAILWAY (3'0")*

Farranfore
Goods

Rathmore
Goods

B
Goods
Killarney

KERRY

LOUGH
LEANE

C

1
2

0   5   10 m.
0   5   10   15 km.

(1:495,000)

89

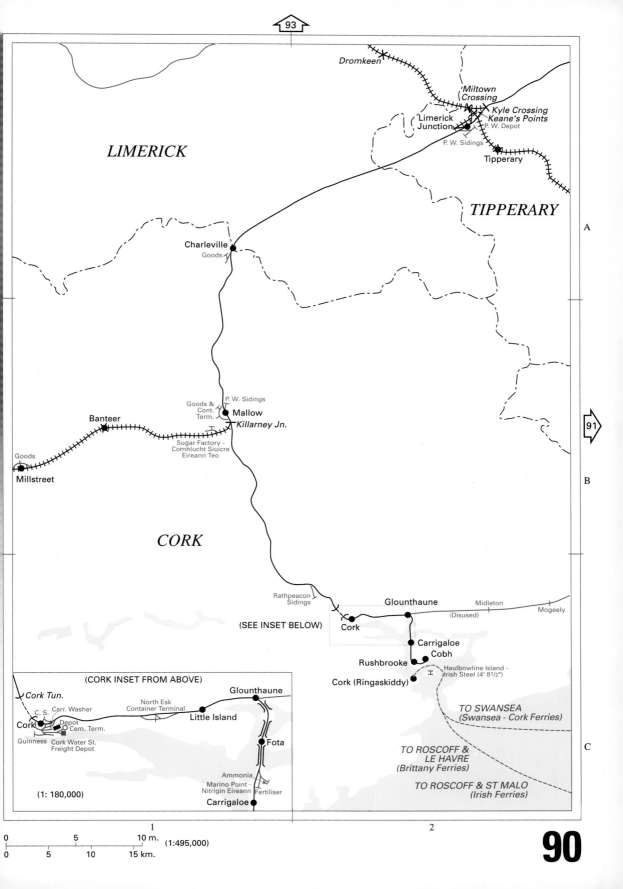

LIMERICK

Dromkeen

Miltown Crossing

Limerick Junction

Kyle Crossing
Keane's Points
P. W. Depot

P. W. Sidings

Tipperary

TIPPERARY

A

Charleville
Goods

91

P. W. Sidings

Banteer

Goods &
Cont.
Term.

Mallow
Killarney Jn.

Sugar Factory -
Comhlucht Siuicre
Eireann Teo

Goods

Millstreet

B

CORK

Rathpeacon
Sidings

Glounthaune

Midleton

Mogeely

(SEE INSET BELOW)

Cork

(Disused)

Carrigaloe
Cobh

Rushbrooke

Cork (Ringaskiddy)

Haulbowline Island -
Irish Steel (4' 8¹/₂")

TO SWANSEA
(Swansea - Cork Ferries)

(CORK INSET FROM ABOVE)

Cork Tun.

Glounthaune

North Esk
Container Terminal

C. S. Carr. Washer

Depot
Cem. Term.

Little Island

Cork

Guinness Cork Water St.
Freight Depot

Fota

TO ROSCOFF &
LE HAVRE
(Brittany Ferries)

C

Ammonia
Marino Point -
Nitrigin Eireann Fertiliser

TO ROSCOFF & ST MALO
(Irish Ferries)

(1: 180,000)

Carrigaloe

1

2

0   5   10 m.   (1:495,000)

0   5   10   15 km.

90

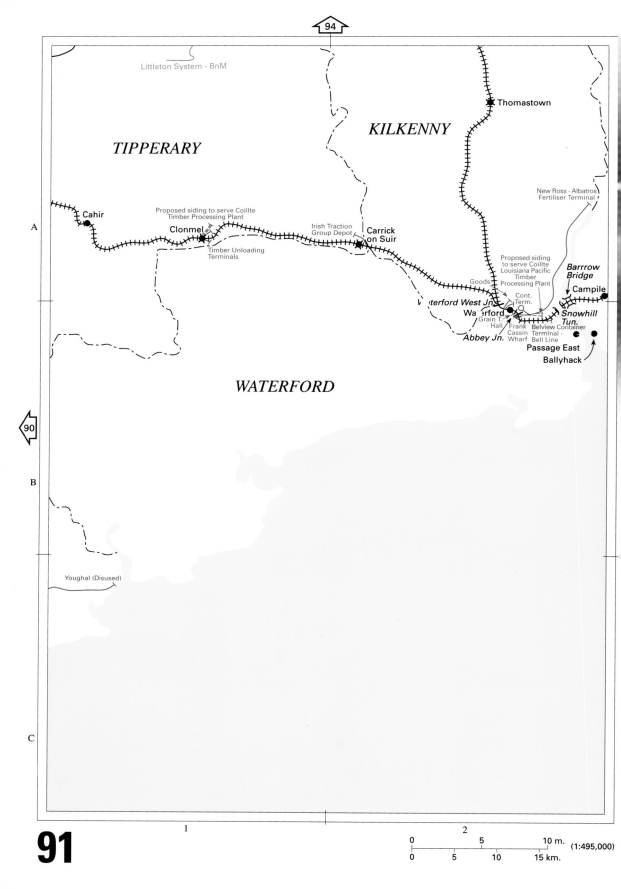

Littleton System - BnM

TIPPERARY

KILKENNY

● Thomastown

New Ross - Albatros
Fertiliser Terminal

● Cahir

A

Proposed siding to serve Coillte
Timber Processing Plant

Clonmel

Irish Traction
Group Depot

Carrick
on Suir

Timber Unloading
Terminals

Proposed siding
to serve Coillte
Louisiana Pacific
Timber
Processing Plant

Barrrow
Bridge

Goods

Cont.
Term.

Campile

Waterford West Jn.

Wa erford

Snowhill
Tun.

Grain T.
- Hall

Belview Container
Terminal -
Bell Line

Abbey Jn.

Frank
Cassin
Wharf

Passage East

WATERFORD

Ballyhack

B

Youghal (Disused)

C

91

0   5   10 m.   (1:495,000)

0   5   10   15 km.

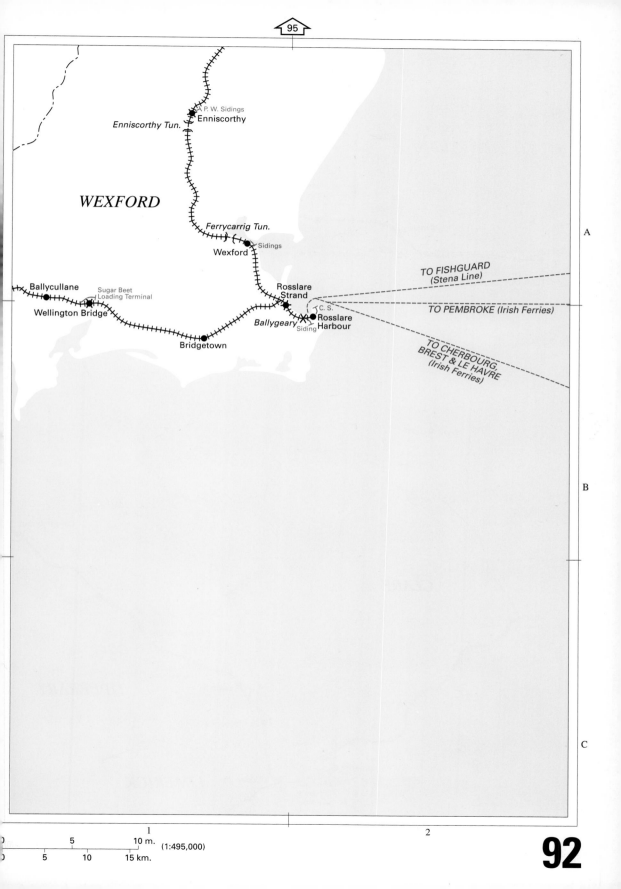

WEXFORD

Enniscorthy Tun.

P. W. Sidings
Enniscorthy

Ferrycarrig Tun.

Wexford
Sidings

Ballycullane

Sugar Beet
Loading Terminal

Wellington Bridge

Rosslare
Strand

TO FISHGUARD
(Stena Line)

TO PEMBROKE (Irish Ferries)

C. S.

Ballygeary
Siding

Rosslare
Harbour

Bridgetown

TO CHERBOURG,
BREST & LE HAVRE
(Irish Ferries)

1

5   10 m.   (1:495,000)

2

0

5

10

15 km.

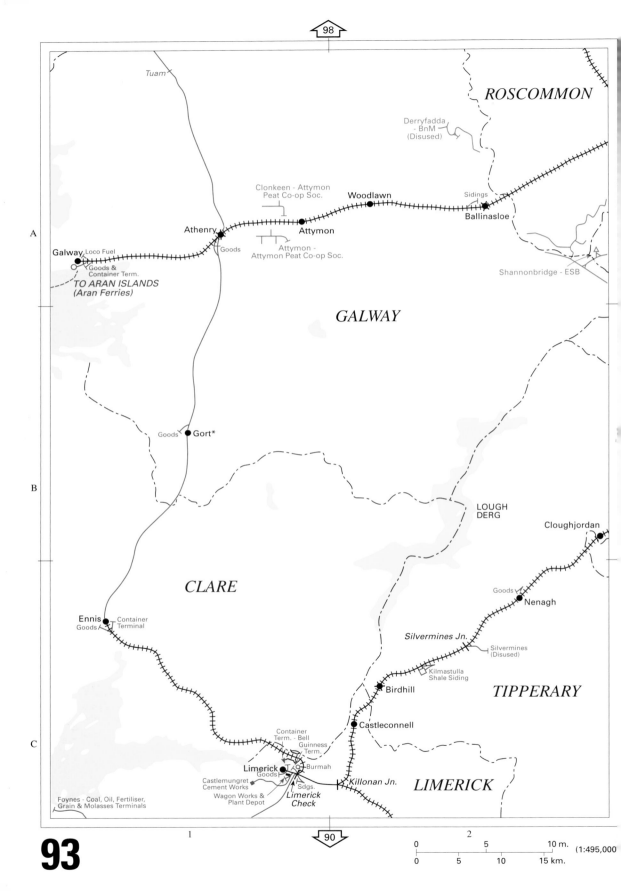

ROSCOMMON

Tuam

Derryfadda
- BnM
(Disused)

Sidings

Clonkeen - Attymon
Peat Co-op Soc.

Woodlawn

Ballinasloe

Athenry

Attymon

Goods

Attymon -
Attymon Peat Co-op Soc.

Shannonbridge - ESB

Galway Loco Fuel

Goods &
Container Term.

TO ARAN ISLANDS
(Aran Ferries)

GALWAY

Goods Gort*

LOUGH
DERG

Cloughjordan

CLARE

Goods

Nenagh

Ennis

Container
Terminal

Goods

Silvermines Jn.

Silvermines
(Disused)

Kilmastulla
Shale Siding

TIPPERARY

Birdhill

Castleconnell

Container
Term. - Bell
Guinness
Term.

Limerick

Burmah

Goods

Castlemungret
Cement Works

Sdgs.

Limerick
Check

Killonan Jn.

LIMERICK

Wagon Works &
Plant Depot

Foynes - Coal, Oil, Fertiliser,
Grain & Molasses Terminals

A

B

C

1

2

5

10 m.

0

5   10   15 km.

(1:495,000

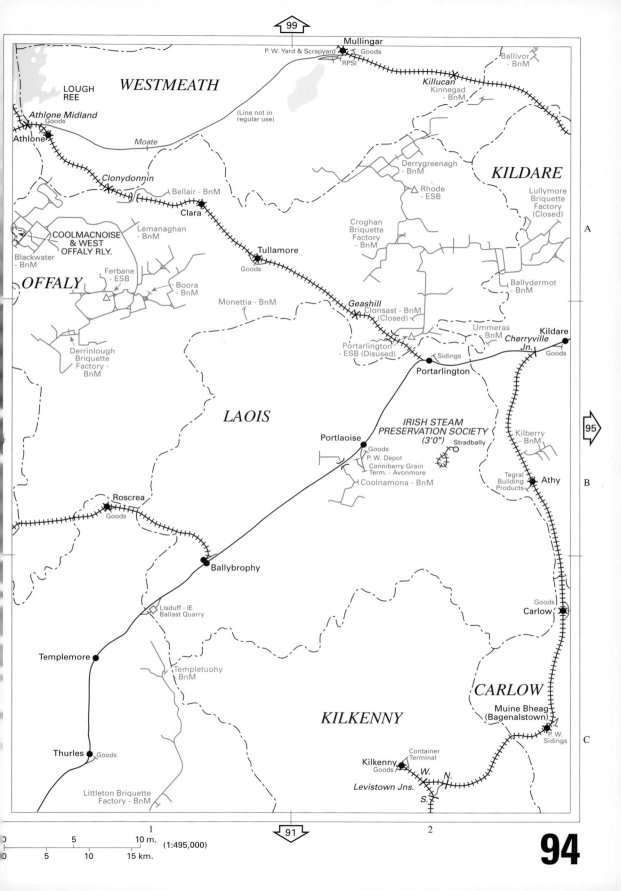

WESTMEATH

LOUGH REE

Athlone Midland
Goods
Athlone
Moate

Clonydonnin

Bellair - BnM
Clara

COOLMACNOISE & WEST OFFALY RLY.

Lemanaghan - BnM

Blackwater - BnM

OFFALY

Ferbane - ESB

Boora - BnM

Tullamore
Goods

Monettia - BnM

Derrinlough Briquette Factory - BnM

Mullingar
P. W. Yard & Scrapyard   Goods
RPSI

Ballivor - BnM

Killucan
Kinnegad - BnM

(Line not in regular use)

Derrygreenagh - BnM

Rhode - ESB

KILDARE

Lullymore Briquette Factory (Closed)

Croghan Briquette Factory - BnM

Ballydermot - BnM

Geashill
Clonsast - BnM (Closed)

Ummeras - BnM

Cherryville Jn.

Kildare
Goods

Portarlington - ESB (Disused)

Portarlington
Sidings

LAOIS

Portlaoise
Goods
P. W. Depot
Conniberry Grain Term. - Avonmore
Coolnamona - BnM

IRISH STEAM PRESERVATION SOCIETY (3'0")
Stradbally

Kilberry - BnM

Tegral Building Products

Athy

Roscrea
Goods

Ballybrophy

Lisduff - IE Ballast Quarry

Carlow
Goods

Templemore

Templetuohy BnM

KILKENNY

CARLOW

Muine Bheag (Bagenalstown)
P. W. Sidings

Thurles   Goods

Littleton Briquette Factory - BnM

Container Terminal
Kilkenny
Goods   W.   N.
Levistown Jns.
S.

A

95

B

C

1   10 m.
5
(1:495,000)
5   10   15 km.

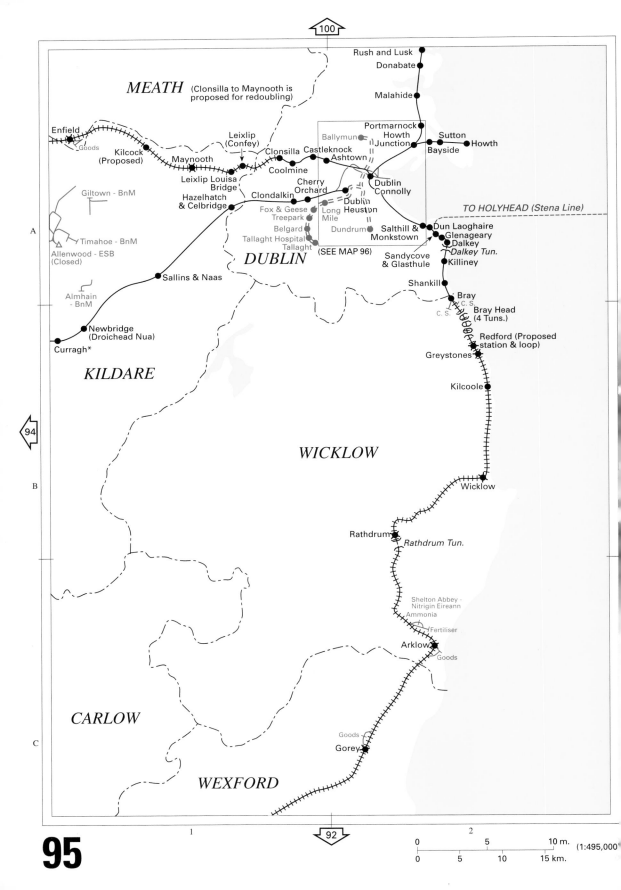

MEATH (Clonsilla to Maynooth is proposed for redoubling)

Rush and Lusk
Donabate
Malahide

Enfield
Goods
Kilcock (Proposed)
Maynooth
Leixlip (Confey)
Clonsilla
Castleknock
Coolmine
Leixlip Louisa Bridge
Ashtown
Portmarnock
Ballymun
Howth Junction
Sutton
Bayside
Howth

Cherry Orchard
Hazelhatch & Celbridge
Clondalkin
Fox & Geese
Treepark
Belgard
Tallaght Hospital
Tallaght

Dublin Connolly
Dublin Heuston
Long Mile
Dundrum

TO HOLYHEAD (Stena Line)

(SEE MAP 96)

Giltown - BnM

Timahoe - BnM

Allenwood - ESB (Closed)

DUBLIN

Salthill & Monkstown
Sandycove & Glasthule

Dun Laoghaire
Glenageary
Dalkey
Dalkey Tun.
Killiney

Sallins & Naas

Almhain - BnM

Shankill

Bray
C.S.
C.S.
Bray Head (4 Tuns.)

Newbridge (Droichead Nua)
Curragh*

Redford (Proposed station & loop)

Greystones

KILDARE

Kilcoole

WICKLOW

Wicklow

Rathdrum
Rathdrum Tun.

Shelton Abbey - Nitrigin Eireann
Ammonia
Fertiliser

Arklow
Goods

CARLOW

Goods
Gorey

WEXFORD

95

0   5   10 m.
0   5   10   15 km.
(1:495,000)

1   2

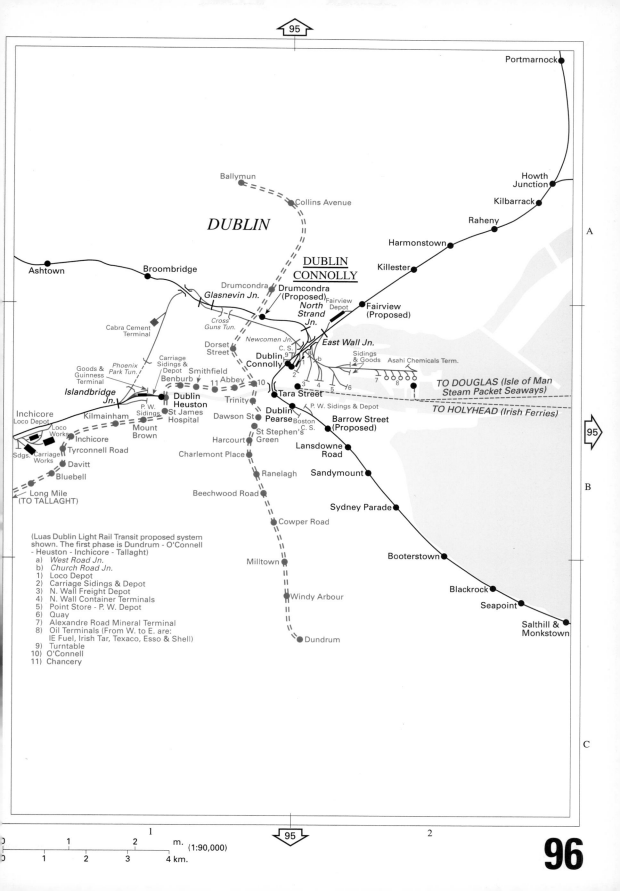

Portmarnock

DUBLIN

Howth
Junction

Kilbarrack

Raheny

Harmonstown

Killester

**DUBLIN
CONNOLLY**

Ballymun

Collins Avenue

Ashtown

Broombridge

Drumcondra
Glasnevin Jn.

Drumcondra
(Proposed)

*North
Strand
Jn.*

Fairview
Depot

Fairview
(Proposed)

Cabra Cement
Terminal

*Cross
Guns Tun.*

Dorset
Street

Newcomen Jn.
C. S.
9 T
a
b

East Wall Jn.

Sidings
& Goods

Asahi Chemicals Term.

Carriage
Sidings &
Depot

Smithfield

Dublin
Connolly

2
1

**TO DOUGLAS (Isle of Man
Steam Packet Seaways)**

Goods &
Guinness
Terminal

*Phoenix
Park Tun.*

Benburb

11

Abbey

10

3

4

5

6

7

8

*Islandbridge
Jn.*

Dublin
Heuston

Trinity

Tara Street

P. W. Sidings & Depot

TO HOLYHEAD (Irish Ferries)

Inchicore
Loco Depot

Loco
Works

Kilmainham

P. W.
Sidings

St James
Hospital

Dawson St

Dublin
Pearse

Boston
C. S.

Barrow Street
(Proposed)

Inchicore

Mount
Brown

St Stephen's
Green

Lansdowne
Road

Sdgs.
Carriage
Works

Tyrconnell Road

Harcourt

Sandymount

Davitt

Charlemont Place

Bluebell

Ranelagh

Sydney Parade

Long Mile
(TO TALLAGHT)

Beechwood Road

Beechwood Road

Booterstown

Cowper Road

Blackrock

Seapoint

Milltown

Windy Arbour

Salthill &
Monkstown

Dundrum

(Luas Dublin Light Rail Transit proposed system
shown. The first phase is Dundrum - O'Connell
- Heuston - Inchicore - Tallaght)
 a) *West Road Jn.*
 b) *Church Road Jn.*
 1) Loco Depot
 2) Carriage Sidings & Depot
 3) N. Wall Freight Depot
 4) N. Wall Container Terminals
 5) Point Store - P. W. Depot
 6) Quay
 7) Alexandre Road Mineral Terminal
 8) Oil Terminals (From W. to E. are:
      IE Fuel, Irish Tar, Texaco, Esso & Shell)
 9) Turntable
10) O'Connell
11) Chancery

A

95

B

C

1

2

m. (1:90,000)

0
1   1   2   3   4 km.

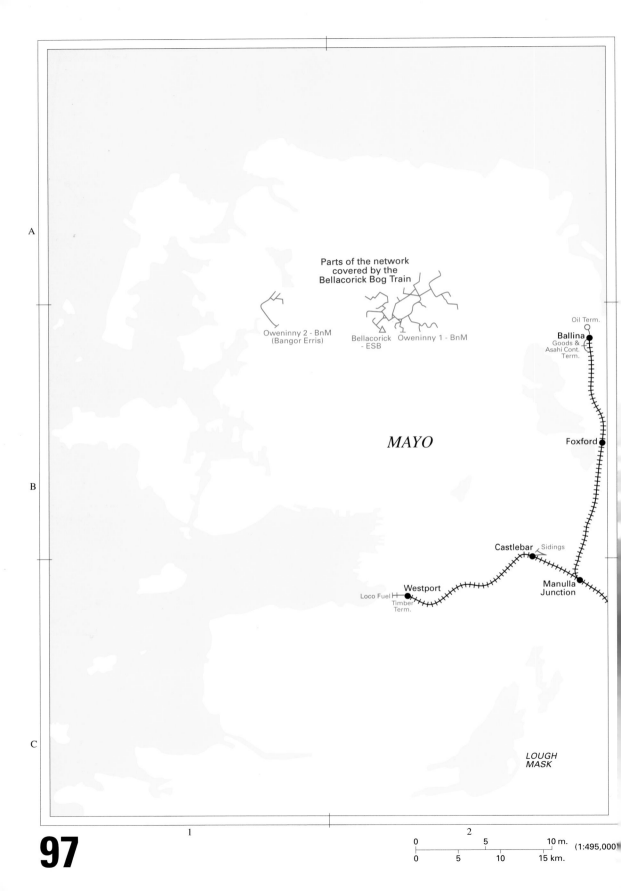

A

Parts of the network
covered by the
Bellacorick Bog Train

Oil Term.

Ballina
Goods &
Asahi Cont.
Term.

Oweninny 2 - BnM
(Bangor Erris)

Bellacorick
- ESB

Oweninny 1 - BnM

MAYO

Foxford

B

Castlebar

Sidings

Manulla
Junction

Westport

Loco Fuel

Timber
Term.

C

*LOUGH
MASK*

97

1

2

0   5   10 m.

0   5   10   15 km.

(1:495,000)

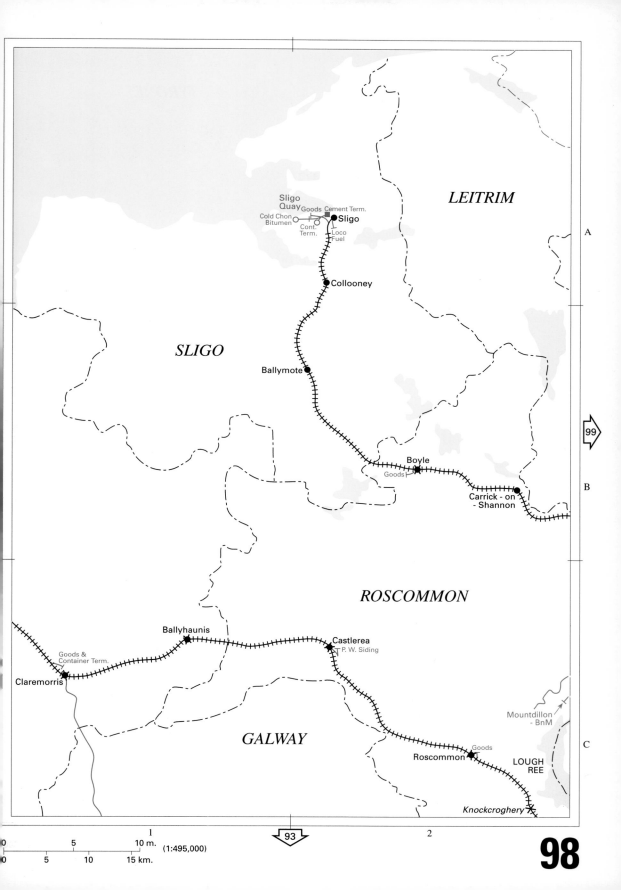

LEITRIM

Sligo
Quay
Cold Chon
Bitumen
Goods
Cont.
Term.
Cement Term.
Sligo
Loco
Fuel

Collooney

SLIGO

Ballymote

99

Boyle
Goods

Carrick - on
- Shannon

ROSCOMMON

Ballyhaunis
Goods &
Container Term.
Claremorris

Castlerea
P. W. Siding

Mountdillon
- BnM

GALWAY

Roscommon
Goods

LOUGH
REE

Knockcroghery

A

B

C

1

10 m.
(1:495,000)

5

5   10   15 km.

93

2

98

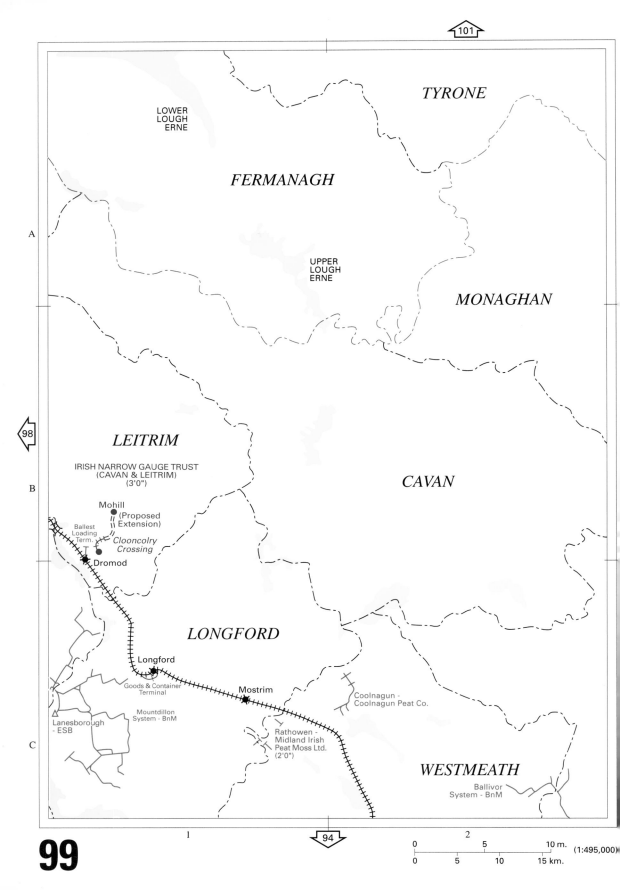

TYRONE

LOWER
LOUGH
ERNE

FERMANAGH

UPPER
LOUGH
ERNE

MONAGHAN

A

LEITRIM

IRISH NARROW GAUGE TRUST
(CAVAN & LEITRIM)
(3'0")

CAVAN

B

Mohill
(Proposed
Extension)

Ballest
Loading
Term.

Clooncolry
Crossing

Dromod

LONGFORD

Longford

Goods & Container
Terminal

Mostrim

Coolnagun -
Coolnagun Peat Co.

Mountdillon
System - BnM

Lanesborough
- ESB

Rathowen -
Midland Irish
Peat Moss Ltd.
(2'0")

C

WESTMEATH

Ballivor
System - BnM

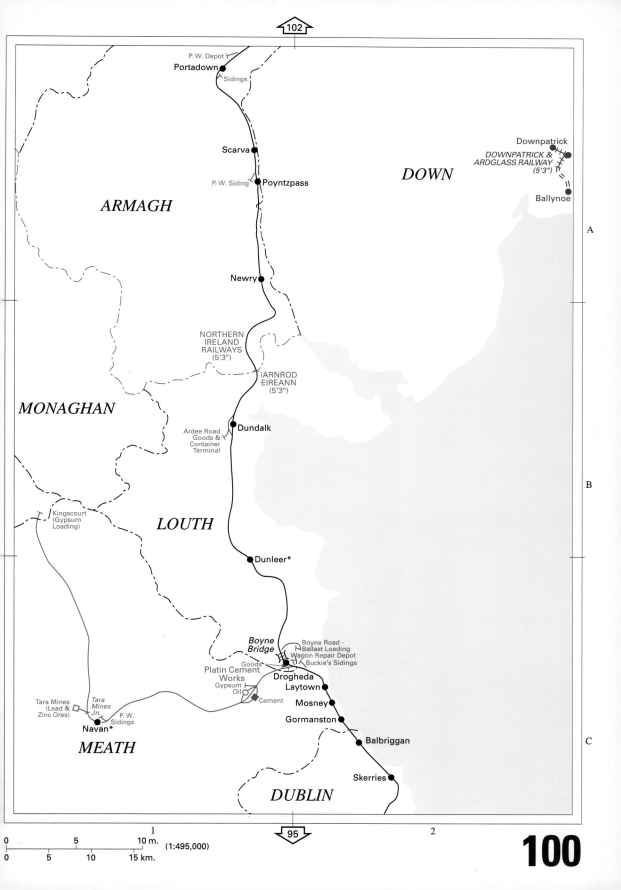

P. W. Depot

Portadown

Sidings

Scarva

P. W. Siding Poyntzpass

Newry

ARMAGH

DOWN

Downpatrick

*DOWNPATRICK &
ARDGLASS RAILWAY*
(5'3")

Ballynoe

A

NORTHERN
IRELAND
RAILWAYS
(5'3")

IARNROD
EIREANN
(5'3")

MONAGHAN

Dundalk

Ardee Road
Goods &
Container
Terminal

B

Kingscourt
(Gypsum
Loading)

LOUTH

Dunleer*

*Boyne
Bridge*

Boyne Road -
Ballast Loading
Wagon Repair Depot
Buckie's Sidings

Goods

Platin Cement
Works

Gypsum

Oil

Cement

Drogheda

Laytown

Tara Mines
(Lead &
Zinc Ores)

*Tara
Mines
Jn.*

P. W.
Sidings

Navan*

Mosney

Gormanston

Balbriggan

C

MEATH

Skerries

DUBLIN

2

100

1

10 m.   (1:495,000)

0   5

0   5   10   15 km.

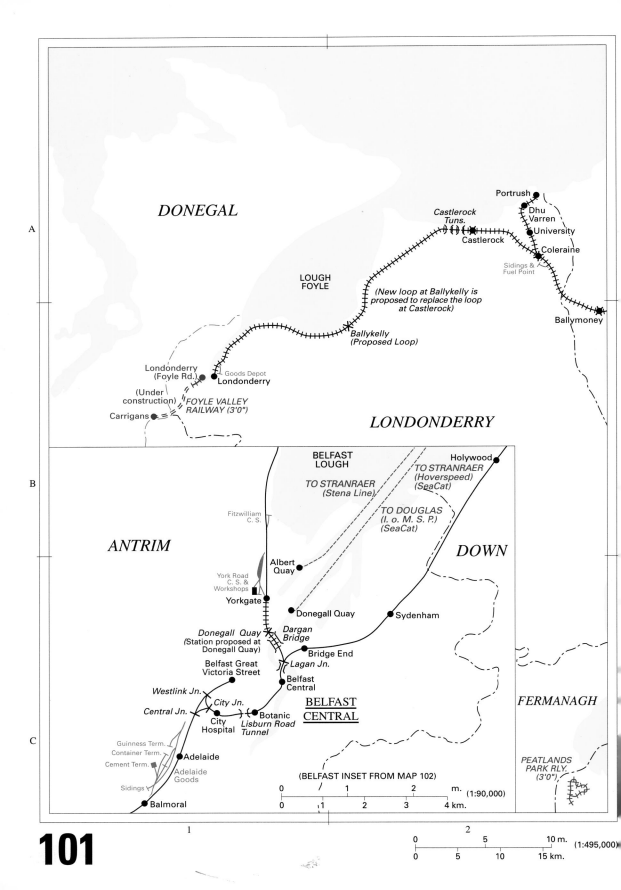

DONEGAL

LOUGH
FOYLE

Portrush

Dhu
Varren

University

*Castlerock
Tuns.*

Castlerock

Coleraine

Sidings &
Fuel Point

*(New loop at Ballykelly is
proposed to replace the loop
at Castlerock)*

Ballymoney

*Ballykelly
(Proposed Loop)*

Londonderry
(Foyle Rd.)

Goods Depot

Londonderry

(Under
construction)

*FOYLE VALLEY
RAILWAY (3'0")*

Carrigans

LONDONDERRY

BELFAST
LOUGH

Holywood

*TO STRANRAER
(Hoverspeed)
(SeaCat)*

*TO STRANRAER
(Stena Line)*

Fitzwilliam
C. S.

*TO DOUGLAS
(I. o. M. S. P.)
(SeaCat)*

ANTRIM

Albert
Quay

DOWN

York Road
C. S. &
Workshops

Yorkgate

Donegall Quay

Sydenham

*Donegall Quay
(Station proposed at
Donegall Quay)*

*Dargan
Bridge*

Belfast Great
Victoria Street

Bridge End

Lagan Jn.

FERMANAGH

Westlink Jn.

City Jn.

Belfast
Central

Central Jn.

City
Hospital

Botanic

*Lisburn Road
Tunnel*

BELFAST
CENTRAL

Guinness Term.

Container Term.

Cement Term.

Adelaide

PEATLANDS
PARK RLY.
(3'0")

Adelaide
Goods

(BELFAST INSET FROM MAP 102)

Sidings

0   1   2   m.

Balmoral

0   1   2   3   4 km.

(1:90,000)

101

1

2

0   5   10 m.

0   5   10   15 km.

(1:495,000)

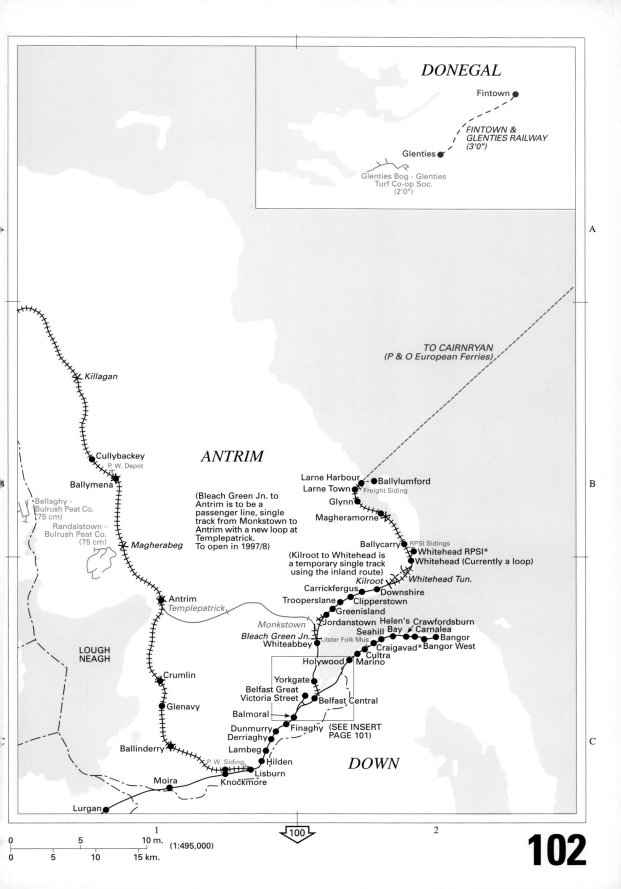

DONEGAL

Fintown

FINTOWN & GLENTIES RAILWAY (3'0")

Glenties

Glenties Bog - Glenties
Turf Co-op Soc.
(2'0")

A

TO CAIRNRYAN
(P & O European Ferries)

Killagan

ANTRIM

Cullybackey
P. W. Depot

Ballymena

Larne Harbour
Larne Town • Ballylumford
Freight Siding
Glynn

Magheramorne

(Bleach Green Jn. to
passenger line, single
track from Monkstown to
Antrim with a new loop at
Templepatrick.
To open in 1997/8.

B

Bellaghy -
Bulrush Peat Co.
(75 cm)

Randalstown -
Bulrush Peat Co.
(75 cm)

Magherabeg

Ballycarry   *RPSI Sidings*
Whitehead RPSI*
Whitehead (Currently a loop)

(Kilroot to Whitehead is
a temporary single track
using the inland route)

Kilroot   *Whitehead Tun.*

Carrickfergus   Downshire
Trooperslane   Clipperstown
Greenisland
Jordanstown   Helen's Crawfordsburn
Seahill   Bay Carnalea

Antrim
Templepatrick

**LOUGH
NEAGH**

Monkstown
Bleach Green Jn. Ulster Folk Mus.
Whiteabbey   Bangor
Craigavad* Bangor West
Cultra
Holywood Marino

Crumlin

Glenavy

Yorkgate
Belfast Great
Victoria Street
Balmoral   Belfast Central

Ballinderry

Dunmurry Finaghy (SEE INSERT
Derriaghy   PAGE 101)
Lambeg
P. W. Siding Hilden   **DOWN**

Moira   Lisburn
Knockmore

Lurgan

C

| 1 | | | | 10 m. | (1:495,000) | | 2 |
0 5   10 m.
0 5   10   15 km.

102

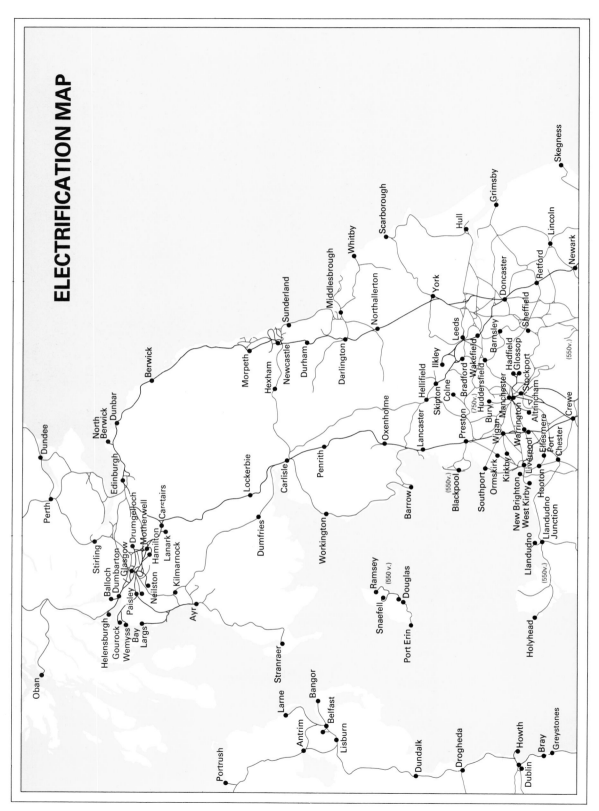

ELECTRIFICATION MAP

103

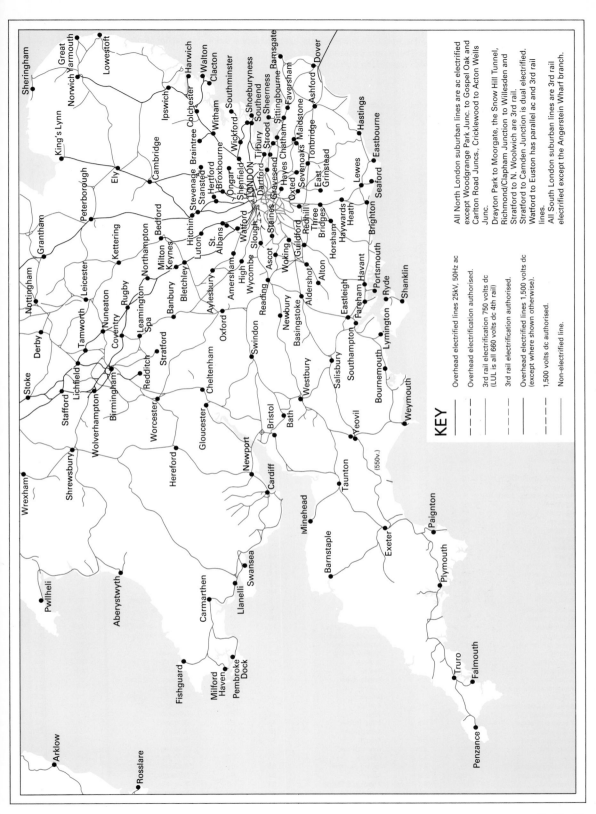

KEY

Overhead electrified lines 25kV, 50Hz ac	
Overhead electrification authorised.	
3rd rail electrification 750 volts dc (LUL is all 660 volts dc 4th rail)	
3rd rail electrification authorised.	
Overhead electrified lines 1,500 volts dc (except where shown otherwise).	
1,500 volts dc authorised.	
Non-electrified line.	

All North London suburban lines are ac electrified except Woodgrange Park Junc. to Gospel Oak and Carlton Road Juncs., Cricklewood to Acton Wells Junc.

Drayton Park to Moorgate, the Snow Hill Tunnel, Richmond/Clapham Junction to Willesden and Stratford to N. Woolwich are 3rd rail.

Stratford to Camden Junction is dual electrified. Watford to Euston has parallel ac and 3rd rail lines.

All South London suburban lines are 3rd rail electrified except the Angerstein Wharf branch.

104

INDEX

All passenger stations are included in this index. Freight terminals, junction names, tunnels and other significant locations are indexed where their names or map references differ from a passenger station.
  * denotes an unadvertised or excursion station. (eg Curragh*)

109

110

Location	Page No.	Page Ref.	Location	Page No.	Page Ref.	Location	Page No.	Page Ref.
Kensington Olympia	21	C1	Kintbury	10	A1	Lawrence Hill	28	C2
Kent House	18	A1	Kippenross Tunnel	84	C2	Laxey	65	C2
Kent Viaduct	66	C2	Kirby Cross	37	B2	Layton	60	B1
Kentish Town	21	A1	Kirby Muxloe (Projected)	42	A2	Laytown	100	C2
Kentish Town West	21	B1	Kirk Sandall	64	A2	Lazonby & Kirkoswald	66	A2
Kenton	20	A1	Kirkby (Merseyside)	59	A2	Lea Brook Road (Proposed)	47	B2
Kents Bank	66	C2	Kirkby Centre (Proposed)	53	B2	Lea Hall	48	C2
Keresley	42	B1	Kirkby Lane End Junction	53	B2	Lea Junction	22	B1
Kernick	1	B2	Kirkby Stephen	67	B1	Lea Wood Tunnel	53	B1
Kettering	43	B1	Kirkby Summit Junction	53	B2	Leadhills	71	A2
Ketton	43	A2	Kirkby Thore	66	A2	Leagrave	35	A2
Kew Bridge	20	C2	Kirkby Tunnel	53	B2	Lealholm	69	B1
Kew Gardens	20	C2	Kirkby-in-Furness	66	C1	Leamington Spa	42	C1
Keyham	2	C1	Kirkcaldy	79	A1	Leasowe	51	A1
Keylands Sidings	12	B2	Kirkconnel	69	A1	Leatherhead	11	A2
Keymer Junction	12	C1	Kirkdale	59	B1	Leckwith Loop Junctions	27	B2
Keynsham	9	A1	Kirkham & Wesham	60	C2	Ledbury	33	A1
Kibworth Summit	42	B2	Kirkhaugh	73	C1	Lee	18	A2
Kidbrooke	22	C2	Kirkhill	82	C2	Leeds	63	A1
Kidderminster	41	B1	Kirknewton	79	B1	Leek Brook Junction	52	B2
Kidderminster Town	41	B1	Kirkwood	78	C1	Leeman Road	62	A1
Kidsgrove	52	B2	Kirton Lindsey	63	C2	Leicester	42	A2
Kidwelly	30	B2	Kitson Wood Tunnel	61	B2	Leicester Forest East	42	A2
Kilbarrack	96	A2	Kittybrewster	86	A1	(Projected)		
Kilberry	94	B2	Kiveton Bridge	53	A2	Leicester Junction	53	C1
Kilburn	21	A1	Kiveton Park	53	A2	Leicester North	42	A2
Kilburn High Road	21	B1	Knaresborough	62	A1	Leicester Square	21	B2
Kilburn Park	21	B1	Knebworth	36	B1	Leigh	12	B2
Kilcock (Proposed)	95	A1	Knighton	40	C1	Leigh-on-Sea	37	C1
Kilcoole	95	B2	Knighton S. Junction & Tunnel	42	A2	Leigham Junction & Tunnels	17	A2
Kildale	68	B2	Knights Hill Tunnel	17	A2	Leighton Buzzard	35	A1
Kildare	94	B2	Knightsbridge	21	C1	Leith	79	B2
Kildonan	88	B1	Knightswood N. Junc. & Tun.	81	A2	Leixlip (Confey)	95	A1
Kilgetty	30	B1	Knockcroghery	98	C2	Leixlip Louisa Bridge	95	A1
Kilkenny	94	C2	Knockholt	12	A2	Lelant	1	A1
Kilkerran	70	A1	Knockmore	102	C1	Lelant Saltings	1	A1
Killagan	102	B1	Knockshinnoch	71	A1	Lenham	13	A1
Killarney	89	B2	Knottingley	62	B2	Lenton Junctions	53	C2
Killarney Junction	90	B1	Knucklas	40	B1	Lenzie	82	A2
Killester	96	A2	Knutsford	52	A1	Leominster	40	C2
Killiecrankie Tunnel	84	B2	Kyle Crossing	90	A2	Leppings Lane	53	A1
Killiney	95	A2	Kyle of Lochalsh	87	C1	Letchworth	36	A1
Killingholme	63	C2	Lackenby	69	A2	Letterston Junction	29	A2
Killoch	77	C2	Ladbroke Grove	21	B1	Leuchars	85	B2
Killonan Junction	93	C2	Ladybank	85	C1	Leven Viaduct	66	C1
Kilmarnock	77	C2	Ladyburn Junction	77	A1	Levenshulme	58	C1
Kilmastulla	93	C2	Ladywell	22	C1	Levisham	69	C1
Kilmaurs	77	C2	Lagan Junction	101	C1	Lewaigue	65	B2
Kilnhurst	62	C2	Laindon	36	C2	Lewes	12	C1
Kilpatrick	81	A1	Laira	2	C2	Lewisham	22	C1
Kilroot	102	C2	Lairg	88	B1	Leyland	60	B2
Kilsby Tunnel	42	C2	Lake	6	A2	Leyton	22	A1
Kilwinning	77	B1	Lakenheath	44	B2	Leyton Midland Road	22	A1
Kimberley C.S.	12	B2	Lakeside	66	C1	Leytonstone	22	A1
Kinbrace	88	A1	Lambeg	102	C1	Leytonstone High Road	22	A1
Kincardine	78	A2	Lambeth North	21	C2	Lichfield City	41	A2
Kineton	42	C1	Lambhill	82	A1	Lichfield Trent Valley	41	A2
King Edward	21	B2	Lamphey	29	B2	Lidlington	35	A2
King Edward Bridge	75	B2	Lanark	78	C2	Lifford Junctions	41	B2
King Street (Blackburn)	61	B1	Lancaster	60	A2	Lillie Bridge	21	C1
King's Cross	21	B2	Lancaster Gate	21	B1	Limbury Road	35	A2
King's Cross Thameslink	21	B2	Lancing	11	C2	Lime Kiln Halt	65	C2
King's Dock	32	A2	Landor Street Junction	48	C1	Limehouse	22	B1
King's Ferry Bridge	13	A1	Landore Junction	31	A2	Limerick	93	C1
King's Langley	23	A1	Landywood	41	A2	Limerick Junction	90	A2
King's Lynn	44	A2	Lanesborough	99	C1	Limpsfield Tunnel	12	A1
King's Norton	41	B2	Langbank	77	A2	Lincoln Central	54	B2
King's Nympton	7	C1	Langho	61	B1	Lindal Tunnel	66	C1
King's Park	82	C1	Langley	35	C2	Lindsey	64	C2
King's Sutton	34	A2	Langley Green	47	C2	Linford Street Junction	21	C1
Kingcraig	84	A2	Langsett	56	B1	Lingfield	12	B1
Kingham	34	B1	Langside	82	C1	Lingwood	46	A1
Kinghorn	79	A1	Langwathby	66	A2	Linkswood	85	B2
Kinglassie	85	C1	Langwith (Proposed)	53	B2	Linlithgow	78	A2
Kingmoor	71	B1	Lansdowne Road	96	B1	Linslade Tunnels	35	A1
Kingsbury (Greater London)	20	A2	Lapford	7	C1	Liphook	11	B1
Kingsbury (Warwicks.)	42	B1	Lappa Valley Railway	1	B2	Lipson Junction	2	A2
Kingscote (Proposed)	12	B1	Lapworth	42	C1	Lisburn	102	C1
Kingscourt	100	B1	Larbert	78	A2	Lisburn Road Tunnel	101	C1
Kingskerswell (Proposed)	3	B2	Largin	2	B1	Lisduff	94	C1
Kingsknowe	79	C1	Largs	77	B1	Liskeard	2	B1
Kingsland Road (Bristol)	28	C2	Larkfield Junction	82	B1	Liss	11	B1
Kingston	16	B1	Larkhall (Projected)	78	B1	Lisvane & Thornhill	27	A2
Kingston Park	75	A1	Larne Harbour	102	B2	Litchfield Tunnel	10	B2
Kingston Tunnel	12	C1	Larne Town	102	B2	Little Barford	43	C2
Kingswear (for Dartmouth)	3	B2	Latchford	51	A2	Little Bispham	60	B1
Kingswinford Junction	47	C1	Latchmere Junction	21	C1	Little Eaton Junction	53	C1
Kingswood	12	A1	Latimer Road	20	B2	Little Hautbois	45	A2
Kingswood Tunnel	84	B2	Launceston	2	A2	Little Island	90	C1
Kingussie	84	A2	Laurencekirk	86	C1	Little Kimble	35	B1
Kinnegad	94	A2	Laverstock Junctions	9	B2	Little Sutton	51	A1
Kinneil	78	A2	Lavistown Junctions	94	C2	Littleborough	61	C2
Kinning Park	81	B2	Law Junction	78	B1	Littlebury Tunnel	36	A2
			Lawley Street	48	C1	Littlehampton	11	C2

116

117

Location	Page No.	Page Ref.	Location	Page No.	Page Ref.	Location	Page No.	Page Ref.
Thameshaven	37	C1	Tower Gateway	21	B2	Upperby	71	C1
Thameshaven Junction	36	C2	Tower Hill	21	B2	Upton	51	A1
Thamesport	37	C1	Town Green	60	C2	Upton Park	22	B2
Thatcham	10	A2	Towneley Tunnel	61	B1	Upwey	5	A1
Thatto Heath	51	A2	Townhead	77	C1	Urmston	57	C1
The Crescent (Proposed)	47	A1	Trafford Bar	57	B2	Usan	86	C1
The Green	66	B1	Trafford Park	57	B2	Uttoxeter	52	C2
The Hawthorns	47	B2	Tralee	89	B1	Uxbridge	19	B1
The Lakes	41	B2	Trawsfynydd	50	C1	Valley	49	A1
The Midden	56	C1	Trefforest	31	C2	Valley Halt	49	B2
The Mound Tunnels	79	C1	Trefforest Estate	31	C2	Vauxhall (Liverpool) (Projected)	59	B1
Theale	10	A2	Trehafod	31	C2	Vauxhall (London)	21	C2
Theobalds Grove	26	A1	Treherbert	31	B2	Ventnor Road	17	C1
Thetford	45	B1	Tremorfa	27	B2	Victoria	21	C1
Theydon Bois	36	B1	Trent Junction and Yard (Scunthorpe)	63	C1	Victoria Sidings	45	A1
Thingley	9	A2	Trent Junctions (Derbyshire)	53	C2	Virginia Water	11	A2
Thirsk	68	C2	Trent Junctions (Lincs.)	54	A1	Voltaire Road Junction	21	C2
Thomastown	91	A2	Trent Yard	63	C1	Waddon	17	C2
Thoresby	53	B2	Trentham	52	C1	Waddon Marsh	17	B2
Thornaby	69	A1	Treorchy	31	C2	Wadhurst	12	B2
Thorne Junction	62	C2	Treverrin Tunnel	2	B1	Wadsley Bridge*	53	A1
Thorne North	63	C1	Treviscoe	1	B2	Wainfleet	55	B2
Thorne South	63	C1	Triangle Sidings	21	C1	Wainhill	35	B1
Thorney Mill	19	C1	Trimley	38	A1	Wakefield Kirkgate	62	C1
Thornford	8	C2	Tring	35	B1	Wakefield Road Tunnel	62	B1
Thornliebank	81	C2	Trinity Way (Proposed)	47	B2	Wakefield Westgate	62	C1
Thornton	85	C1	Troed-y-Rhiw	31	B2	Walkden	57	A1
Thornton Abbey	63	C2	Troon	77	C2	Walkergate	75	B2
Thornton Fields	22	B1	Trooperslane	102	C2	Walkeringham	54	A1
Thornton Gate	60	B1	Trostre	30	B2	Wallasey Grove Road	59	B1
Thornton Heath	17	B2	Trowbridge	9	A1	Wallasey Village	59	B1
Thorntonhall	78	B1	Trowell Junction	53	C2	Wallers Ash Tunnel	10	B2
Thorpe Bay	37	C1	Trowse	45	A1	Wallingford	34	C2
Thorpe Culvert	55	B2	Truro	1	C2	Wallington	17	C1
Thorpe Junction	45	A1	Tuam	93	A1	Wallneuk Junction	81	B1
Thorpe-le-Soken	37	B2	Tufnell Park	21	A1	Wallsend	76	B1
Thorpes Bridge Junction	58	B1	Tullamore	94	A1	Wallyford	79	A2
Three Bridges	12	B1	Tulloch	84	A1	Walmer	14	A1
Three Oaks	13	C1	Tulse Hill	17	A2	Walsall	47	A2
Three Spires Junction	42	B1	Tunbridge Wells	12	B2	Walsden	61	B2
Thrislington	68	A1	Tunbridge Wells West	12	B2	Walsingham	56	C1
Thurgarton	54	B1	Tunnel Junction (Salisbury)	9	B2	Waltham Cross	26	A1
Thurles	94	C1	Tunnel Junction (Worcester)	41	C1	Walthamstow Central	22	A1
Thurnscoe	62	C2	Tunstall Road (Hunslet)	63	B1	Walthamstow Queens Road	22	A1
Thurso	88	A1	Tunstead	52	A2	Walton (Merseyside)	59	A2
Thurston	45	C1	Turkey Street	26	B1	Walton Old Junction	51	B1
Thurstonland Tunnel	62	C1	Turnchapel Branch Junction	2	C2	Walton Street Junction	63	B2
Tidal Yard	27	B2	Turners Lane Junction	62	C1	Walton-on-Naze	37	B2
Tidenham	32	C2	Turnham Green	20	C2	Walton-on-Thames	15	C2
Tidworth	10	A1	Turnpike Lane	25	C2	Wanborough	11	A1
Tilbury Town	38	C2	Tursdale Junction	68	A1	Wandsworth Common	17	A1
Tile Hill	42	B1	Tutbury and Hatton	53	C1	Wandsworth Road	21	C2
Tilehurst	34	C2	Tweedmouth	80	B2	Wandsworth Town	21	C1
Tilmanstone (Proposed)	14	A1	Twerton Tunnel	9	A1	Wanlockhead (Proposed)	71	A2
Timahoe	95	A1	Twickenham	16	A1	Wansbeck Road	75	A2
Timperley	57	C2	Twyford	35	C1	Wansford	43	A2
Tinsley	56	B2	Ty Croes	50	A1	Wanstead	22	A2
Tipperary	90	A2	Ty Glas	27	A2	Wanstead Park	22	A2
Tipton	47	B1	Tye Green Junction	36	A2	Wapping	22	B1
Tir-phil	32	B1	Tye Lane	4	A1	Wapping Wharf (Bristol)	28	C2
Tisbury	9	B2	Tygwyn	49	C2	Warblington	11	C1
Tiverton Parkway	7	C2	Tyndrum Lower	84	B1	Warcop	67	B1
Toadmoor Tunnel	53	B1	Tyne Dock	76	B2	Wardley	76	C1
Tod Point Junction	69	A2	Tyne Yard	75	C2	Ware	36	B1
Toddington	33	A2	Tynemouth	48	C2	Wareham	5	A2
Todmorden	61	B2	Tyneside Central Freight Depot	75	B2	Wargrave	35	C1
Tolworth	16	B2	Tyseley	41	B2	Warham Halt	56	C1
Tomatin	88	C1	Tytherington	33	C1	Warminster	9	B1
Ton Pentre	31	C2	Tywyn	38	A2	Warnham	11	B2
Tonbridge	12	B2	Tywyn Pendre	38	A2	Warren Hill Tunnel	44	C2
Tondu	31	C2	Tywyn Wharf	38	A2	Warren Street	21	B2
Tonfanau	37	A2	Uckfield	12	C2	Warrington Bank Quay	51	B1
Tonypandy	31	C2	Uddingston	82	C2	Warrington Central	51	B1
Tooting	17	A1	Ulceby	63	C2	Warsop Junction	53	B2
Tooting Bec	17	A1	Ulleskelf	62	B2	Warwick	42	C1
Tooting Broadway	17	A1	Ulster Folk Museum	102	C2	Warwick Avenue	21	B1
Topley Pike	52	A2	Ulverston	66	C1	Washford	7	B2
Topsham	3	A2	Umberleigh	7	C1	Washwood Heath	48	B2
Torness	80	A1	Ummeras	94	B2	Waste Bank Tunnel	66	A2
Torosay Castle	83	B2	University (Birmingham)	48	C1	Watchet	7	B2
Torpantau (Proposed)	31	B2	University (Coleraine)	101	A2	Water Orton	42	B1
Torquay	3	B2	University of Sheffield	53	B1	Water Orton West Junction	48	B2
Torre	3	B2	Up Empty Carr. Line Tunnel	22	C2	Waterbeach	44	C2
Totley Tunnel	53	A1	Uphall	78	A2	Water Street (Cork)	90	C1
Totnes	3	B1	Uphill Junction	8	A1	Waterfall Halt	49	B2
Totnes (Littlehempston)	3	B1	Upholland	60	C2	Waterford	91	B2
Toton Yard	53	C2	Upminster	36	C2	Wateringbury	12	A2
Tottenham Court Road	21	B2	Upminster Bridge	36	C2	Waterloo (London)	21	B2
Tottenham Hale	21	A2	Upney	36	C1	Waterloo (Merseyside)	59	A1
Tottenham North Curve Tunnels	21	A1	Upper Halliford	15	B2	Waterloo Goods (Aberdeen)	86	B1
Totteridge & Whetstone	25	C1	Upper Holloway	21	A2	Waterloo Loop Junction	32	B2
Totton	9	C1	Upper Tyndrum	84	B1	Waterside	70	A2
Tower (Blackpool)	60	B1	Upper Warlingham	12	A1	Waterston	29	B2
Tower (Mid Glamorgan)	31	B2				Waterthorpe	56	C2

INDEX TO LOCOMOTIVE STABLING POINTS, CARRIAGE DEPOTS AND RAILWAY WORKS